ETHNICITY IN THE SUNBELT:
A HISTORY OF MEXICAN AMERICANS
IN HOUSTON

by
Arnoldo De León

Mexican American Studies
Monograph Series No. 7

Mexican American Studies Program
University of Houston
Houston, Texas 77204-3783

CONTENTS

TABLES

ACKNOWLEDGEMENTS

This monograph resulted from research I conducted during a year-long tenure as Visiting Scholar in the Mexican American Studies Program at the University of Houston, 1986–1987. Most helpful in giving form and direction to the book were discussions with Dr. Tatcho Mindiola, Jr., Director of the Mexican American Studies Program at the University of Houston, Dr. Thomas H. Kreneck, Associate Director of the Houston Metropolitan Research Center in Houston, and Dr. Nestor Rodríguez, Department of Sociology, University of Houston.

As is invariably the case, one incurs numerous debts in the course of writing a book, and I freely acknowledge my gratitude to those institutions and people who contributed to the finished work. Foremost are the staffs at the M. D. Anderson Memorial Library at the University of Houston and at the Texas Room of the Houston Metropolitan Research Center, Houston Public Library, who graciously lent me their assistance. Enthusiastic endorsement of the project as it proceeded came from members of the administration at the University of Houston, namely, Senior Vice President for Academic Affairs A. Benton Cocanaugher, and Dr. James H. Pickering, Dean of the College of Humanities and Fine Arts. Dr. Lloyd D. Vincent, president of Angelo State University where I teach, happily granted me a leave of absence so that I could undertake the research and writing.

But my special thanks for unflinching support go to the colleagues I worked with at the University of Houston, namely Professors Mindiola, Kreneck, Rodríguez, and my research assistant Roberto R. Treviño, who made my stay in Houston worthwhile. Dr. Kreneck's critical pen and vast knowledge of the Houston Chicano experience sharpened interpretations and corrected potentially embarassing factual errors. His input made the final product all the better. Last, my gratitude is extended to Mario T. García (University of California, Santa Barbara), Albert Camarillo (Stanford University), and Alex M. Saragoza (University of California, Berkeley), who read the entire manuscript and offered invaluable suggestions for revisions. Of course, any errors of fact or interpretation are solely mine.

TEXAS GULF COAST

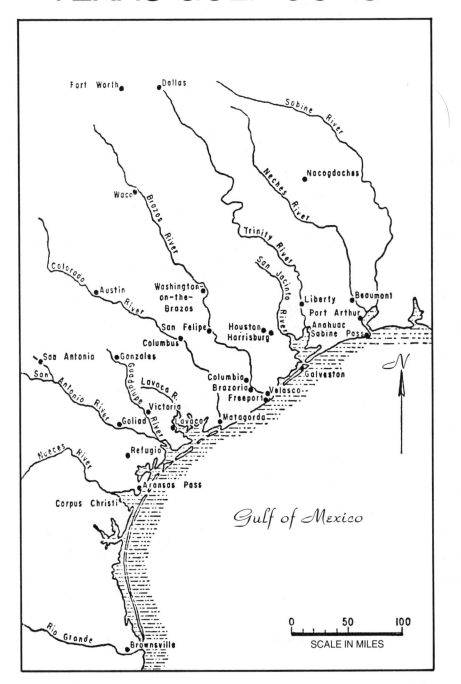

Source: Marilyn McAdams Sibley, *The Port of Houston: A History* (Austin: University of Texas Press, 1968, page 6). Reprinted by permission of the Port of Houston.

HOUSTON - GALVESTON BAY AREA

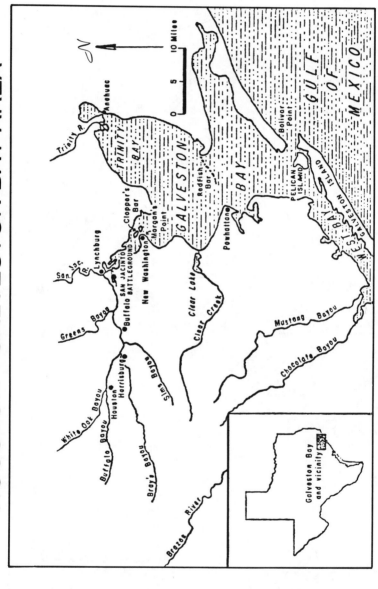

Source: Marilyn McAdams Sibley, *The Port of Houston: A History* (Austin: University of Texas Press, 1968, page 7). Reprinted by permission of the Port of Houston.

PREFACE

Early books on Chicano urban history were products of doctoral dissertations written in the 1970s. Among other things, these early monographs sought explanations for an immediate question: what accounted for the historic subordination of Mexican Americans in United States society? The prevailing answer of social scientists, that Mexican Americans descended from a backward, traditional culture, seemed unsatisfactory. Better answers appeared essential, and they were found in the absence of opportunity which characterized Chicano city life. A common theme which marked the books of historians Richard Griswold del Castillo, Albert Camarillo, Mario T. García, and Ricardo Romo was that lack of social mobility in the city was due to such forces as political disfranchisement, residential segregation, discrimination, and labor segmentation.[1] More recent books like Rodolfo F. Acuña's *A Community Under Siege* and Thomas E. Sheridan's *Los Tucsonenses* have similarly focused on trying to explain the process of institutionalized subordination.[2]

To be sure, all of the books mentioned above did not limit themselves to treating Chicanos as objects being acted upon by historical forces. To the contrary, they astutely informed us how Chicanos created constructive responses to the forces they faced. The urban setting was a place where Mexican Americans lived in a familiar surrounding and where they could both identify with the traditions of the homeland while accepting tenets of the host society on their own terms. Not surprisingly, scholars like Mario T. García now investigated culture and community more carefully, noting varied strains within communities that manifested themselves socially, politically, and intellectually.[3] A host of other historians—among them Richard A. García, Mario Barrera, Manuel Peña, David Montejano,

Alex M. Saragoza, Guadalupe San Miguel, Jr., and F. Arturo Rosales—also delved into the study of Mexican American communities in the United States in efforts to determine change in ideological currents.[4]

In a similar vein, this monograph on Mexican Americans in Houston, Texas, seeks to determine historical flux in ethnic identity and culture. A first aim of this monograph, therefore, is to address some of the issues raised by the recent writings. For instance, when specifically and to what degree do "communities" (instead of individuals) begin accepting the ethos of the host society? In what precise historical eras can change be detected? Are there "watershed" periods in history which account for new directions? What forces in particular alter the cultural makeup of a community?

Furthermore, what path does acculturation take? Do members of the immigrant community accept the trappings of the new environment at a uniform or disparate rate? Do such variables as urbanization, economic opportunity, and Americanization influence everyone in a community similarly? If not, do differences/clashes develop between those tied to the old milieu and the new emerging one? As acculturation occurs, does the community remain ideologically unified given the common problems it faces or is internal division manifest? Do the philosophical positions that the community takes in one era remain constant across time, or may differences be detected from one generation to the next?

As this monograph will show, the Houston Tejano community has historically exhibited diverse, sometimes conflicting nationalist, class, and ethnic sentiments. Cultural change did not affect everyone in the same form. Degrees of acculturation have ranged a wide gamut: residents of the community have remained loyal to Mexican music, films, and Spanish-language radio and newspapers; others have maintained a happy balance with Mexican and United States culture; others have become completely assimilated. Intellectual and ideological currents, appropriate in one era, have been replaced by others more in step with the changing of times. Feelings towards specific issues, furthermore, have not remained constant. The way the Houston community felt towards the foreign born in the 1950s and the issue of "color identification," for example, reversed itself in the 1970s and 1980s.

A second goal of this book is to provide a framework within which to understand the process of Chicano urban community development. To facilitate such an inquiry, the book is broken down into three parts, each focusing on different historical generations from the early twentieth century to the present. By an overview/survey approach, it traces a community through several decades, focusing on generational, ideological, and cultural change. Moreover, it ferrets out other forces that compel evolution—the job, the Catholic Church, the educational system, the level of immigration, or the impact of economic decline or growth, of increased urbanization and of the impact of consumer culture. The study describes the Houston Mexican American community's internal dynamics as it undergoes an Americanization process, but also documents patterns of oppression that may explain adaptation.

As I see it, Houston's Chicano history conforms to the general outlines of development which the above mentioned historians have sketched out for twentieth century Chicano history. In such a schema, the nineteenth century Mexican American community assumed an immigrant condition when overwhelmed by thousands of refugees and exiles fleeing the troubles in Mexico during the early decades of the 1900s. The newcomers dominated the Mexican American *colonias* to the extent that the look for many *barrio* residents was to Mexico instead of the United States. This historical generation up to circa 1930 is referred to as the "Immigrant Generation." I cover it in Part I, called "Arrival and Consolidation."

In Part II, Chapters III to VII, I deal with what recent Chicano scholars such as Rodolfo Álvarez, Richard A. García, and Mario T. García identify as the "Mexican American Generation."[5] Sometime around the late 1920s and continuing into the 1930s, these students note, a new historical cohort emerged. Elements of *"lo mexicano"* persisted within communities for several reasons: racism and segregation isolated barrio residents from American society, strong nationalist currents emanating from Mexico sustained the old allegiance, while others simply preferred adherence to immigrant culture. But birth in the United States, time of residence in this country, and contact with American institutions won over a corps whose allegiance shifted to the United States. This element represented a stage of cultural assimilation within Texas-Mexican culture which, while loyal to immigrant traditions and attached to working class roots, espoused an ideology more in consonance with their conditions in the United States. This sentiment of *"lo americano"* was most readily accepted by members of the League of United Latin American Citizens (LULAC), who in the 1930s, came from a incipient middle class comprised partly of the sons and daughters of the Immigrant Generation. LULACers heartily expressed their admiration for American institutions while demanding their rights as United States citizens.

Tremendous changes spurred by World War II further reshaped the Texas-Mexican community socially and ideologically. It is at this historical moment, according to Manuel Peña (*The Texas Mexican Conjunto*), that a greater social division within the Tejano community became manifest. The war, writes Peña, was a "watershed marking an important turning point in the history of Tejanos." Several variables transformed a Tejano society already in flux, among them a demographic shift from rural to urban living and a change from agricultural to nonagricultural occupations. As Tejanos moved into new socioeconomic fields, they "became irrevocably split between middle class and working class."[6]

A third purpose of this book is to scrutinize this subject of social differentiation in the historical experience of Chicanos. Too often, writers have conceptualized Chicano history as one of conflict with mainstream American society. Such a perception has tended to flatten the diversity within the Chicano community and create the impression of a homogeneous Mexican American community ("us") versus white society ("them, the Anglos"). I challenge such a view throughout the manuscript, posing questions which other students have asked. For instance, at what point in the community's history does class difference surface? Does nationalist or ethnic friction accompany uneven class development? Do members of varied socioeconomic classes within the community express different ideologies, either towards each other or against mainstream society? Do members of the rising, more acculturated middle class within the enclave forefeit or gain the right to speak in behalf of the interests of the *colonia*? In Part III, titled "Many Mexicanos," Chapters VIII to XII, I probe deeply into the current era (since the 1960s), using such episodes as the Chicano Movement of the 1960s and the early 1970s as examples underlying the historic social complexity of the Tejano community.

Thus, at this point I offer a caveat. Obvious from the onset is the absence of commonality within the Houston Chicano community. This in no way distinguishes Houston's Mexican American history from any other. Rather it shows the fundamental diversity of the Chicano experience which other historians have documented elsewhere. It is to underscore the fact that people of Mexican descent have responded in diverse ways to the conditions they have faced.

While the goals I've enumerated above serve as the primary incentives for writing this book, I have a few other objectives in mind. First, I try to rectify the lacunae that exist in Texas Chicano urban history. A Mexican American community of the size that exists in Houston would be expected to attract academic attention, yet scholars have neglected the Mexicans of Houston. The bulk of the scholarly writing on Texas Mexicans deals with those parts of the Lone Star State which historically and culturally have had a highly visible Tejano presence. The region from a

line south of Béxar County, therefore, receives most attention. Dispropor-
tionately neglected are the Mexicanos from the rural vastness of West
Texas (save perhaps for El Paso) and the urban regions of North and East
Texas.[7] Little of Houston is found in the traditional literature, therefore.
Even the latest edition of Rodolfo F. Acuña's *Occupied America: A History of Chicanos* (3rd ed.; New York: Harper and Row, 1987), has only
passing references to the Mexican presence in Houston. Those wanting to
write on Houston's Chicanos have practically no body of secondary literature to draw upon.[8] Hopefully, some will find merit in this monograph
which lays the groundwork for more specialized studies on Mexican
Americans in Houston.

Another intent of this book is to place the experience of the Mexicans of Houston within the context of an urban setting. Historians are well
aware that a multitude of factors determine the manner in which people
adjust to a setting of their choosing. In the case of Mexican Americans in
the United States, several variables may play a part in that adaptation: the
age of the settlement, the flow of immigration, the presence of a landed
class or a petite bourgeoisie, the geographic location of the *colonia,* the
ethnic makeup of the population with which the inhabitants of the *barrios*
associate, the degree or interaction with mainstream institutions, or the
structure of the economic lifeblood of a region (whether it be rural-
commercial- or industrial-based). These are forces that historically have
acted to distinguish, say, the rural Mexicanos of South Texas from their
counterparts in West Texas, or the urban Chicanos of El Paso from those
of Houston.

Certainly, there are singular features about the city of Houston which
might contribute to the commonly recognized diversity of Mexican American residents of the United States. Not the least of these distinctions
would be the city's demographic development. Founded in 1836 along
Buffalo Bayou (some fifty miles from the Gulf of Mexico) by August C.
and John K. Allen, the city's population has experienced growth of at
least 20% in every decade since 1850. In the early decades of the twentieth century, the percentage growth rate was even greater and no lull has
appeared in more recent times. During the boom years of the 1970s, indeed, some 1,000 people streamed into Houston per week. By 1980, the
metropolis had 1.6 million within its expanded borders and ranked as
the fifth largest city in the country. By 1983, it surpassed Philadelphia in
estimated population to become fourth largest.

Spatially, Houston's enlargement is equally striking. By means of
annexation, the incorporated city expanded from nine square miles in

HOUSTON 1980

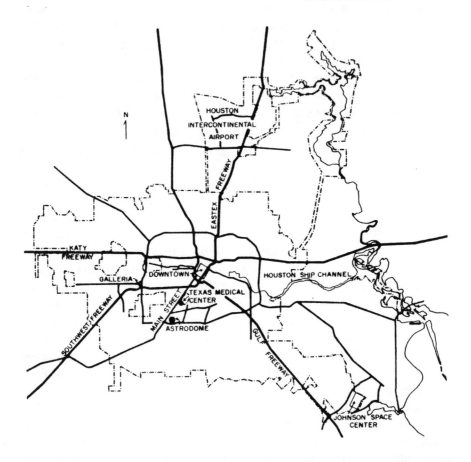

Source: David G. McComb, *Houston: A History* (Austin: University of Texas Press, 1981, p. 140). Reprinted by permission of University of Texas Press.

1900 to 556 square miles in 1980. Presently, Houston stretches some twenty-five miles in each direction from a downtown section of awesome skyscrapers. Spaghetti freeways link diverse neighborhoods and suburbs, taking people to their places of work and business, including the various corporate offices dispersed throughout the urban giant. The same freeways act as arteries to the industrial east side where oil and gas refineries and ancillary companies go on and on for forty miles all the way to the Gulf coast.[9]

Few, if any, cities in Texas owe their growth to the same factors which allow Houston to claim the sobriquet of the "Golden Buckle of the

Sunbelt.'' In part, the city has profitted from the national flow of capital toward the Sunbelt and the Third World, a trend that began in the 1940s and continues until the present.[10] But the growth of the oil industry and relatively unchallenged local control by the local business community seem more significant in molding the city's transformation.

Houston began the twentieth century auspiciously when a well gushed oil at Spindletop near Beaumont in 1901. With more oil discoveries closer to the city (in the next thirty years or so, nearly a score of new fields were found within a fifty-mile radius of Houston) corporate enterprises, among them Gulf Oil and Standard Oil, transferred their offices to the Houston area. The impact of boom was profound.[11] Thereafter, Houston experienced sustained growth in its oil-petrochemical industry. Over the years, the metropolitan area became an important center of oil technology specialization in the world economy. It established links to regions throughout the world—among them Latin American areas in the 1950s and 1960s, Middle European regions in the 1960s and 1970s, and deepwater areas in the Gulf of Mexico, the North Sea, and the Yellow Sea in the 1970s and 1980s—as sources of petroleum for refining in Houston or as markets for Houston's oil and petro-chemical technology. As this phenomenon unfolded, a combination of forces stimulated the city's economic development: federal intervention in the economy during and after World War II, quotas on oil imports in the 1960s, national recentralization in the late 1960s and 1970s, and even the Arab oil embargo of the 1970s.[12]

Such an economy, integrally tied to the capitalist world system, has manifested an insatiable demand for all types of labor. As the oil-petrochemical sector expanded, it generated growth in a variety of supportive industries. Literally thousands of jobs were made available by this trickle-down effect, both in the primary sector (white or blue collar jobs) as well as the secondary sector (jobs with little skill, low pay, and employment insecurity). In the early years, openings developed among the railroad construction and ship-channel related industries, restaurants, laundries, and factories. In more recent times, demand has expanded to car washes, cleaners, construction workers, personal service, and other low-wage occupations. Often, these types of works have been temporary—Houston's economy resembles other advanced capitalist economies which obtain labor from foreign migrant workers, then release them in times of economic distress.[13]

Encouraging Houston's boomtown success has been an ideological climate that is anti-government, anti-regulation, anti-union, anti-planning, anti-taxes or anti-any of the things that violate the doctrine of laissez-faire capitalism. Houston's business community has carefully cultivated such a notion, boasting that the city's free market economy accounts for growth and prosperity. In actuality, however, the business community has invited close cooperation with government and tolerated intervention into the free market economy when it serves its needs. As indicated above, for example, federal funds accessed by the local business community have been major stimuli to Houston's economic growth. Still, the facade of free enterprise persists and serves the function of legitimizing private sector domination.[14]

In reality, wealth and economic progress has accrued more to the city's middle and upper class residents. Hence, social problems abound in Houston, while community organizing to address major social problems has been generally weak.[15] Observers of Houston's structural life have advanced a number of reasons for the relative absence of organizational activity. The city's individualist philosophy, the accent on "free enterprise" to solve problems, the dominance of business groups in city politics, the largely disenfranchised minority population, and the absence historically of a "left tradition" are offered as possible explanations.[16] "In Houston," one historian writes, "where government has been kept small and limited in power, where power has been concentrated in private, extra-political bodies, where the political culture opposed all forms of leftwing dissent as fundamentally treasonous and un-American, it has been near impossible to mount anything bordering on an effective challenge to the dominant directive of economic development or, on a more limited scale, a challenge for greater equity in service delivery which might raise the issue of city priorities."[17]

Certainly, the several features I have associated with Houston might act to differentiate somewhat the experience of Mexican Americans in Houston from those of the state and nation, but so may the city's geographical setting. As a culture region, in fact, its history is more closely tied to the South than to that of the more "frontier" expanses of southern or western Texas. Situated in East Texas, its past is grounded on the political and social mores of the southern Black Belt dating to urban slavery and Reconstruction. The perseverence of such a tradition is evidenced in that streets and schools—including new ones—bear the names of Confederate heroes. Business signs are known to display the word "Dixie" in their name. The Sons of Confederate Veterans and the United Daughters of the Confederacy sponsor a "Confederate Ball" which attracts dignitaries, among them city officials. Houston, furthermore, contains a black population with historical roots in ante-bellum servitude; it is presently the largest Negro concentration in the South, exceeding that of either New Orleans or Atlanta. More than one-fourth of Houston's population is black. While the city's size, economic orientation, and urbanized environment temper its southern tradition,[18] the fact remains that in no other similar place in Texas have Tejanos established roots.

And those of Mexican origin who have made Houston and its surroundings their home number somewhere between 250,000 to 500,000 in the 1980s. Table P.1 breaks down the number of the population of the city according to the three major ethnic groupings. As in the case of the black population which ranks high among cities in the country (in the 1970s, it was the eighth largest black population in the United States), so also the Mexican population figure is prominent statistically. Today, only Los Angeles, Chicago, and San Antonio contain more inhabitants of Mexican origin than does Houston.

Table P.1
1980 Houston Metropolitan and City Populations

	SMSA	City of Houston
Total	2,905,353	1,595,138
Hispanic	424,903	305,170
White	1,888,003	936,676
Black	528,510	441,303

Source: Beth Anne Shelton, et al., *Houston: Growth and Decline in a Sunbelt Boomtown* (Philadelphia: Temple University Press, 1989).

Houston, thus, seems to be a non-traditional laboratory to study Tejano history. With a reputation as a prime frontier for those on the make, speculators, wheeler-dealers, Horatio Algers, and builders of tomorrow, it is a setting offering seemingly unbounded opportunity. How do Mexican Americans fare therein? Have they integrated an ethic that likes to display its Jaguars, Mercedes Benz's, and BMW's? Such propensities might be one to emanate from a city tied to the world economy and not from another where things are more provincial and where pickups and western wear are the measures of one's aspirations. The Houston economy today has room for the emergence of several Chicano capitalists and millionaires (of which there are several)—this would be an impossibility in the economies of the Rio Grande Valley and parts of West Texas.

Finally, a word on terminology. I consistently alternate the terms Mexicanos, Mexicans, and Mexican Americans as catch-all terms when speaking of the Mexican-origin population as a community. I have tried to distinguish the Mexican-born residents of the colonia by using a variety of labels which indicate their status: among such descriptions employed are "foreign-born," "Mexican nationals," and "undocumented." From the 1930s through the 1950s, the term Latin American was in vogue both by Mexican Americans and Anglo Americans, and I restricted its usage to my discussion of the history of that period. Similarly, I tried to contain the word Chicano to my coverage of the era of the 1960s and 1970s. I began using the word Hispanic towards the latter part of the book which deals with the current period of the 1980s.

NOTES

[1]Richard Griswold del Castillo, *The Los Angeles Barrio, 1850–1890: A Social History*; Albert Camarillo, *Chicanos in a Changing Society: From Mexican Pueblos to American Barrios in Santa Barbara and Southern California, 1848–1930*; Mario T. García, *Desert Immigrants: The Mexicans of El Paso, 1880–1920*; and Ricardo Romo, *East Los Angeles: History of a Barrio*.

[2]Rodolfo F. Acuña, *A Community Under Siege: A Chronicle of Chicanos East of the Los Angeles River, 1945–1975*; Thomas E. Sheridan, *Los Tucsonenses: The Mexican Community in Tucson, 1854–1941*.

[3]Examples are Mario T. García, "Mexican Americans and the Politics of Citizenship: The Case of El Paso, 1936," *New Mexico Historical Review*, LIX (April, 1984); Mario T. García, "Americans All: The Mexican American Generation and the Politics of Wartime Los Angeles, 1941–1945," *Social Science Quarterly*, LXV (June, 1984); Mario T. García, "La Frontera: The Border as Symbol and Reality in Mexican-American Thought," *Mexican Studies/Estudios Mexicanos*, I (Summer, 1985).

[4]Selected studies include Richard A. García, "The Making of the Mexican American Mind, San Antonio, Texas, 1929–1941: A Social and Intellectual History of an Ethnic Community" (Ph.D. Dissertation, University of California at Irvine, 1980); Richard A. García, "The Mexican American Mind: A Product of the 1930s," in Mario T. García, *History, Culture, and Society: Chicano Studies in the 1980s*; Mario Barrera, "The Historical Evolution of Chicano Ethnic Goals: A Bibliographic Essay," *Sage Race Relations Abstracts*, X (February, 1985); Manuel Peña, *The Texas Mexican Conjunto: A History of a Working-Class Music*; David Montejano, *Anglos and Mexicans in the Making of Texas, 1836–1986*; Alex M. Saragoza, "The Significance of Recent Chicano-related Historical Writings: An Appraisal," *Ethnic Affairs*, No. 1 (Fall, 1987); Guadalupe San Miguel, Jr., "The Struggle Against Separate and Unequal Schools: Middle Class Mexican Americans in the Desegregation Campaign in Texas, 1929–1957," *History of Education Quarterly*, XXIII (Fall, 1983); and Francisco Arturo Rosales, "Shifting Self Perceptions and Ethnic Consciousness Among Mexicans in Houston, 1908–1946," *Aztlán*, XVI (1985).

Preface

[5]Rodolfo Álvarez, "The Psycho-Historical and Socioeconomic Development of the Chicano Community in the United States," *Social Science Quarterly*, LIII (March, 1973); and citations in note # 4.

[6]Peña, *The Texas-Mexican Conjunto*, p. 117.

[7]See my article, "Tejano History Scholarship: A Review of the Recent Literature," *West Texas Historical Association Yearbook*, LXI (1985).

[8]Published works include articles in the special issue of *The Houston Review*, III (Summer, 1981), which includes F. Arturo Rosales', "Mexicans in Houston: The Struggle to Survive, 1908–1975," and; Margarita Melville, *Mexicans in Houston*. Also see the article by Rosales, "Shifting Self-Perceptions and Ethnic Consciousness Among Mexicans in Houston, 1908–1946," which appeared after the first draft of this book was finished.

[9]Joe R. Feagin, "The Socioeconomic Base of Urban Growth: The Case of Houston and the Oil Industry," pp. 2–3 (unpublished paper); Robert Fisher, "Houston, Texas: A Working Paper on the Interrelation of Economic Growth, Ideology, Power, and Community Organization Since 1920," pp. 4, 12 (unpublished paper).

[10]Fisher, "Houston, Texas," p. 6.

[11]Ibid, pp. 7–11.

[12]Nestor P. Rodríguez, "Patterns of Race and Ethnic Disparity and Conflict: Hispanic Communities," pp. 9–10 (forthcoming); and, Fisher, "Houston, Texas", pp. 7–11.

[13]Rodríguez, "Patterns of Race and Ethnic Disparity and Conflict," pp. 6, 11–13, 17.

[14]Fisher, "Houston, Texas", pp. 13–17. More extensive discussion of the above is in Feagin, "The Socioeconomic Base of Urban Growth," pp. 10 passim.

[15]Fisher, "Houston, Texas", p. 3.

[16]Joe R. Feagin and Beth Anne Shelton, "Community Organizing in Houston: Social Problems and Citizen Response," p. 1 (unpublished paper).

[17]Fisher, "Houston, Texas," p. 33.

[18]Chandler Davidson, *Biracial Politics: Conflict and Coalition in the Metropolitan South*, pp. 12–13, 17, and 18.

PART I:
ARRIVAL AND CONSOLIDATION, 1528–1930

CHAPTER I
THE MAKING OF A *COLONIA*

The antecedents of the twentieth century Texas-Mexican population of Houston date to the earliest years of the European discovery of the western hemisphere. Spaniards first moved into the region around the Houston area out of military and political necessity. Mexicans during the period between 1821 to 1836 took an interest in that part of the Texas province because from there emanated the most annoying troubles with Anglo American colonists. Mexican and Mexican American migrants who made their way to Houston towards the latter nineteenth century and most noticeably in the early twentieth century had more immediate reasons for entering the city. They sought a place of residence where a decent livelihood might be wrenched.

Background, 1528–1880

The history of Spain and México in the periphery of modern day Houston may be traced to the earliest Old World presence in Texas. Indeed, the first person from the Old World known to have passed through the vicinity of Houston was no less than the first literate European ever to set foot on Texas soil: the shipwrecked Spaniard Alvar Núñez Cabeza de Vaca. As the crown pushed into East Texas in efforts to secure the region from French encroachment in the eighteenth century, the presidio San Agustín de Ahumada, founded in 1756 (but abandoned in 1772) on the lower Trinity River, became an outpost for the defense of the coast.[1] During the decade of the 1810s, while Mexico fought to gain independence from Spain, Galveston Bay attracted Spanish/Mexican activity. From there, Francisco Xavier Mina launched an abortive attack against the

3

Spaniards in Mexico. While at Galveston Bay, however, one of Mina's men is said to have named Point Bolívar for the South American hero, Simón Bolívar.[2] Still, after almost three centuries of activity around the modern-day Houston area, Spain's impact on the region was mainly peripheral.

During the Mexican period of Texas history, 1821–1836, the region surrounding the future city of Houston was the stage for significant events between Mexico and Anglo Americans. It was to that area that the Mexican government permitted Stephen F. Austin to bring and settle 300 families; as a matter of fact, Austin's first grant encompassed the entire length of Buffalo Bayou.[3] The decision to allow foreigners into the province proved a fateful one for the Mexican government, a fact which became evident when troubles between Anglo Americans and the Mexican commander at Anáhuac on Galveston Bay broke out in 1832. Once more, Anáhuac became the scene in July 1835 of what one historian has termed "the first act of violence in the Texas revolution"—an insurrection led by none other than William Barrett Travis. With distrust mounting in the summer of 1835, Mexico dispatched troops to Texas.[4]

As fate had it, the major episodes of the Texas Revolution, save for the Battle of the Alamo, occurred around the Houston area. Harrisburg, at the junction of Buffalo and Braes bayous, became the seat of the *Ad Interim* government elected at Washington-on-the-Brazos when President David G. Burnet and Vice President Lorenzo de Zavala retreated there for their safety and that of their families.[5] Antonio López de Santa Anna set fire to the town when unable to apprehend the two leaders. It was, needless to say, at the San Jacinto River/Buffalo Bayou battlefield where Santa Anna lost to Sam Houston in the decisive battle that made Texas independent from Mexico.

The Mexican presence around the Houston area continued into the post-Mexican period, albeit less conspicuously. The most prominent figure living there was Lorenzo de Zavala, the federalist liberal from Yucatán who had fled to Texas to escape the Centralists in Mexico and to tend to his land possession in East Texas. In 1835, the future Vice-President of the *Ad Interim* government had bought land on the north bank of Buffalo Bayou, close to where the Battle of San Jacinto was fought, and settled there with his American wife and new family.[6] Lesser figures residing in the region were members of Santa Anna's defeated army who, on the reasoning that the expense of holding them prisoners was too much for the Texas government, were allowed to become servants for Texians in every part of the country including Galveston.[7] Given land by the Texas government in Harris County for service rendered to it during the Revolution were several Texas Mexicans—whether these veterans took up residence therein remains to be confirmed.[8] No Mexican in nineteenth century Harris County, however, came to make a mark on Texas history (although a dubious one) as did the Texas-Mexican Joseph Rodríguez, a Travis County resident who somehow wound up voting twice in Harris County in 1873. In the celebrated case of *Ex parte Rodríguez*, the Texas Supreme Court declared the election of 1873 invalid because the polls had not been kept open four days as stipulated by the Constitution of 1869.[9]

In the city of Houston proper, Mexicans were apparent since its earliest days—in fact they helped develop it. According to Dr. O. F. Allen's recollections, Texians in 1836 put some of Santa Anna's prisoners to clearing the swampy grounds around the city when it was founded; the Mexicans, along with black slaves, endured insect stings and malaria, snake bites, impure water, and other hardships which no white man could have endured, Allen asserted.[10] During Houston's days as the seat of Texas government between 1836–1839, moreover, some 100 of the same prisoners acted as servants in the young town, mixing "on an equal footing," one traveler observed, with government officials, lawyers, gamblers, tradesmen, artisans, and adventurers.[11] The Mexicans mixed on an "equal footing" because Houston during that early period was a crude, bawdy, violent town where abusive language, brawls, and alcoholic consumption abounded—for certainly, Mexicans were not treated as social equals. In a statement of public resentment, an unknown writer signing himself "A Sufferer," complained to the editor of the Houston *Morning Star*:

> It is presumed that Editors know every thing—then will you be so good as too inform me how long we are to see a parcel of idle, thieving Mexican vagabonds prowling about our streets without any ostensible means of support, before the proper authorities will take it into their hands to investigate the matter? Hardly a day passes over our heads that we do not hear complaints made against that degraded class of our citizens. I myself have seen them at noon-day hurrying around the outskirts of the corporation, playing their national game of Monte, and idling away their time until night closes upon them when they may be found clustering at every turn of the streets.
>
> Were they *white men*, the law would long since have visited them, but we are to apt to look upon them with contempt because they are a miserable remnant of our conquered enemy—until even now their conduct has become insufferable, and unless the law will take hold of them the citizens must take the matter in their own hands, and the transgressors must abide the consequences.[12]

What eventually became of these men in Houston is unknown. It had always been understood that citizens who had taken the Mexicans in as servants were to re-deliver them to the Texas government upon demand. It is clear, however, that the number of Mexicans in the city declined during the 1840s. The federal census of 1850, the first taken of Texas, enumerated just six Mexican-born persons and that of next decennium in 1860, counted eighteen; in both cases, most of those enumerated were males.[13] In 1880, the census rolls show no major increases in the Mexican population: less than ten people of Mexican-origin resided within the city limits.[14] Why was Houston unenticing to Mexican laborers? Perhaps because in the nineteenth century Houston's economy was oriented toward servicing an agrarian economy of lumber, grain, and cotton. To that end, it had developed an important infrastructure of bankers, railroads, warehouses, and cotton gins.[15] Save for its financial institutions, the city and its surrounding counties (most of which were rural) could turn to their large black population for a cheap source of labor. While Mexicans during that period were sought after in the farmlands of South Texas, the ranchlands of West Texas and the urban economy of San Antonio, no equivalent calls were initiated from East Texas.

The Lure of the Bayou City, 1880–1910

In the last two decades of the nineteenth century, however, Mexican American activity resurfaced in Houston. Some seventy-five Mexican Americans were brought in as strikebreakers in October 1880 when black laborers struck at the Direct Navigation Company wharves, at the several cotton compresses in Houston, and on different railway lines. The Mexican role in the city's history was short lived, however, for they were "shipped up the central road" once the black strikers gave in to management.[16] Mexicans must have drifted into the city in the 1880s, nevertheless, for a correspondent for *Harper's New Monthly Magazine,* in 1890, noticed Mexican vendors during the city's "Market Day," although he was more struck by the other nationalities represented at the square.[17] The city directories of the 1890's list the small Mexican American population of Houston as making its living primarily as peddlers (mainly *tamale* vendors), though a few claimed occupations as tailors, barbers, and shoemakers.[18] In 1900, the somewhat less than 500 Mexicans living in Houston[19] performed similar tasks, though the categories of "laborer" and "railroad hand" were more noticeable.[20]

The major push into Houston did not occur until the city's metamorphosis into a metropolis commenced early in the twentieth century. Sometime between the 1890s and about 1910, the modern day Houston Mexican American community began taking shape. By the time that the Mexican Revolution started, a viable colonia of approximately 2,000 Mexicans existed in the city. Henceforth, the growth of the Mexican American population would accompany Houston's own twentieth century expansion into urban stardom.[21]

The major catalyst transforming the city from one dependent on an economy based on lumber, grain, and cotton into a major oil and gas production center was the discovery of oil ninety miles east of the city at Spindletop in 1901. Several things fell Houston's way in rapid succession. First, Houston's other competitors in the region faced unique problems. Though Galveston had a larger population and an excellent port, a massive hurricane in 1900 devastated the city and made owners of oil-related companies reluctant to consider its exposed coastal location. Beaumont, although closer to some major oil fields, did not have the railroad and banking infrastructure that Houston had already developed as a center for agricultural commerce.[22] Further enhancing Houston's position in the race to host the oil industry were oil discoveries closer to Houston following the Spindletop bonanza.

In this early period, Houston's local growth coalition played an intimate role in helping the companies expedite and solidify their decision to choose Houston as a base of operations. Local bankers, real estate investors, and other business leaders, for instance, lobbied for state subsidies to improve Houston's deficient port facilities. In 1910, they successfully won a large $1.25 million grant to deepen the Houston ship channel, the largest federal grant to a local government up to that time. With improved port facilities, oil-related companies flocked to the greater Houston area.[23] The new economic orientation also beckoned for laborers of all sorts, including those to meet the demand for low wage, unskilled positions in the supportive and service categories.

The movement of Mexican labor towards the Houston regions became apparent to Victor S. Clark, writing for the Department of Commerce and Labor in 1908. "In southern Texas," noted Clark, "Mexican labor is everywhere preferred to negro labor, and is supplanting it upon public works on many places, including some of the larger cities along the Gulf coast and in central Texas."[24] In Houston, furthermore, public advertisments could be found specifically designating Mexicans as desirable hands, even for jobs previously the domain of blacks, such as pickers for the cotton district in the Brazos bottom.[25] The labor agent Martín Jiménez in 1904 openly advertised his employment company on Congress Street as able to "furnish all kinds of Mexican laborers for farms, railroads, and plantations."[26]

Those responding to the lure of Bayou City during the early years of the twentieth century arrived in Houston to find an environment different than that which other Mexican immigrants into Texas had encountered in the nineteenth century. Mexicans did not find familiar surroundings as did migrants who entered in older Hispanic regions. They found no remnants or restored reminders of the Spanish and Mexican past. No missions or *presidios* existed in Houston. The familiar plazas characteristic of California and New Mexican towns were non-existent. The same applied to street names in Spanish, a situation so familiar in South Texas. Ranches were not a part of Houston's immediate surroundings for Tejanos to use time-tested work skills. Furthermore, since most descended from rural areas of the state or from farm and peasant villages of Mexico, they were encountering an urban setting with its affiliated evils—congested housing, factories, and population density—for the first time.

Settlement, 1900–1910

To be sure, Houston did not compare with the larger cities of the north and its demographic structure retained the small town pattern. As of 1910, even as its population increased to 78,800, its downtown areas included homes integrated among emerging buildings. It was into the fringes of the downtown district where Mexican immigrants responding to Houston's call for workers gravitated. It is there where Mexicans were dispersed as of 1910.

Still, no specific clustering pattern is apparent according to plotting done from the city directories of the era. The locations of Mexican households as of 1910 give vague indications of the greater outlines that Houston's barrios would take later. Indeed, Houston as late as 1910 did not have any "ethnic enclaves." Foreign-born Houstonians could be found in several sections of the city and even blacks, who dealt with a racial order indigenous to a Southern town, were relatively evenly distributed throughout the six wards.[27]

So, why specifically did Mexican immigrants congregate in those regions all around the central city? First of all, Houston lacked established Mexican settlements as was the case in other towns where Mexicans had lived for many years before the twentieth century. As in other towns born in the nineteenth century, furthermore, industries in Houston had localized a few blocks from the central city. In Houston, the center of town was just south of the confluence of Buffalo and White Oak Bayous where Congress Street running parallel to Buffalo Bayou intersected Main Street. In each direction from the downtown district were located railroad yards and railroad shops which tied Houston to the aforementioned lumber, grain, and cotton enterprises of East Texas and the interior of the state. Houston, therefore, was still a "walking city" as business people, shoppers, shopkeepers, and workers got to their destinations by foot.

According to the 1910 *Directory of the City of Houston*, almost 25% of some 100 Spanish-surnamed persons listed worked in one capacity or another with the railroad lines. Conveniently enough, some type of railroad work was easily accessible to Mexicans regardless of what part of the town they lived in. Those residing west of the downtown area in the First and Sixth wards walked to the H. & T. C. shops, those on north side of the Bayou in the Fifth Ward worked at the S & P yards, and others inhabiting homes to the southeast portion of the town south of Buffalo Bayou turned to the I & G. N. line close to their homes.

Others unable to find work in the railroads were not disadvantaged by distance, for they could easily walk to their workplace. Another 25% of the people listed in the city directory of 1910 earned their livelihood as "laborers," an all encompassing term that may have included workers of varying skills employed outside the city as easily as it could have applied to those working close to their residence. Other jobs listed included waiter, dishwasher, cook, tailor, clerk, and barber, all occupations which would have permitted Mexicans to stroll daily to the downtown area. Tamale, chile, and candy peddlers ostensibly joined them in this daily sojourn to sell their wares at the City Market located just a block away from where Congress and Main intersected. What we see, then, is the growth of a working class population taking root near downtown, an ironic phenomenon where people lured by the city's boom lived in poverty just a stone's throw from the center of wealth that touched other capitalists thousands of miles away.

Notwithstanding its embryonic stage, the Mexican colonia in Houston during the first decade of the twentieth century showed signs of stability and permanency. Fragmentary evidence indicates at least some kind of teaching representation in the Houston school system (as teachers of Spanish), the most prominent appointment being Professor J. J. Mercado, a Spanish instructor in the High School since the early 1900s who would play a leading part in the interests of Houston's Mexican colonia for years thereafter.[28] But men residing within the community were more concerned with ensuring the welfare of those around them. For one thing, they had gotten the city to meet their need for preserving the peace, this in the form of a special officer attached to the police department and assigned to do duty among the Mexicans.[29]

Equally necessary to the inhabitants were organizations or institutions which might come to their aid in critical times. The earliest known group to have met this demand was *El Campamento Laurel* #2333, a lodge founded in 1908. As a chapter of the Woodmen of the World (in Spanish, *Los Leñadores del Mundo*, or, *Hacheros*), it offered limited security in the form of life insurance, recreation, fraternal companionship, and cultural reinforcement.[30]

More of a sign that the community in Houston had taken roots in the Bayou City was the commemoration of the Mexican national holiday of the *Diez y Seis de Septiembre*, starting in 1907. The next year, Professor J. J. Mercado took the lead as the president of the *Junta Patriótica* in Houston to organize a grand spectacular of music and speech at the hall of the Woodmen of the World, 205 San Jacinto Street. A row, unfortunately, dampened the night of patriotic and soul inspiring exercises of the *Grito* when a disagreement between Professor Mercado (also a Methodist minister) and the labor agent Martín Jiménez, treasurer of the Junta Patriótica, arose over whether or not a dance should be given. The episode notwithstanding (Jiménez was charged with disturbing the peace), the fiesta ended successfully, having attracted the Mexican consul at Galveston as well as several members of Galveston's Junta Patriótica.[31]

El Segundo Barrio Takes Shape, 1910–1920

During the 1910s, Houston's Mexican community continued expanding. Opportunities opened up in occupations generated by the oil-related industries lured more Mexicans to the city, especially after the completion of the Ship Channel in 1914. Simultaneously, the revolution then raging in Mexico compelled immigrants to flee north to Texas and seek a livelihood wherever available. Some chose Houston.

Almost certainly, not all those who arrived in Houston during this period came directly from Mexico. It is probable that many were Texas-born, picking up roots from other parts of the state (South Texas, for example), and that others were of first-generation, already exposed to acculturating American institutions. But at the same time, the budding Mexican community became a refuge for working class immigrants as well as upper class exiles from Mexico. The historian F. Arturo Rosales has been able to trace the place of origin of many of the inhabitants of the 1910 Houston colonia to the Mexican states of Coahuila, Nuevo León, Tamaulipas, San Luis Potosí, and Zacatecas;[32] oral interviews deposited at the Houston Metropolitan Research Center substantiate Rosales' findings.[33] Those of peasant origins left their homeland "porque no había trabajo" (there was no work)[34] in their war-torn country, but others fled to avoid the wrath of *campesinos* bent on revenge for years of subordination under the Porfiriato. Wealthy Mexican refugees, according to a story in the Houston *Chronicle,* found the city a safe haven from the turmoil of the Revolution. "While a great many are here but a few weeks," observed the paper, "others have made permanent residence here and have brought their servants and enough furniture to 'weather the revolution out' in safe surroundings."[35] The presence of these *"rico"* element stood in stark contrast to the way of the *pobres* and attested to the existence of at least two social classes within the Spanish-speaking Houston community during the 1910s.

With population increases occurring through the 1910s, Houston's barrios begin to take shape with recognizable boundaries setting them apart from other portions of the city. Their development did not differ much from the ways in which ethnic enclaves in other cities took shape about the same time. With increased wages caused by the oil boom and the establishment of the streetcar as a means of transportation, an age in Houston's urban evolution waned. The walking city disintegrated as wealthy and the middle class citizens encouraged by the street car abandoned the central core as a place of residence. Simultaneously, the urban working class, Mexicans, and other poor folks began occupying the vacated housing. Large homes, already undergoing a process of subdivision into small apartments or a transformation into boarding houses, also took in new tenants.[36] Ethnic communities which had been absent before this time (the need to be close to work had produced some degree of integration before) now became visible. The Fourth Ward turned primarily into a black quarter as were parts of the Third and Fifth Wards.[37] The inner city now showed signs of income disparities and manifestations of segregation based on race and status.

One of the sections left to the Mexicans was the Second Ward. Here, some of the poverty-stricken newcomers staked claim to vacant lands, neglected there by municipal government. According to a survey conducted there in 1911:

In Houston, too, are found the *jacales* of San Antonio. There is a row of them along the banks of the bayou not a remote distance from the heart of the city. They have been constructed of tin, sheet iron, barrel staves, boxes and any other available material which the junk heaps of the dumping ground have provided. The little shacks have been in existence a long time.

....

[One] long-time resident told the writer that the city owned the land on which the shacks were built. No restrictions were placed upon occupancy. A family could enter the lot and build its own dwelling place under the common acceptance, perhaps, of squatter rights.[38]

This, however, did not describe the essence of the Second Ward proper, for this part of town had previously been a fashionable neighborhood with good homes, fine gardens and shady streets. According to a settlement worker, the neighborhood in 1910 consisted of three-fifth Jews, one-fifth black, and the remainder Germans, Irish, native Americans (Anglos), and Mexicans.[39] Transformed into a working class district, it came to mirror the poverty of its new inhabitants, for the incomers improvised for their livelihood in ways that deteriorated the area further. These were the early origins of *El Segundo Barrio,* as the Mexicans labeled the old Second Ward neighborhood.

By 1920, this section of Houston starting from the downtown area and extending beyond it for about one mile began assuming its place as a future, if not temporary, "heart" of the Mexican community in the city. Buffalo Bayou defined its boundary on the north and Congress Avenue marked it on the south. Within these confines, social institutions arrived to work with the Mexicans, among them the Catholic Church. In 1912, a frame church and school combination was built on Marsh and Runnels (Navigation) streets and the first Mass was celebrated in the new Our Lady of Guadalupe Church on August 18, 1912.[40] As part of its religious work, the Church undertook education in El Segundo Barrio through Our Lady of Guadalupe School which opened on September 12, 1912, under the direction of the Sisters of the Divine Providence. Originally, classes were taught in English but the Mexicans preferred Spanish, a concession the Church made by assigning Sister Benitia Vermeersch as principal in 1915. "La Madre Benita," as she affectionately came to be called, was to perform all sorts of good work for the school and parish for years to come.[41]

At the same time that Sister Benitia ran her classes in Spanish, Rusk Elementary at 1701 Maple Avenue, previously an Anglo school for the children of the most prominent families of Houston (as many as twenty-five nationalities attended Rusk at one time before the 1910s), gradually was made into the school for Mexican children. Attendance was sporadic to be sure (many of the children could not afford lunches so they stayed at home), but those taking advantage of the gesture were the first wave of Mexican children exposed to an American ethos from which an endogamous culture would spring.[42] Further socializing the people of El Segundo Barrio were the efforts of the Houston Settlement Association which worked out of the Rusk Settlement House located next to Rusk School. With typical Settlement commitment, Anglos at Rusk Settlement assisted with the problems of the neighborhood, seeking to reduce disease by holding classes on hygiene and providing basic medical information, offering youths an outlet in sports, establishing a day nursery for children, and training young women in craft skills.[43]

Ideologically, the Houston Mexican community early on manifested an awareness of the social ills Mexicanos elsewhere in Texas confronted. In 1911, for example, a delegation from the city attended the *Primer Congreso Mexicanista*, a meeting being hosted in Laredo for the purpose of discussing and acting upon the common problems of Mexican Americans in the state. There, J. J. Mercado played a leading role in the deliberations, denouncing judicial injustice against Mexicans in Texas and expressing concern over the linguistic deterioration occurring within the Texas Mexican community. Accompanying Mercado from Houston were representatives of the *Agrupación Protectora Mexicana*, an association dedicated to the defense of Texas Mexicans, especially on the issue of lynchings. During the discourses of the convention, the Houston delegates discussed the notion of teaching children in their native language first and urged the Congreso to protest school discrimination to the State Superintendent of Schools.[44] The interests that the Houston community maintained in the welfare of fellow Tejanos is further seen in the assistance it and Professor Mercado extended to getting accused slayer Gregorio Cortez paroled from Texas prison. Indeed, Cortez felt obliged to journey to Houston and thank his supporters there following his release in 1913. Sizeable crowds received him.[45] Also, Mexican Houstonians extended financial support to Aniceto Pizaña and Luis de la Rosa, two Cameron County Mexicanos who organized attacks from Mexico against symbols of Anglo American dominance in the Lower Rio Grande Valley during the years of the Mexican Revolution. Both figured closely with the *Plan de San Diego*, a manifesto for a popular insurrection issued from Duval County, Texas, in 1915.[46] Considering the influx of immigrants into Houston, on the other hand, it is not surprising to find the colonia taking an interest in the revolution then raging in the homeland. The look to Mexico was displayed in the role local groups took in partisan politics back in the old country. *La Sociedad Mexicana "Vigilancia,"* organized in Houston on May 24, 1914, for instance, pledged its support to Venustiano Carranza, the leader of the Constitutionalist forces in northern Mexico seeking to oust the tyrant Victoriano Huerta, who in 1913 had usurped the presidency from Francisco I. Madero.[47]

Fragmentation

Other lesser barrios began taking form to the north and west of the downtown region as El Segundo Barrio grew. The birth of a small isolated community in the Houston Heights is unique—there *obreros* lived in Factory Village while working at the Oriental Textile Mills making cloth from camel hair.[48] For the most part, however, neighborhoods took root around the aforementioned railroad yards in the First and Sixth Wards and in the Northside (Fifth Ward) as people moved into deserted homes, or built their own houses, or as in the case of the Second Ward, took refuge in box car arrangements provided by the railroad companies; there is repeated mention in the directories of Mexicans residing in S. & P. Place, I. & N. G. Place, and the like.[49] By 1920, institutions such as churches were beginning to tend to the people in the several barrios. The Mexican Methodist Episcopal Church was established at 1020 McKee on the northside enclave and by 1917 was observing the Diez y Seis de Septiembre with religious services.[50]

In reality, such barrios were adjacent to El Segundo Barrio but Buffalo Bayou acted as a natural boundary to separate one community from the other. Thus, early in its history, the Houston colonia found itself fragmented in a way not seen in other Texas cities. Warehouses and other physical structures situated amid immense railroad yards acted as further psychological barriers separating one component settlement from another. By the late 1910s, indeed, two separate celebrations of the Diez y Seis were being held.[51]

Meantime, a new barrio sprouted amidst the previously all white neighborhood of Magnolia Park. This suburb of Magnolia Park took form in 1911 as people from other states began settling near the basin readying for work on the enlargement of the Ship Channel.[52] The origins of the barrio in this southeastern part of Houston some four miles from the downtown area, and about two miles from the nearest Mexican barrio, lay apparently in the call for workers at the Houston Ship Channel, completed

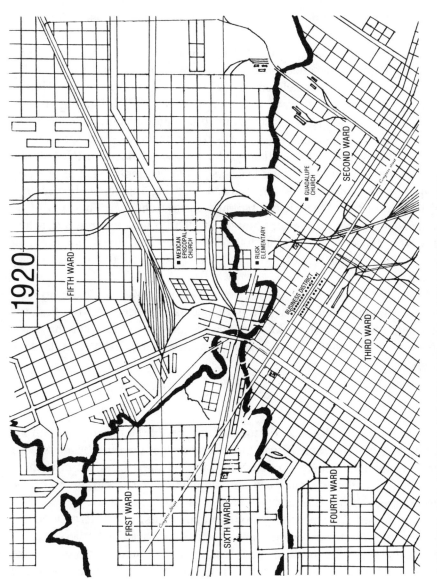

1920

FIFTH WARD

MEXICAN
EPISCOPAL
CHURCH

RUSK
ELEMENTARY

GUADALUPE
CHURCH

SECOND WARD

BUSINESS DISTRICT

THIRD WARD

FIRST WARD

SIXTH WARD

FOURTH WARD

MEXICAN SETTLEMENTS IN HOUSTON, 1920

in 1914. Its first settlers improvised their housing just as others were doing elsewhere in Houston. Some established residence in that part of Magnolia (Avenue K and Avenue L and 77th Street) filled in by sand dredged from the turning basin. Appropriately, they referred to it as *"El Arenal"* ("the Sands").[53]

Anglo residents of Magnolia Park, mostly of the middle class, tolerated the Mexican presence since it was a labor source, but feared seeing the neighborhood overwhelmed. In 1920, indeed, trustees of the Harrisburg school district had plans underway to erect a brick building at 75th Street and Avenue H because about 100 children were attending the schools of Magnolia and Central Parks. None of the teachers spoke Spanish, and to overcome the difficulty, the trustees decided on the separate school where Spanish-speaking teachers would be employed. But property owners in the neighborhood threatened to bring injunction proceedings against the trustees to halt the building of the school.[54] This was of no avail, however, for during the summer of 1920, a neat two-room structure of white stucco was built at 700 75th Street and given the name of Lorenzo de Zavala school. At that time it belonged to the Harrisburg District.[55]

At that early period, the barrio of Magnolia was too young to have its own Church. Situated there was Immaculate Conception, but this was an Anglo church in which Mexicans were not allowed to enter the pews. Those who did attend mass had to remain standing even if seats were available.[56]

Obreros

Within easy distance of the barrios established near the railroad yards (Magnolia excepted) was to be found a germinating business zone along Congress Avenue. From what can be gleaned from the city directory of 1920, the nascent business community was small, most of the businesses probably being only a few years old. Also, there seems not to have been much competition among entrepreneurs; one enterprise seems to have met the needs of the Spanish-speakers, save for barbers. Lastly, the businesses were more or less located in the same vicinity near or within the central city. Such patterns foreshadowed the future emergence of Congress Avenue as the "commercial district" of the colonia.

That the business community during this early era was not large is reflective both of the nascent development of the Hispanic colonia and the aforementioned poverty of its inhabitants. Though there were some who were fortunate in finding a niche in the professions—a Mrs. E. M. Tafolla and Professor J. J. Mercado were teachers of Spanish in the public schools of the 1910s[57]—the mass of Mexicanos was kept from the more lucrative occupations generated by Houston's good fortune. Instead, they were relegated to low-grade occupations. "When I arrived in Houston in 1913," recalled Juan C. Hernández, an immigrant from Piedras Negras, "the most available jobs for Mexicanos were in *'el sure'* (sewerage), *'el traque'* (railroad), and *'la labor'* (the fields)."[58]

This was another way of saying that the good jobs opening up for other Houstonians escaped the newcomers. The directories of the era indicate high representation in blue collar, low-paying occupations, with railroad work being among those jobs most available. More telling of such conditions was the presence of a good percentage of the Mexican labor force in the category of "laborer," the catch-all term that identified *jornaleros* (day laborers) who did everything from construction work to laying track. But essential as the labor of Mexicans was to the railroad companies, remuneration was hardly commensurate with the toil. Juan C. Hernández elaborated:

> En los 1910s, los sueldos eran muy pequeños. Los mecanicos de primera ganaban cuarenta centavos la hora por diez horas de trabajo. Yo comencé de aprendiz de herrero por veinte y cinco centavos la hora, por diez horas.[59]

> In the 1910s, the salaries were very low. Mechanics of first class earned forty cents an hour for ten hours of work. I started as a blacksmith apprentice for twenty-five cents an hour, for ten hours.

In the cotton compresses, textile mills, and construction companies, pay could not have been much more of an improvement. Moreover, Mexicans faced job insecurity. Organized labor refused to countenance any threats from competitors. In April, 1914, for example, a delegate from the Sheet Metal Workers remonstrated before the Houston Labor Council that "Mexican and other foreign" labor was being used in city work.[60] Later that month, the Labor Council complained to the county judge and commissioners' court that public improvements should be reserved "to the citizens of this community . . . [who] should not be compelled to stand in enforced idleness and want while watching this work being done by a horde of Mexican laborers . . . who are fast driving white and black labor to want and poverty. . . ."[61] Mexican workers were practically powerless against such attitudes for there is little indication of labor organizing efforts involving Mexicanos in Houston during this period. There did exist, however, some representation in local unions.[62]

A Budding Colonia

In the first score of years of the twentieth century, thus, Mexicans whose interest in Houston had been seemingly peripheral for so long, entrenched themselves permanently in this southeastern Texas city. In that time, during which the community consisted so heavily of *inmigrantes* from Mexico, survival seemed the issue of most urgent concern. Disadvantaged in language and technical skills, newcomers survived by taking whatever jobs availed themselves. Forced to assume the less desirable occupations in the economy's secondary sector, they were thrust into a position which would lead to uneven growth between themselves and those profiting from Houston's bountifulness. Those chancing their own future as entrepreneurs might have fared better, but their dependence on consumers from the colonia restricted them to an economy outside the one gradually becoming part of an international economic order.

A colonia of *inmigrantes*, comprised of both exiled *ricos* and lower-class common folks, quite naturally maintained an interest in the affairs of Mexico. Thus, the budding colonia's consciousness during this time period was much Mexican and less American. But as noted, Houston Mexicanos simultaneously kept abreast of events transpiring in the state. Their interest in the Primer Congreso Mexicanista, in the imprisoned status of Gregorio Cortez, and in the Plan de San Diego indicate political transition. It also shows a willingness to take active roles in efforts to improve conditions for their fellow man. That similar expressions of dissent were not displayed in Houston proper may have been in keeping with the city's history of activist silence. In general, the early history of Mexicans in Houston was a prelude to an experience of constant cultural change and a cautious confrontation with institutions they both respected and distrusted.

NOTES

[1]Marilyn McAdams Sibley, *The Port of Houston: A History,* pp. 12–13.
[2]Eldon Stephen Branda (ed.), *The Handbook of Texas: A Supplement,* III, p. 740.
[3]Sibley, *Port of Houston,* p. 15.
[4]David J. Weber, *The Mexican Frontier: The American Southwest Under Mexico, 1821–1846,* pp. 155–156.
[5]Sibley, *Port of Houston,* pp. 23–24.

[6]Ibid., pp. 23–24; Raymond Estep, *Lorenzo de Zavala: Profeta del Liberalismo Mexicano*, p. 295.

[7]Andrew Forest Muir (ed.), *Texas in 1837: An Anonymous Contemporary Narrative*, pp. 6–7.

[8]Thomas Lloyd Miller, *Bounty and Donation Land Grants of Texas, 1835–1888*, pp. 187, 258, 433, 628, 629; and, Thomas Lloyd Miller, "Mexican Texans in the Texas Revolution," *Journal of Mexican American History*, III (1973).

[9]George Shelley, "The Semicolon Court of Texas," *Southwestern Historical Quarterly*, XLVIII (April, 1945), 457.

[10]Dr. O. F. Allen, *The City of Houston From Wilderness to Wonder*, pp. 1–2.

[11]Max Freund (ed.), *Gustav Dresel's Houston Journal: Adventures in North America and Texas, 1837–1841*, p. 33.

[12]*The Morning Star*, Houston, Texas, September 26, 1839, p. 2.

[13]Mary Susan Jackson, "The People of Houston in the 1850s" (Ph. D. Dissertation, Indiana University, 1974), p. 61.

[14]Hand count of the census made by the author.

[15]Feagin, "The Socioeconomic Base of Urban Growth," p. 19.

[16]Robert E. Zeigler, "The Workingman in Houston, Texas, 1865–1914" (Ph. D. Dissertation, Texas Tech University, 1972), pp. 124–127.

[17]Lee C. Harby, "Texan Types and Contrasts," *Harper's New Monthly Magazine*, vol. 81 (June, 1890), 230–232.

[18]*Directory of the City of Houston, 1894–1895*.

[19]The estimate is made from scrutinizing the hand count made by students at the University of Houston. See "Hispanic Persons in the Federal Census of 1900, Harris County, Texas," held in Houston Public Library, Houston Metropolitan Research Center (hereinafter referred to as HMRC).

[20]*Directory of the City of Houston, 1900*; and, "Hispanic Persons in the Federal Census of 1900, Harris County, Texas."

[21]The estimate is made from scrutinizing the hand count made by students at the University of Houston. See "Hispanic Persons in the Federal Census of 1910, Harris County, Texas," held in Houston Public Library, HMRC.

[22]Harold L. Platt, "Houston at the Crossroads: The Emergence of the Urban Center of the Southwest," *Journal of the West*, XVIII (July, 1979), 53–56.

[23]Feagin, "Socioeconomic Base of Urban Growth," pp. 10–11.

[24]Victor S. Clark, "Mexican labor in the United States" (from Department of Commerce and Labor, Bureau of Labor *Bulletin*, No. 78, Washington D.C., 1908) reprinted in Carlos E. Cortes (ed.), *Mexican Labor in the United States*.

[25]Houston *Chronicle*, Houston, Texas, August 10, 1908, p. 5; January 22, 1906, p. 8; May 10, 1910, p. 12.

[26]Ibid., November 11, 1904, p. 22.

[27]Zeigler, "Workingman in Houston," p. 53.

[28]Houston *Chronicle*, January 16, 1906, p. 5; September 9, 1906, p. 16. Notice of Mercado's death is announced in ibid., October 14, 1950, p. 7A.

[29]Ibid., May 1, 1908, p. 11.

[30]*Campo Laurel*, #2333 W. O. W., Marzo 2, 1908, typescript, Small Collection, HMRC. Also, HMRC Oral History Collection, Juan C. Hernández, November 19, 1978, interview with Thomas H. Kreneck. Unless otherwise stated, all interviews used in this

text were conducted by Thomas H. Kreneck and are part of the HMRC Oral History Collection, Houston Public Library.

[31]Houston *Chronicle,* September 17, 1907, p. 11; September 16, 1908, p. 3; September 17, 1908, p. 5.

[32]Rosales, "Mexicans in Houston: The Struggle to Survive," p. 227.

[33]See for example, HMRC Oral History Collection, interviews with Juan C. Hernández; Rodrigo García, July 10, 1979; and Ralph and Mary Villagómez, April 16, 1979.

[34]Ibid., Juan C. Hernández interview.

[35]Houston *Chronicle,* April 14, 1914, p. 2.

[36]Corrinne S. Tsanoff, *Neighborhood Doorways,* p. 1.

[37]Barry J. Kaplan, "Race, Income, and Ethnicity: Residential Change in a Houston Community, 1920–1970," *The Houston Review,* III (Winter, 1981), 185.

[38]*Galveston Daily News,* Galveston, Texas, December 10, 1911, p. 26.

[39]The study of Elaine H. Maas, "The Jews of Houston: An Ethnographic Study" (Ph. D. Dissertation, Rice University, 1973), p. 50, however, places the Jewish population in the Third Ward.

[40]Sister Mary Paul Valdez, *The History of the Missionary Catechists of Divine Providence,* pp. 2–4.

[41]Ibid., pp. 3–4, 5, 8–9.

[42]Tsanoff, *Neighborhood Doorways,* p. 7; Lynne W. Denison and L. L. Pugh, "Houston Public School Buildings: Their History and Location" (n. p., 1936), p. 133.

[43]Ibid., pp. 1–7.

[44]José E. Limón, "El Primer Congreso Mexicanista de 1911: A Precursor to Contemporary Chicanismo," *Aztlan,* V (Spring and Fall, 1974), 89, 104, 92–93, 95, 96.

[45]Américo Paredes, *"With His Pistol in His Hand": A Border Ballad and Its Hero,* p. 100.

[46]Rodolfo Rocha, "The Influence of the Mexican Revolution on the Mexico-Texas Border, 1910–1916" (Ph. D. Dissertation, Texas Tech University, 1981), 287, 291, 324, 344–345.

[47]Juan Gómez-Quiñones, "Piedras Contra La Luna, México en Aztlán y Aztlán en México: Chicano-Mexican Relations and the Mexican Consulates, 1900–1920," in James W. Wilkie, et al., *Contemporary Mexico: Papers of the IV International Congress of Mexican History,* pp. 516–517.

[48]Sister M. Agatha, *The History of Houston Heights, 1891–1918,* p. 30.

[49]Also, HMRC Oral History Collection, interview with Rodrigo García.

[50]Houston *Chronicle,* September 15, 1917, p. 4.

[51]Ibid., September 17, 1917, p. 5.

[52]Valdez, *History of Missionary Catechists,* p. 1.

[53]HMRC, Oral History Collection, interviews with Ralph and Mary Villagómez and Rodrigo García; "Detalles Generales del Poblado de Magnolia Y Su Incorporación a La Ciudad de Houston," HMRC, Mexican American Small Collection; *Magnolia Park Neighborhood Plan,* p. 2.

[54]Valdez, *History of Missionary Catechists,* p. 1; Houston *Chronicle,* March 1, 1920, p. 2.

[55]Denison and Pugh, "Houston Public School Buildings," p. 87.

[56]Valdez, *History of Missionary Catechists,* p. 6; HMRC Oral History Collection, interviews with Ralph and Mary Villagómez; and María Puente, October 26, 1978.

[57]Houston *Chronicle*, August 27, 1915, p. 11.

[58]HMRC Oral History Collection, interview with Juan C. Hernández, November 29, 1978.

[59]HMRC Oral History Collection, interview with Juan C. Hernández, November 29, 1978.

[60]Zeigler, "The Workingman in Houston," p. 186.

[61]James C. Maroney, "Organized Labor in Texas, 1900–1929" (Ph. D. Dissertation, University of Houston, 1975), p. 37.

[62]See for example, Emilio Zamora, "Mexican Labor Activity in South Texas, 1900–1920" (Ph. D. Dissertation, University of Texas at Austin, 1983), p. 204.

CHAPTER II
HOUSTON'S "LITTLE MEXICO":
A CITY WITHIN A CITY, 1920–1930

Refugees and exiles from Mexico and Texas-Mexican migrants solidified their presence in Houston during the 1920s. Increased numbers of immigrants and United States-born Mexicans streamed into the oil city during the decade to enlarge the flowering colonia. Many arrived forseeing a temporary stay. As the tailor Isidro García, who arrived in Houston in 1920, reminisced:

> At that time, many of us thought we would someday return to Mexico. We didn't want to become American citizens. Many of us also carried the idea with us that Mexico is wherever there's a Mexican and we didn't want to be disloyal to our fatherland.[1]

García and many others stayed permanently. The boom of the era seduced them with rising expectations, though in the end, that prosperity deceived them.

But the promise Houston held out seemed propitious, at least in comparison to the settings from which Mexicans departed. By the beginning of the decade, the city was well on its way to becoming an oil capital. Prodding it in that direction was the growing popularity of the automobile among Americans. Before the car emerged as a standard of American culture, crude oil had served mainly for kerosene, fuel oil, and lubricants. But with some eighteen million vehicles registered in the country by the mid-1920s, the demand for motor fuel rose dramatically. The more Detroit mass-produced cars, the more rapidly the major oil companies around Houston were inspired towards further development.

Other industries simultaneously came to rely on fuel oil and lubricants. Locomotives and industrial plants switched from coal to oil, for example. With new capital made available from gasoline and fuel oil sales, oil companies built numerous refineries and other oil-related industrial facilities in the Houston area in order to be near critical raw materials and to reduce transportation costs. From 1920 onward, the Gulf Coast oil economy had integrated itself into the national economy. The new job opportunities created by the expansion attracted workers from everywhere, including Mexico.[2]

Not surprisingly, the most rapid growth in the city's history occurred during this era. Between 1920 and 1930, the city grew by more than 111 percent, from 139,000 to 292,000 people.[3] A parallel increase in the Mexican population also took place; it is estimated that the number of Mexican-origin people jumped from 6,000 to about 15,000 in 1930, an intercensal increase of some 150%, greater than the rest of the city's overall population and still a record for intercensal increase as of the 1980s.[4]

In actuality, forces pushing people from Mexico and pulling factors from within the city account for this dramatic rise of population. Though the warring dimension of the Mexican Revolution had ceased by 1920, aspects of *La Tormenta* (as the storm or "reign of terror" in Mexico's Revolution is referred to) persisted as the new leaders in the country sought to implement the different goals of the Revolution. Efforts at carrying out land reform and the anti-clerical provisions of the Constitution of 1917 perpetuated an unstable environment which disrupted life and dislodged many from the most affected area.

Into Houston, therefore, streamed Tejanos from other parts of the state. Accompanying them in greater proportions were Mexican immigrants from both the middle and working classes. The majority trekked toward Houston by whatever means; people from the populous west central states of Guanajuato, Jalisco, and Michoacán were highly represented among the immigrant population.[5] A report on illiteracy issued in 1923 determined that the foreign-born Mexican population of Harris County in 1920 was approximately 5,500.[6] There is, of course, need to use caution with such figures, but even with that consideration, it is obvious that an overwhelming majority of those in the Houston area were not of native birth.

Contemporaries of the period, furthermore, verified such a fact. As the *Gaceta Mexicana*, a Spanish-language newspaper in the city noted in 1928 about *"La Librería Hispano-Americana,"* a local business: "está relacionada con las luchas y sacrificos de tantos y tantos compatriotas que han salido de la patria a causa de la guerra civil'' (it is related to the struggles and sacrifices of so many of our compatriots who have left the nation [Mexico] due to the civil war [created by the aforementioned causes].[7] The Catholic Church, experiencing parish increases, especially in Our Lady of Guadalupe Parish, also recognized the origins of the new arrivals, perceiving the flow as made up of exiles fleeing religious persecution in Mexico. It sought to accommodate them by finding housing for them, improving facilities at Our Lady of Guadalupe School, and assuring them of their right to practice their Catholicism without the problems Mexico was encountering.[8]

Dispersals

As they arrived in Houston, the immigrants gravitated toward the nascent enclaves which had formed in the 1910s. In the Second Ward where Anglos had continued to live throughout the 1910s in fine homes within the area embracing Commerce, Congress, and some of the adjoining streets, Mexicanos took over vacated homes and turned them into rooming houses. With consolidation taking place there, the real push of the neighborhood was in a direction away from the downtown district and Guadalupe Church.[9] The Northside or Fifth Ward saw increased density but growth occurred away from the place of the early settlements around the railroad yards toward the northeast between White Oak Bayou on the west and Buffalo Bayou on the south.

To the west of this Northside barrio, filling in occurred along both sides of Washington Avenue as this Mexican neighborhood pushed away from the downtown district and into homes which had become the residences of eastern and southern Europeans in the 1880s. In the Houston Heights addition, a barrio continued growing as some 100 families lived around the Oriental Textile Mills. It was augmented by other families that made their living in other mills that produced cotton oil and peanut oil. This particular enclave was isolated not only in distance but in that it did not have churches nor schools specifically intended for its Spanish-speaking inhabitants.[10]

Greatest growth, perhaps surpassing that in El Segundo Barrio, took place in Magnolia. During the early years of the 1920s, it remained a fledgling barrio of unpaved streets and homes which lacked water, light, and gas service. But by the time the Magnolia suburb was incorporated into Houston on October 18, 1926, Magnolia was well on its way to containing "the largest of the local Mexican settlements," as a local newspaper article put it.[11]

By the 1920s, therefore, the pattern of today's major barrios in Houston had taken form and future immigrants into the city came to live within these settlements. While a common culture bound Mexicans together throughout the city, division of the several neighborhoods caused by distance as well as physical and psychological barriers caused people to identify more closely with their immediate neighborhoods and to differentiate themselves from others. As two Houstonians recalled about their days in Magnolia Park during the 1920s:

> The Second Ward people attended their own theatre on Congress Avenue. The Second Ward people were different. Most were native born. They were "Tejanos" as we used to call them. Their ways were different. We were from Mexico. They were of a different type.[12]

Demographically speaking, such a statement may have been unfounded. But those in Magnolia saw things otherwise.

Comerciantes and Obreros

But among the things which the several barrios had in common during the 1920s was the downtown commercial district. As already noted, this business section was within walking distance of each central city barrio despite the divisions created by Buffalo Bayou and the railroad yards. Its anchor points were the 1700 and 2100 blocks of Congress Avenue. There, Mexicano businessmen attended to "the inhabitants of this part of 'Little Mexico'," noted the Houston *Chronicle* in 1930. "There are drug stores, hotels, cafes, doctors' offices, dentists' offices, dry goods stores, jewelry shops, filling stations, grocery stores, bakery shops and innumerable other small shops."[13] Economically, they serviced a clientele ignored by Anglo merchants; socially, they filled a need as places of association.

By the latter 1920s Magnolia itself had developed a business district. "Its 'Avenida Madero' is Navigation Boulevard," noted the *Chronicle*. Business houses there included drug stores, restaurants, private offices, filling stations, grocery stores, bakeries, a Spanish talkie theatre, barber shops, furniture and dry goods stores, "all named in Spanish and conducted by Mexicans," the paper observed.[14]

Those who patronized the business districts were usually common folks present in Houston as part of a working force occupying those low-grade occupations generated by the city's booming oil economy. As in the

1910s, the railroads continued being among the major recruiters of Mexican workers. Also hiring Mexican help were the several companies affiliated with the Houston Ship Channel. Those living in the Magnolia Barrio worked in nearby refineries, compresses and other wharf and Ship Channel industries. The women were employed in textile mills, factories, and stores.[15]

Houston businesses by the 1920s desired Mexican labor not only for its cost but because of the virtues *obreros* displayed in the work place. As the Mexican consul in Houston reported to his superiors in late 1921: "One of the most prominent city officials indicated to me that Houston ought to congratulate itself on having at its disposal, for such a low wage, the necessary Mexican workers to perform public works of great utility and urgency."[16] A survey done by the National Urban League in 1929 found similar attitudes among employers. According to the final report, Mexicans were noticeably replacing blacks in unskilled and semi-skilled jobs. In part, this was due to the fact that blacks in Houston had experienced an improvement in jobs during World War I and were now leaving dirty jobs and hard work to Mexicans and recent arrivals. But more significantly, said the report, the rise in Mexican population indicated that there were many employers who preferred Mexican labor because of its reliability, dependability, and punctuality.[17]

Social Conditions

Such accolades hardly made up for the social conditions Mexican Houstonians faced. For as contemporaries recalled, racial prejudice during the period was as prevalent in Houston as anywhere else and Jim Crow codes applicable to black people extended to Mexicans. Mexican Americans in the 1920s were denied access to nearly all public and private establishments owned by Anglos, from restaurants to ballrooms.[18]

Institutionalized segregation, furthermore, resembled that documented for other parts of the state.[19] Originally, housing segregation grew out of the circumstances wherein Mexicans came into neighborhoods and through a process of encroachment in a period of economic prosperity displaced Anglos already prepared to leave the inner city for emerging suburbs. Once left in the several barrios, however, Mexicans were kept there through a variety of forces, including tacit agreements by real estate developers not to sell or rent to Mexicans, perhaps a personal preference to live among those who shared a common culture, and poverty which limited their resources to purchase a home outside the inexpensive homes of the barrios.

Whatever the causes of segregation, the neighborhoods wherein Mexicans lived were spotted by deplorable conditions which were described by social reformers, journalists, policemen, and casual observers of "Little Mexico" as among the worst to be seen in any major city. In contrast to the frame houses and paved streets of the Anglo neighborhoods, Mexicans lived under distressing conditions in El Segundo Barrio. There, some inhabitants lived without privacy and proper sanitary conditions in homes converted into boarding home arrangements or in makeshift homes erected along the banks of Buffalo Bayou. In the middle of the 1920s, the area behind Rusk Settlement consisted of slums, among them the notorious "Schrimpf Alley."[20]

In the rest of the colonia, residents fared little better. In Magnolia, dusty streets of clay or gravel stretched away from the paved boulevards. There inhabitants lived for the most part in crowded substandard dwelling units which were scantily furnished and surrounded by outside privies.[21]

Socializing Institutions

Amidst these dire conditions, Houston's Mexicans became active in community institutions which extended them a hand for self-improvement. Schools, religious organizations and voluntary associations played active roles in the barrios and attempted the residents' enculturation into mainstream traditions. Youngsters hardly lacked for education, although the institutions they attended were invariably substandard. In the course of demographic change, white schools had been left behind to Mexicans; consequently, school buildings were second-class and normally segregated. Thus, every barrio had the presence of a local "Mexican School" which generally serviced only the younger children, for in Houston as elsewhere, unwritten rules discouraged promotion into the junior high schools.

In the 1920s, those living in El Segundo Barrio continued attending the three-story red brick Rusk School on Maple Street.[22] In the Northside, children went to the old Elysian Street School, or Jones Elementary at 914 Elysian.[23] In the First and Sixth Wards, school children received instruction at two schools: the Dow Elementary School at 1912 Lubbock and the Hawthorne Elementary School at 1417 Houston.[24]

Magnolia's elementary students attended the Mexican school built for them in 1920. As the barrio grew, expansion became necessary. In the latter part of the decade, more classroom space was added and additional playground space provided in order to accommodate the expanding student body.[25] There were those in Magnolia, however, who preferred private education and so, a private school also functioned there. Named *La Escuela Mexicana "Hidalgo,"* it was supported by families desiring to see their children maintain ties to their native culture.[26]

While Mexicans appreciated the learning opportunities extended to them in Houston, at the same time they were not oblivious to the fact that facilities were inferior and segregated; many resented the degrading policies such as "no Spanish" rules. Thus, as an Americanizing agency, the Houston schools taught not only the positive aspect of the American culture, but simultaneously indoctrinated newcomers on the uglier dimensions of American life.

The work of the Catholic Church also exposed Mexicans to the ways of the new setting. In the Second Ward, work continued to be carried on at Our Lady of Guadalupe where brisk expansion took place in the first half of the decade. The same kind of growth extended to Our Lady of Guadalupe School, still under the tutelage of Sister Benitia. More nuns were added to the staff. With the building of the new church, the original frame church-school building was remodeled and used for school and social purposes. By 1929, more than 400 children were taught by eight sisters. There they submitted to socialization as the language of instruction was English.[27]

In Magnolia, people were without a church during the early 1920s and rode the streetcars into Our Lady of Guadalupe. In 1925, however, the Segundo Barrio Church Parish was divided and, thus, bore the new church when a priest from Guadalupe was assigned to begin a congregation in Magnolia. Initially, a two-story private home located on 71st and Navigation served as a temporary chapel. Ultimately, enough funds were raised to build another two-story building at 700 75th Street. On November 8, 1926, it became the place of worship and was given the name of Immaculate Heart of Mary. Two years later, the new parish acquired a parochial school.[28]

Several Protestant churches were also active in the barrios. A Mexican Baptist Church, located at 2505 Canal, held many social and religious activities. In Magnolia Barrio, a Mexican Presbyterian Church, 7535 Avenue L, and a Mexican Holy Roller Church (Pentecostal) were active. Elsewhere, a Mexican Presbyterian Church was located at 915 Houston, and on the Northside, the Mexican Methodist Episcopal Church at 1110 McKee carried on proselytizing activities.[29]

Also an arm of mainstream society was the Rusk Settlement Association which increased its involvement and continued its Americanizing

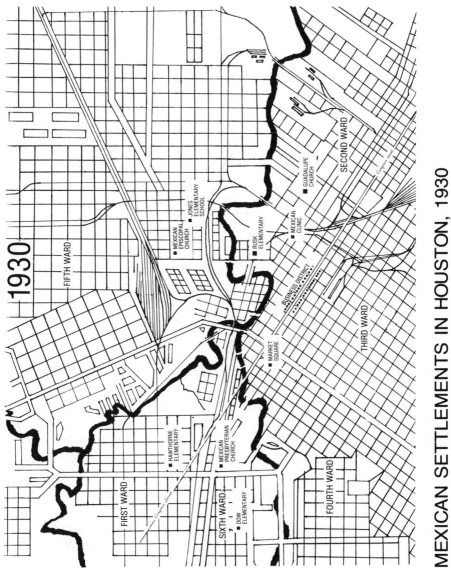

1930

FIFTH WARD

SECOND WARD

FIRST WARD

SIXTH WARD

FOURTH WARD

THIRD WARD

HAWTHORNE ELEMENTARY

MEXICAN PRESBYTERIAN CHURCH

DOW ELEMENTARY

MARKET SQUARE

BUSINESS DISTRICT

MEXICAN EPISCOPAL CHURCH

JONES ELEMENTARY SCHOOL

RUSK ELEMENTARY

MEXICAN CLINIC

GUADALUPE CHURCH

MEXICAN SETTLEMENTS IN HOUSTON, 1930

drive in the barrios. As an institution dedicated to helping the underprivileged, the Association made available numerous facilities. The Settlement Home, situated next door to Rusk School, offered a playroom, kitchen, club rooms, and a library. For girls and women, there were cooking classes which taught American methods of homemaking, cooking, cleaning, sewing and family rearing. For all, lessons in Americanisms were stressed, especially English writing—night classes were for men and afternoon classes for women. For the mothers, practical things were emphasized—learning names of foods, clothing, furniture, or how to ask for prices. For the young, Girl Scout and Boy Scout troops were organized. Additionally, free baths were given, a nursery school made available, and recruitment drives undertaken to keep children in school. For the other barrios, the Association opened clubs in Jones, Hawthorne, and Dow Schools in the 1920s.[30]

To what degree the Association succeeded in its work is difficult to gauge. There was always too much work to be done and the Settlement workers were too few in numbers. With new people entering the barrios so regularly, moreover, the Settlement could only reach a small percentage of the target group. But while its social impact may have been slight, its presence loomed prominently as a symbol of Americanization.

Further extending a helping hand and bringing Mexicans in contact with mainstream life was a free clinic established in El Segundo Barrio. Founded in 1924 as a response to the alarming mortality rate among Mexican infants, it was maintained by the National Council of Catholic Women. The Mexican Clinic first opened in a rented building in the 1900 block of Franklin Street with local doctors donating their services and Catholic parishes and individual donating funds. From there, however, the Mexican Clinic was transferred to 1909 Canal and by the late 1920s had won support from charitable organizations. It was a non-profit organization for rendering medical aid and services to indigent persons, regardless of race, color, or creed.

Several doctors worked out of the clinic, treating infirmities of every sort, even performing operations. Prenatal care was available and nurses spent much time visiting homes attending to sick babies, taking milk and medicine to homes lacking them, and suggesting ways of taking proper care of infants.[31]

The impact that these and other mainstream institutions had on Mexicans may have been slight as of the 1920s, but it was apparent to outsiders. A reporter for the Houston *Chronicle* already saw a distinction between the older generation and the new in 1930. While the older women might have worn a *mantilla,* the young girls wore the "same chic styles in vogue among American girls," he noted. The older inhabitants born in Mexico may have liked lotteries and the other amusements of their native land, but their sons and daughters went in for the American equivalents with the same enthusiasm that their parents displayed for the old customs. "The young generation," the journalist elaborated, "educated in the city public schools, playmates with the Americans, have learned the American ways. The younger residents of Little Mexico have become little Americans."[32]

Self-Help Organizations

Even as adjustment to American customs and traditions occurred, the generation of folks that resided in the several barrios were too closely tied to the past to forsake the values of the mother country completely. Throughout the 1920s, therefore, Mexicans in Houston regularly expressed concern for the welfare of *"la patria"* and its people, and despite their displacement, sought to perpetuate old ways. In January 1920, for instance, the colonia formed an association in efforts to raise funds for the relief of survivors of an earthquake which had just hit Mexico. Dances and entertainments were planned and the proceeds were forwarded to the temblor's victims.[33] Also, the message of *"la patria querida"* was received with attention even as many settled into Houston's American life. The Mexican consul carried on that message as did other emissaries from the Mexican government who periodically journeyed to Houston on official business and took time off to address the Mexican colony. So it was when Señor Luis Montes de Oca, representing the president of Mexico, spoke before the Mexican colony in late 1920. He felt comfortable in inviting the Mexicans to return to their native country now that things were pacified. However, he urged those who preferred to stay in the United States to so live and act as "to hold the friendship of Americans and gain their friendship *for your native land."* Assistance was readily available to Mexicanos, de Oca noted, from the Mexican consul in Houston.[34]

Further emphasizing the attachment that the Mexicans of Houston retained with Mexico were social associations organized throughout the 1920s, among them mutual aid societies. Such mutual aid and fraternal insurance companies were not restricted to Houston Mexicanos, nor for that matter, Mexicanos throughout the United States. Rather, they were part of a widespread movement involving many different nationalities which was begot by industrialization and the migration of people from the

31

countryside to the cities. Cut off from traditional networks of support, immigrants and urban-dwellers replaced old supportive systems with such organizations as fraternal societies, for these helped them survive in an alien and often hostile environment.[35]

In Houston proper, only one fraternal organization existed before the late 1910s, that being the aforementioned Campo Laurel No. 2333, and which, according to some of its founding members, went on to become "el decano de todas las organizaciones de habla española en el Condado de Harris" (the dean of all Spanish-speaking organizations in Harris County) for having spurred other W.O.W. lodges (by 1920, there existed another lodge in Houston, El Campo Roble, No. 6, *Leñadores del Mundo*) as well as other civic and social groups.[36] However, there existed in the city a desperate need for a mutual aid society which placed greater emphasis on *"lo mexicano."* Apparently, the WOW did not appeal to the new arrivals as would a Mexican oriented mutual aid society. According to a recent study, the *Leñadores* was a bit more attractive to those of middle income status. "Those who wore the Masonic ring always had 'good jobs.'"[37] Most obreros in Houston were not that fortunate.

Such an association with a Mexican orientation was established in May 1919 when sixteen Mexicans met in Magnolia Park to found the *Sociedad Mutualista Mexicana "Benito Juárez"* (whether its members previously had any ties with Campo Laurel #2333 is unknown). Expressive of their cultural allegiance were several distinctive features of the Mutualista "Benito Juárez." First, it carried the name of a national hero from Mexico: Benito Juárez was the great president who held the country together during the 1850s and 1860s despite civil turmoil and invasion by the French. Moreover, Juárez was the "Mexican" personified: an Indian from the state of Oaxaca who embodied the idealism of Mexico's new revolutionary order. Second, the society's specific purpose was to assist other "mexicanos" in the functions of mutualistas elsewhere: caring for members during times of illness or death, encouraging intellectual inquiry and stimulation within the group, and working for the betterment of the community (as time would show, this meant sponsoring or supporting social activities such as dances, barbecues, and celebration of fiestas patrias).[38] Third, the language preferred by the group was Spanish—a tongue with which the members felt quite comfortable, judging from the lofty tone employed in writing the *Reglamento*. Specifically, the emblem would be a banner with the picture of Benito Juárez and the group's motto *"Unión y Progreso."*

32

Further manifest of the society's Mexican links were those things the Mutualista "Benito Juárez" did not represent. Its Mexican organizers were not interested in assimilation: they did not display an incipient Americanization; instead the stress was on Mexican ideals and values. Nor were they confrontationalist in their philosophy. To the contrary, the mutualist was basically defensive: it sought to look out for its own, tried to establish a degree of social cohesion, offered spiritual reinforcement to a working-class people, and provided some sense of familiarity in an adopted world.[39]

Equally expressive of the Houston Mexican community's ties to roots in Mexico were cultural and recreative clubs, the most prominent and successful during the 1920s being the *Club Cultural Recreativo "México Bello."* Its origins go back to 1924 (it still exists today) when a handful of young men came together in the Northside (Fifth Ward) barrio to discuss the notion of a social club intended to fill a void arising from a "nostalgia for their native country." The very name of the club "México Bello" ("Beautiful Mexico") revealed the members' sentiments. So did its goals: through "México Bello" the traditions and customs of the mother country would be preserved and the name of Mexico kept sound and safe. The motto of the organization also held up tradition and name: *Raza, Patria, e Idioma* (Race, Country, and Language). The green, red and white colors of Mexico for the club's emblem would reinforce heritage and allegiance. To emphasize the link to a true Mexico, furthermore, cultural affairs would be put together *"para defundir el idioma castellano"* (to perpetuate the "Castillian" language). In addition to its cultural objectives, Club "México Bello" intended to look after the physical welfare of its members, organize recreational activities (in the 1920s, this included presenting dramas, holding picnics, and going on boatrides out at the Ship Channel), and sponsor dances on a periodic basis.[40]

In actuality, the club was born not only from nostalgia for the old country, but also from the racism of the 1920s. Not only did it try to preserve the good attributes of Mexico, but also to present an appearance of "civility" among the people of Mexico residing in Houston; this would be done by "nuestros actos, nobleza e irreprochable conducta" (our acts, nobility, and irreproachable conduct). "There was a great deal of discrimination in those days and we wanted to do something to benefit the Mexican American community," recalled an early member. "We wanted to present our culture and our heritage to Anglo-Saxon society." Thus, cultural activities would be vehicles by which stereotypes and prejudice might be combated, and to that end, Club "México Bello" in 1927 began holding formal black and white dances in prominent halls as an effort to display the "proper behavior" of Mexicans. Once Anglos saw Mexicans for what they really were, they would accept Mexicanos on their own terms, according to this logic. In a similar vein, the club sought to direct its efforts of comportment to the barrio community. By flaunting their own Mexicanness, they hoped to remove the stigma of shame felt by fellow Mexicanos as a result of the blatant discrimination. There was nothing shameful about *"México Bello."*[41]

The founders and members of Club "México Bello" were hardly upper class elites attracted to each other by their social standing. In fact, many were working class folks, some from the railroad yards, attracted to the club primarily because of its emphasis on "lo mexicano." Others were of more prominence, attracted by its cultural and nationalistic theme.[42]

Other organizations co-existed with Club "México Bello" as recreative groups, mostly catering to young men and boys. That was the case with the *Club Deportivo Azteca,* an athletic club which met in the Second Ward near Rusk School and emphasized baseball and soccer. As in the case of "México Bello," the name "Azteca" was a throwback to the homeland, as was the emphasis of the club rules that business be conducted in Spanish.[43]

La Patria Querida

Also oriented towards their native land were a group of businessmen, most of them concentrated in the commercial district around Congress Avenue, who were conspicuous by their open proclamation as "Mexicans." Most probably, they were middle class refugees. Part of what is known about them comes from the *Gaceta Mexicana.* Published by José Sarabia, himself an immigrant from Mexico, the paper in September 1928 issued a special edition which gave tribute to the work and achievements of the business community of immigrants and exiles who had recently left continued troubles in Mexico and come to Houston. According to the descriptions provided by the *Gaceta,* the community of men who managed enterprises ranging from commercial establishments, pharmacies, and medical practices, consisted of well-educated proprietors and managers, some having received their education in well-respected universities in Mexico. At least a part of them considered their presence in Houston as temporary; commenting about Sr. Pánfilo Tellez, proprietor of the El Fenix restaurant, the *Gaceta* noted: "Tellez es de los compatriotas que al regresar a la Patria pueden decir con orgullo: 'Fuí a luchar y luché; me hice el propósito de triunfar y triunfé' " ("Mr. Tellez is one those compatriots who, upon returning to Mexico, may say with pride: 'I went to struggle and did; I made it a point to triumph, and did' ").

By the very nature of their business, the community of recently arrived Mexicans fostered and carried on "lo mexicano." Despite the qualifications of many, there were limits to what they could do in Houston: namely, they could not penetrate the greater city's commercial circle. Not integrated into the class structure of Anglo society, they directed their services instead to the colonia. Advertisement was in Spanish—"La Botica Guadalupana," "La Panadería Cuauhtemoc," "Teatro Azteca" read some of the business signs. Doctors (the *Gaceta* profiled five of them) attended a Mexican clientele. In its *departamento bancario*, "La Sultana" of Sr. Gonzalo Mancillas, sold bank drafts from several foreign exchange markets in Mexico and bought and sold Mexican currency, services crucial to those in Houston wanting to send money to their folks back in Mexico. Similarly, "La Librería Hispano-Americana" (a combination curio shop, library, and printing establishment at 1811 Congress owned by the four Sarabia brothers from the valle de Santiago in the state of Guanajuato, México), which was closely connected (as it put it), "to the struggles and sacrifices of so many of our compatriots who have left our country due to the civil war," sold a variety of literary works including magazines, Spanish-language newspaper weeklies, but most importantly *El Universal* and *Excelsior* of Mexico City.

Ideologically, the above men of business and education proclaimed their Mexicanismo by their actions and demeanor. Some assumed leadership roles in the colonia, others displayed it by taking important positions in the patriotic committees entrusted with the responsibility of commemorating significant national holidays of Mexico. Others expressed it by their comportment. As the *Gaceta* noted of one of the persons it profiled:

> Su carateristica principal es la firmeza con que sostiene su nacionalidad, pues él como sus hermanos aquí radicados son mexicanos puros y los proclaman con orgullo.

> His principal characteristic is the firmness with which he bears his nationality, for he, as his brothers residing here, are true Mexicans and proclaim it with pride.[44]

As refugees, some of these men felt a duty to look out after their working class compatriots. They were pleased with the reaffirmation given them by the Chief of Police Tom C. Goodson during the course of an interview with the *Gaceta* in 1928. "I've always had a good concept of the Mexicans in Houston," the police chief commented. "According to our statistics, it is a small percentage of them who are involved in delinquency, though this is not true in the real sense of the word, for a good part of these are *American citizens* [they are Mexican Americans]." Apparently in response to problems with the authorities in Houston, but more specifically the police, Mexican leaders founded La Asamblea Mexicana in 1924. The organization, led by Fernando Salas and several other new arrivals, worked closely with the Mexican consul and sought to ensure that the proper guarantees were extended to Mexicans and that justice was given to those who for whatever reasons faced problems before the law.[45]

That the Asamblea worked closely with the *Consulado de México* pointed to still another Mexican connection; to wit, the uprooted saw in the consulate an institution which functioned as a source of protection— an accurate judgment, for indeed, Mexican consuls had been assigned to Houston since the beginning of the decade as the Mexican population increased. The consul for his part, labored assiduously in behalf of the interests of colonia residents.[46] He worked closely with the comite patrióticos in putting up the fiestas patrias and took a leading part in the holidays' commemorations, organized delegations of people from the barrios to receive officials visiting from Mexico, but more importantly,[47] tried to insure the well-being of those of Mexican birth. In response to recommendations made by Houston's mayor in 1921 that unemployed Mexicans in Houston should be repatriated in light of the fact that they were a burden on the city and the colonia, for example, Consul L. Garza Leal conducted a careful study of the employment status of Houston Mexicans. In his view, the Mexicans of Houston were doing well for themselves (the unemployment referred to by the mayor was temporary due to the winter). The only concern for the mother country ought to be for those living in extreme poverty. For their own well being, the consul advised, expatriation seemed a correct solution.[48]

More of a sense of how this element of refugees looked to Mexico for reinforcement comes from the philosophy found in the editorial comments of the *Gaceta Mexicana*. The gazette proclaimed itself as being a vehicle by which those commercial establishments in the city with a Mexican clientele might be given needed attention and publicity[49] and thus, it did little investigative reporting; as part of its limited format, it did print news about weddings, baptisms, anniversaries, and upcoming social events in the colonia. Occasionally, however, its publishers provided commentaries that revealed the spirit of "lo mexicano" felt by others in the 1920s.

The *Gaceta* employed the word "exile" freely as if to emphasize the understanding that Mexicans would still be in Mexico were circumstances different. Not surprisingly, therefore, constant references were made to Mexico as a point of reference for proper conduct, behavior, patriotism, and the like. Children were to be taught values the same as if they were in Mexico: to be good citizens, to earn their bread honorably, to respect the law, to take pride in their heritage and language, and to behave as educated individuals. The *Gaceta* understood the Americanizing effects that schools and other institutions had on children, but those things taught at home would temper that assimilation. Hence, Mexican Americans would retain the precious values of the motherland and ever project a favorable image of the Mexican character before American society.

Thus, like the members of Club "México Bello," the *Gaceta* sought to have Mexican Americans preserve and emphasize their Mexicanness. Those who violated the true values of the old country were unrepresentative of the Mexican character. This was a position that the publishers took in several of its commentaries, particularly one in June 1928 involving a recent conviction. The Mexican perpetrator, it stated, had committed an action that was not reflective of *"el carácter del mexicano."* Lest the wrong impression be given to the Anglo American community, steps had to be taken to distant the convict from *"los mexicanos honrados y trabajadores."* The *Gaceta* supported such efforts wholeheartedly.[50]

Whether other Spanish-language newspapers revealed a similar kind of sentiment is difficult to determine. Some six such newspapers reportedly serviced the colonia in Houston during the late 1920s, among the most prominent being the semi-weekly *El Tecolote* edited by Rodolfo Ávila de la Vega. This particular newspaper had been founded on December 24, 1924, and it continued production until the late Depression years; in 1930, its circulation was reported as averaging 3,000. Its columns carried political notes, songs and short stories, in a vein, perhaps, as the *Gaceta*. But like the rest of the newspapers, it is no longer extant.[51]

Helping further to perpetuate the spirit of Mexico in the 1920s was the existence of a Spanish-language theatre. "El Teatro Azteca," also owned by José Sarabia and located next to "La Librería Hispano-America," hosted plays of drama and comedies put on by traveling companies from Mexico. It was also a movie theatre where some of the more spectacular features in Spanish (according to its advertisement) were exhibited.[52]

National Holidays

Commemoration of the national holidays of Mexico, the *Cinco de Mayo* and the *Diez y Seis de Septiembre,* was continued with increased enthusiasm during the 1920s. The rise in population, for one thing, made available more people who would lend spiritual support to the festivities. Also, the presence of a consul to work closely with the Mexican colonia gave the patriotic committees and organizers the moral uplift which they had previously lacked. Then, the establishment of newspapers such as *El Tecolote* and the *Gaceta Mexicana* made possible the dissemination of information for the necessary preparations throughout the several barrios. Furthermore, the emergence of lodges, the Sociedad Mutualista "Benito Juárez," and Club "México Bello" could call upon their members to get involved in a cause dear to their heritage. The 1920 Diez y Seis, for example, was staged by the juvenile department, El Campo Roble No. 6, Leñadores del Mundo.[53] Soon thereafter, the Sociedad Mutualista Benito Juárez became closely involved in the fiestas, opening up its hall to the *comite patriótico del Parque Magnolia* so that the committee could prepare its plans for the fiestas. Other groups helping that year included the Campo Laurel #2333.[54]

So, by the latter half of the decade, the fiestas patrias—commemorated simultaneously by different groups in the several barrios—had become major attractions in Houston. City officials came to recognize them as a legitimate expression of ethnicity. The local newspapers publicized their commemoration in places other than the barrios, including Hermann Park, and the Mayor Oscar Holcombe gave enthusiastic support to it. By the mid-twenties, organizers had little difficulty receiving permission to hold the festivities at the City Auditorium. In 1925, some 4,000 Mexicanos were reported to have attended the Diez y Seis celebration at the Auditorium, this after a huge parade through downtown Houston. The Mexican consul that year took the opportunity to announce the founding of a Mexican library in the city, stocked by "a considerable number of volumes given by a group of compatriots."[55]

The Colonia on the Eve of the Depression

On the eve of the Great Depression of the 1930s, the Mexicans of Houston had consolidated their arrival. Ethnic institutions were in place, ways of making a living were found, and the necessary first steps toward adjusting to American ways had been taken. Within a bit more than a score of years, Mexicans had cut a trail to Houston and established themselves as a permanent community.

Despite this, the Immigrant Generation of that period had not advanced much beyond the entrenchment of the 1910s. The community was completely powerless in face of the city's political structure. No leading figure had emerged to voice the needs of the colonia vis-a-vis white society, either as a spokesperson or as an elected official. Confrontation or protest was absent; those taking leadership roles within barrio organizations preferred concentrating on creating associations that would meet the needs of folks still attached spiritually to the old ways. Overt dissent was not manifest, but this was not unusual, for it was not heard from the many other disadvantaged groups in the city, either.

As a community, the colonia was still a transplant of a culture imported from Mexico. Both the handful of *rico* exiles and the mass of laboring poor perpetuated a common milieu. True, the young came in touch with institutions which enculturated them and there were those individuals who were Americanized, but the community was not. Evidence of this is seen in the several organizations which sought the resurrection of older ways from Mexico. Practically no Mexican organizations, newspapers, or business establishments could be found within the boundaries of the barrios which reflected biculturation. Houston was unlike other parts of Texas where Texas-Mexican communities had existed throughout the nineteenth century. There, Mexicanos had already undergone a degree of assimilation and some of those communities saw themselves as Mexican American. The titles of mutualistas (*Sociedad México-Texana*), the names of newspapers (*El Mexicano de Texas*), the designation of political clubs (*Club Republicano México Texano*) reveal the sentiments of those other communities.[56] But Houston was a different setting as of the late 1920s and the community still identified with "lo mexicano." White society disparagingly called barrio residents "Mexicans," yet, Mexicanos did not reject the term. With an entirely different notion of themselves, they proclaimed the concept of "Mexican" proudly and sought to carry on dearly held traditions of "la patria querida."

NOTES

[1]*El Sol*, Houston, Texas, March 21, 1969, p. 1.

[2]Feagin, "The Socioeconomic Base of Urban Growth," pp. 11–12.

[3]Ibid., p. 3.

[4]Rodríguez, "Patterns of Race and Ethnic Disparity and Conflict," p. 5, Table 3; and, U. S. Department of Commerce, Bureau of the Census, *Fifteenth Census of the United States, 1930: Population*, vol. 3, pt. 2, p. 1015.

[5]Francisco A. Rosales, "The Mexican Immigrant Experience in Chicago, Houston, and Tucson: Comparisons and Contrasts," in Francisco A. Rosales and Barry J. Kaplan, *Houston: A Twentieth Century Urban Frontier*, p. 60.

[6]University of Texas Bulletin, No. 2328: July 22, 1923, *A Report on Illiteracy in Texas*, Bureau of Extension, pp. 8–12.

[7]*Gaceta Mexicana*, Houston, Texas, September 15, 1928, p. 22.

[8]Valdez, *The History of the Missionary Catechists of Divine Providence* (n.p., 1978), pp. 11–17.

[9]Tsanoff, *Neighborhood Doorways*, p. 1; Houston *Chronicle*, November 9, 1930, p. 1 ("Editorial and Features" Section).

[10]Houston *Chronicle*, November 9, 1930, p. 1 ("Editorials and Features" Section).

[11]"Detalles Generales Del Poblado de Magnolia y Su Incorporación A La Ciudad De Houston," HMRC, Mexican American Small Collection; HMRC Oral History Collection, interview with Rodrigo García and John J. Herrera, May 22, 1981; Houston *Chronicle*, August 17, 1960, p. 2 (Section 8). The description of the 1920s barrios borrows heavily from Houston *Chronicle*, November 9, 1930, p. 1 ("Editorials and Features" Section).

[12]HMRC Oral History Collection, interview with Ralph and Mary Villagómez.

[13]Houston *Chronicle*, November 9, 1930, p. 1 ("Editorials and Features" Section).

[14]Television interview with Alfredo Sarabia, HMRC, Mexican American Small Collection; Houston *Chronicle*, November 9, 1930, p. 1 ("Editorials and Features" Section).

[15]Houston *Chronicle*, November 9, 1930, p. 1 ("Editorials and Features" Section).

[16]L. Garza Leal, Consul de México, December 30, 1921, to Presidente de la República, México, D. F., in HMRC, Mexican American Small Collection.

[17]Jesse O. Thomas, *A Study of the Social Welfare Status of the Negroes in Houston, Texas*, pp. 12–15, 18.

[18]Houston *Post*, Houston, Texas, January 21, 1979, p. 8D; and, "Resumé of Juvencio Rodríguez," HMRC, Juvencio Rodríguez Collection; *El Sol*, March 21, 1969, p. 1.

[19]See Montejano, *Anglos and Mexicans in the Making of Texas*, pp. 157–254; and, *El Sol*, March 29, 1969, p. 1.

[20]Tsanoff, *Neighborhood Doorways*, p. 17.

[21]Houston *Chronicle*, November 9, 1930, p. 1 ("Editorials and Features" Section).

[22]Denison and Pugh, "Houston Public School Buildings," p. 122; Houston *Chronicle*, November 9, 1930, p. 1 ("Editorials and Features" Section); L. H. Weir, "Public Recreation in Houston" (Houston: Houston Recreation Department, 1927), p. 3, puts the school census at 1,108.

[23]Houston *Chronicle*, November 9, 1930, p. 1 ("Editorials and Features" Section); Denison and Pugh, "Houston Public School Buildings," p. 111; Weir, "Public Recreation in Houston," p. 3, puts the school census at 982.

[24]Houston *Chronicle*, November 9, 1930, p. 1 ("Editorials and Features" Section); Denison and Pugh, "Houston Public School Buildings," pp. 34 and 99; Weir, "Public Recreation in Houston," p. 4, puts census at Dow at 1,106 and at Hawthorne at 534.

[25]Denison and Pugh, "Houston Public School Buildings," p. 87; Houston *Chronicle*, November 9, 1930, p. 1 ("Editorials and Features" Section), May 2, 1925, p. 14; Weir, "Public Recreation in Houston," p. 3, says the school census was 576 in 1927.

[26]*Gaceta Mexicana*, June 1, 1928, p. 9.

[27]"Boletín Parroquial," HMRC, Juan P. Rodríguez Collection; "History of Our Lady of Guadalupe Parochial School, Houston, Texas" (Houston: Centennial of Sisters of Divine Providence, 1966), pp. 3, 4; Valdez, *The History of the Missionary Catechists of Divine Providence*, pp. 12–15.

[28]*Immaculate Heart of Mary, Houston, Texas: Directory*, unnumbered pages; Valdes, *The History of the Missionary Catethists of Divine Providence*, pp. 12, 23; HMRC Oral History Collection, interview with María Puente.

[29]Houston *Chronicle*, November 9, 1930, p. 1 ("Editorials and Features" Section).

[30]Ibid., May 23, 1920, p. 26; Tsanoff, *Neighborhood Doorways*, pp. 15–17.

[31]"San José Clinic," HMRC, Mexican American Small Collection; Sister Mary Brendan O'Donnell, "Annunciation Church—Catholic Mother Church of Houston" (M. A. Thesis, University of Houston, 1965), pp. 93–94.

[32]Houston *Chronicle*, November 9, 1930, p. 1 ("Editorials and Features" Section).

[33]Ibid., January 18, 1920, p. 15.

[34]Ibid., November 22, 1920, p. 16. Emphasis mine.

[35]Sheridan, *Los Tucsonenses: The Mexican Community in Tucson*, pp. 107–108.

[36]Campo Laurel #2333, W.O.W., Marzo 2, 1908, typescript, HMRC, Mexican American Small Collection; HMRC Oral History Collection, interview with Juan C. Hernández. Further mention of Campo Laurel #2333 is found in HMRC, Newspaper Microfilm Collection, *Gaceta Mexicana*, undated, p. 10; Houston *Chronicle*, May 4, 1925, p. 19.

[37]See José Amaro Hernández, *Mutual Aid for Survival: The Case of the Mexican American*, p. 66.

[38]Barrera, "The Historical Evolution of Chicano Ethnic Goals," p. 5.

[39]"Reglamento de la Sociedad Mutualista Mexicana 'Benito Juárez,' " HMRC, Mexican American Small Collection.

[40]"50th Anniversary Program," HMRC, Club México Bello Collection; "Estatutos Club Cultural Recreativo México Bello," HMRC, Carmen Cortez Collection; HMRC Oral History Collection, interviews with Primitivo Niño, March 16, 1979 and Isidro García and Primitivo L. Niño, April 9, 1969; Houston *Chronicle*, January 21, 1979, p. 8D.

[41]Houston *Chronicle*, January 21, 1979, p. 8D; "50th Anniversary program," HMRC, Club "Mexico Bello" Collection.

[42]Ibid.

[43]HMRC, Oral History Collection, interview with Santos and Ester Nieto, July 7, 1983.

[44]Entire issue of *Gaceta Mexicana*, September 15, 1928.

[45]Ibid., pp. 16, 20, 30; June 1, 1928, p. 15.

[46]Ibid., September 15, 1928, p. 30; Houston *Chronicle*, November 22, 1920, p. 16; November 9, 1930, p. 1 ("Editorials and Features" Section); Denison and Pugh, "Houston Public School Buildings," p. 87.

[47]Houston *Chronicle*, May 4, 1925, p. 19; August 30, 1925, p. 31; May 8, 1925, p. 1.

[48]L. Garza Leal, Consul de México, December 30, 1921, to Presidente de la República, México, D. F., in HMRC, Mexican American Small Collection.

[49]*Gaceta Mexicana*, February 15, 1928, p. 1.

[50]Ibid., April 15, 1928, n.p.; May 1, 1928, n.p.; June 1, 1928, p. 1; Pam Pennoni, "Archival Project for History 3333," University of Houston term paper, May, 1986.

[51]Houston *Chronicle*, November 9, 1930, p. 1 ("Editorials and Features" Section). *El Tecolote* carried the date of the paper's founding in its masthead. See, for example, issue No. 276, Año VI, Semana de Mayo de 1930.

[52]*Gaceta Mexicana*, February 15, 1928, p. 15, May 1, 1928, p. 26.

[53]Houston *Chronicle*, September 16, 1920, p. 1.

[54]Ibid., May 4, 1925, p. 19.

[55]Ibid., September 17, 1925, p. 13; August 30, 1925, p. 31. Also see, *Gaceta Mexicana*, May 15, 1928, p. 14; September 15, 1928, p. 15.

[56]Arnoldo De León, *The Tejano Community, 1821–1900*, p. 206.

PART II:
THE MEXICAN AMERICAN GENERATION, 1930–1960

CHAPTER III
"LA CRISIS," 1930–1940

Current historical assessments hold that the Great Depression did not afflict Houston as it did other larger American cities. As this line of thinking goes, the city's specialization in oil production and its ties to the world economy helped it weather the worst of the Depression. Part of the city's good fortunes lay on continued discoveries of oil fields in East Texas; in due time, these new finds came under the influence of oil companies with subsidiaries in Houston. As a center for shipment, also, Houston expanded greatly: by 1935, just under half of all Texas oil passed through the Port of Houston. By then, Houston had climbed to the nation's sixth largest port, supplanting New Orleans as the premier Gulf Coast port.

Federal investments into the Houston economy and the mobilization of the war years helped mediate disaster. With money from the Reconstruction Finance Corporation, the National Recovery Administration, and the Works Progress Administration, the city built parks, monuments, schools, roads and public buildings such as the City Hall. Several million dollars in federal funds were provided for more improvements to the Houston ship channel. Not surprisingly, therefore, the 1930s and 1940s were an era of uninterrupted growth in jobs, people, office buildings, residential subdivisions and in relative prosperity. Houston's economic strides were impressive enough that a national magazine in the late 1930s called it "the city that never knew the Depression."[1]

Mexicans in Houston fared less well. Poverty, repatriation, and occupational stagnation loomed over many. Still, the Mexican community of some 20,000 inhabitants as of 1940 showed staying power. The development of culture and of barrio institutions continued to unfold and mainstream institutions further converted many. Social classes within the colonia became more apparent. A new generation of Mexican Americans appeared, proclaiming themselves as American instead of Mexican citizens.

La Crisis

While the Depression of the 1930s failed to make the inroads in Houston that it did in other cities, it still touched the town, as witnessed by the attention relief agencies bestowed on it. For Mexicans specifically, the economic downturn became an unfortunate reversal which exacerbated already dismal conditions. The Depression, therefore, impacted on Mexicans. Of course, it did not bring down thriving businesses nor dismiss workers from lucrative employment, for Houston's Mexican colonia was essentially a community comprised of low-paid blue collar workers that in turn supported Mexican businessmen whose survival rested on this weak purchasing power. What the Depression did do was worsen the degree of poverty. Also, it imposed upon Mexicans a new identity as *obreros*: from laborers previously useful, they became economic liabilities. Lastly, it compelled them to come to terms with their dilemma and accept assistance from whatever source made help available.

By the early 1930s, the Depression wreaked havoc upon the Houston colonia. Among children, it was clearly displayed in the misery of their condition. With parents unable to speak English or unwilling to ask for aid from welfare agencies, many Mexican youngsters came to rely on the free meals offered in the several schools or by church groups as the only means of daily sustenance.[2] Adults, meanwhile, found themselves less desirable in the work place as industrial concerns released workers. By the winter of 1930–1931, hundreds were unemployed, according to some reports. Guardians of Americanism, moreover, refused to assist Mexicans on the pretext that they were outsiders. In 1931, local labor unions organized the Home Labor Association of Houston and Harris County with the intent of protecting the city from becoming a magnet for "loafers, idlers, snowbirds, and drifters." Without much struggle, the Association successfully persuaded the city and county to adopt rules requiring all employees, laborers, and subcontractors to be bona fide residents of six months standing in Houston in order to be employed on public works. The spirit of debate that preceded the acceptance of the policy by the city and county, however, made it obvious that Mexicans were not regarded as "residents," even if they had been in the city for years.[3]

Time did not greatly improve conditions. According to one member of the Houston Settlement Association in 1935: "No group of people in Houston are greater sufferers from the present economic situation than members of the Mexican colony."[4] With some of the businesses compelled to reduce their work forces or limit their hiring, preference was given to white workers. Industry and labor unions, therefore, guarded the blue collar occupations in which Anglos were entrenched. Mexican dock workers, plumbers, electricians, carpenters, painters, boiler makers, brick layers, or artisans faced diminishing demands for their skills.[5]

Aside from financial difficulty, Mexicanos in the colonia faced racist attitudes that went back for years. Discrimination was expressed just about everywhere in the workplace: the bakeries, breweries, and the oil companies (where the better jobs were located) displayed signs reading "No Mexicans Hired," "No Mexicans Need Apply," "No Mexicans, for White Only," "No Chili, Mexicans Keep Out." This urban situation in the 1930s, scholars note, was not starkly different than that found in the rural areas.[6]

Such long standing sentiments were coupled with a reality only faintly remembered by Mexicans in Houston. While so many had responded to the Bayou City's beckons for laborers before, they now contended with deportation and repatriation pressures. These movements germinated both from local interests wishing to be rid of the new liabilities and from the Mexican government which worked closely with local Mexican and Mexican American groups in wanting to relocate the repatriates in Mexico where they might find better conditions. Two historians have estimated that at least 2000 Texas Mexicans, or approximately fifteen percent of Houston's Mexican population in 1930, left in the early Depression years.[7]

The movement to relocate Mexicans occurred with haste, indicating that the initial shock of the Depression touched Anglo Houstonians deeply enough to undo their previous perceptions they held of Mexicans as providers of cheap labor. By the first eleven months of 1930, some 333 Mexican families repatriated from Houston according to reports from the Mexican consul. But this may have been conservative figures reflecting only those families who registered with the Mexican consulate before leaving Houston, for the American consul at Nuevo Laredo stated that 895 former Houston residents entered Mexico at Laredo during the last half of 1930.[8] Local Mexican American organizations wishing to see the conditions for those without means of support be improved in Mexico, assisted the Mexican consul in the deportation. A *Comité Pro-Repatriación* composed of members from the *comisión honorífica* and other social and recreative clubs coordinated the efforts of raising funds from the proceeds of entertainment given in Mexican centers and from private subscriptions.[9] That efforts from within the colonia to have members lacking claim to American citizenship be deported were signs of a rift, either incipient or well-entrenched, between native and foreign born. In an ironic twist, Mexican Americans worked alongside Anglo Americans to see "Mexicans" sent back to where they came from.

By May 1932, three shipments had been financed from the Rusk Settlement, 301 Gable, with the assistance of the colonia. The trips to the border brinked on the perilous: an old truck which depended on luck for its journey as it did anything else (its major expense was the gas and oil it consumed) had the task of delivering the repatriates to the Mexican government. Luggage was piled on the truck, and then men, women, and children made themselves as comfortable as possible atop the load. Passengers and driver found quarters as best they could and ate their meals on the roadside. On the return expedition the truck driver took on freight to help pay expenses.[10] Trips financed by the Mexican consul were not any more comfortable. In one case, the trucks were so overloaded that the returnees were forced to make the entire trip standing up from Houston to Mexico—a distance of about 350 miles.[11]

Such shipments as made through the efforts of the Mexican colonia apparently ended by the end of 1932—difficulties in financing the trips prevented their continuation—but other means of underwriting the cost of the repatriates' return were pursued. In 1933, for example, the Houston Settlement Association negotiated with the city's unemployment relief organization to provide transportation to the Mexican border for more than a hundred destitute Mexican families. Repatriation was to be made both as a humanitarian act and as a measure of ultimate economy to the relief organization.[12]

Whether the repatriates looked upon their relocation with apprehension or anticipation is difficult to discern. The Comité Pro-Repatriación apparently felt it as being for the repatriates' own good; many Mexican immigrants returned to Mexico voluntarily in the face of economic failure or the fear of it and in some cases on the promise of government aid in Mexico, and it was said, others were anxious to return to surroundings where relatives and friends could be counted upon—an ambient lacking in Houston. Also, the Houston Settlement Association noted that no family or individual was to be returned to Mexico "who did not volunteer to go."[13]

Yet, much evidence points to a picture of forced deportation and repatriation. Periodically, immigration officials raided private construction job sites where companies were suspected of employing Mexicans. In 1931, such raids netted 152 deportations from the city. Two students of repatriation in Houston who made an examination of U.S. district court records in Immigration and Naturalization Service files from 1929–1933 found a considerable number of imprisonment and deportation actions in Houston district courts against Mexicans arrested for violation of the immigration acts.[14]

Furthermore, oral history interviews with Mexican Houstonians who experienced repatriation first hand indicate that trauma and distress accompanied the removal of Mexicans and Mexican Americans. The young ones born in the United States, particularly, found it difficult to adjust in Mexico. In some cases, families were separated from loved ones during the process of repatriation. The fact that so many returned to Houston casts doubts on the argument of "voluntary" repatriation.[15]

Relief Withheld, Succor Extended

The Great Depression in Houston also threw many Mexicans into a somewhat unaccustomed situation of relying on established, poverty-assistance oriented agencies for survival. Though by the early 1930s thousands of Mexicans in the city were suffering from extreme privation, relief from city and federal groups was not forthcoming. While the schools provided free lunches for hungry children, they did not function as a welfare agency.[16] City authorities refused to provide work relief for indigent Mexicanos; about the only assistance available to them was in the form of used clothing and food. Applications for unemployment relief were not accepted, and Houston Mexicans were asked to shift for themselves according to testimony given before a U.S. Senate Committee on relief in 1932.[17] Some assistance did come from New Deal programs enacted after 1933 to those who could prove their citizenship, but overall, New Deal relief agencies neglected the colonia. Aliens, indeed, were barred from receiving work on public works projects, according to rules established by Civil Works Administration (C.W.A.) directors in Texas; this meant that many born in Mexico had limited recourse for relief. Enabling legislation also restricted non-citizens from working on local Works Progress Administration jobs, and in Houston as late as 1937, some 2,700 Mexicanos were removed from the agency's rolls. Private charity such as that available from the

Community Chest was so strained that it could hardly help anyone by 1933.[18]

Mexicans, therefore, turned to the churches, the Settlement Association, and their own mutual aid societies as recourses for aid. Such groups had historically attended to the disadvantaged anyway, but the list of service seekers during the 1930s increased. Desperately poor families from all over Houston trekked to Our Lady of Guadalupe Church where the Sisters of Divine Providence provided a semblance of help, including feeding many children twice a day with donations from local companies and revenue provided from carnivals and street fairs.[19] The Methodist Church through its Women's Board of Missions also extended social services to the needy,[20] as did the Presbyterian Church Women working through the community centers situated in the several barrios during the 1930s.[21]

The Rusk Settlement House also came to the forefront, carrying on its previous work among the disadvantaged. An integral part of the Segundo Barrio since the Association's start in the early years of the century, Rusk Settlement met the burden of the Depression years not only by dipping into the budget of those agencies that subsidized it (like the Community Chest and the Houston Social Service Bureau) but also by finding faithful participation among members of the colonia. Regularly, throughout the 1930s, Rusk Settlement held Mexican fiestas and dinners to continue the programs which otherwise would be curtailed through the lack of funds. Newspaper accounts report several thousands attending these fiestas; the people were charged no fee for general admissions but they supported the Settlement's efforts by patronizing the concessions.[22]

The colonia's belief in the Settlement's work is manifest in actions other than attendance at fiestas. When the Houston Social Service Bureau announced that the Settlement's budget in 1931 had to be reduced, a committee of concerned members of the colonia promised to persuade sixty-five "influential Mexicans" to donate $1.00 per month for eight months in order to insure that a children's worker was kept on staff.[23] Also, barrio groups worked closely with the Settlement in repatriating the indigent. Both the Settlement and its Mexican American supporters apparently carried out these plans on the premise that they were working for a common good: to wit, find help in Mexico for those who could not find it in Houston.

Several other charitable agencies beside the Houston Settlement Association (which, incidentally, established an unsuccessful center at Magnolia Park in 1933)[24] tended to the needs of the disadvantaged in the

Houston colonia. In 1930, the Wesley Community House was opened at 1815 North San Jacinto by the Methodist Church to serve the recreational and educational needs of the Mexican settlement.[25] In the northside, the city recreation department operated a community center at Jones School, where interested Mexican residents learned handicrafts, engaged in playing a variety of games, and presented Mexican plays.[26] More importantly, the Mexican Clinic at 1909 Canal Street continued its critical work in the colonia. It treated approximately 1,000 patients per month, filled over 1,200 prescriptions, and dispensed much milk, special baby food, eye glasses and some clothes. Supported by the 1930s by the Community Chest, it still depended on the volunteer services of nurses and doctors (of which there were eight). By the war years, the Mexican Clinic had been in operation long enough that mothers who as little girls had benefitted from the services of the clinic were now back with their own children.[27]

Poverty on the Eve of WW II

For the large portion of the Mexican community in Houston, the 1930s were more an intensification of poverty than they were a new experience. Poor before the Depression, Mexicans entered the 1940s in much the same standing. The Census of 1930 gives a graphic depiction of the occupational distribution of Mexicanos as the Depression took hold in Houston. As Table 3.1 shows, a bit more than 60% of workers held jobs of a "low blue collar" nature; together with those in "high blue collar" jobs, Mexican obreros were in positions which offered paltry wages and similar hopes for economic improvement, at best.

Ten years later, circumstances could hardly have improved. The 1940 census did not acquire socioeconomic information on Mexicans to allow for a breakdown of occupations such as that which the 1930 census did, but it is safe to state that the colonia was not in a better standing. As one newspaper account put it in 1940, "many of Mexicans in Houston are of the very poorest laboring class."[28] A survey conducted by the Works Progress Administration (sponsored by the Houston Housing Authority— HHA) in 1939 corroborates the existence of such conditions, at least among a portion of the colonia. The report revealed that 25,680 Houston families lived in dwellings classed as substandard (i.e., the houses lacked running water, proper ventilation and space, inside toilets, baths, electricity, among other things). Of this total, 12,666 were white families, 10,277 were black, and 2,787 were Mexican. This means that 11.0% of those living in substandard housing were Mexicans, a figure twice the size of the percentage of Mexicans in Houston (the total population of the city is put at 384,514 in 1940). These Mexican families living in substandard housing had incomes of less than $600 per year.[29]

To correct such a situation as existed in Houston, the HHA planned to demolish the blighted sections and replace them with dwellings that met the standards of modern living at rentals these families could afford. The projects were to be financed through funds allotted by one of the New Deal programs, the United States Housing Authority. As of 1940, the HHA had planned the development of seven slum clearance projects: the Mexican project to contain twenty-two buildings and 260 dwellings was to

Table 3.1
Selected Occupations*
of the Mexican Population in Houston,
10 Years and Older 1930**

	Males	Females
High White Collar	3.6%	1.9%
retail dealer	2.8%	1.1%
restaurant, cafe, and lunch room keeper	0.8%	0.8%
Low White Collar	2.9%	7.8%
sales person	1.2%	4.8%
clerks in stores	0.7%	3.0%
musicians and music teachers	0.3%	
other	0.6%	
High Blue Collar	13.9%	30.6%
carpenter	2.1%	
tailor	1.4%	
baker	1.2%	
machinist	1.2%	
mechanic (car)	0.8%	
mechanic (other)	0.6%	
shoemaker	0.7%	
painter (bldg)	0.6%	
painter (factory)	0.5%	
brick/stone mason	0.5%	
Operatives		
car/r.r. shops	0.5%	
food/allied indust.	0.7%	7.6%
other industries	2.9%	11.0%
textile industries		13.0%

Table 3.1 (Continued)

	Males	Females
Low Blue Collar	62.3%	53.4%
servants	5.7%	9.7%
waiters/waitresses	2.8%	4.1%
porters (domestic/personal)	0.6%	
chauffeurs/truck drivers	1.4%	
barbers	1.1%	0.4%
deliverymen	1.0%	
boarding and lodging housekeepers		8.6%
laundress (not in laundry)		10.0%
laundry operatives		4.3%
laborers		
steam railroad	12.4%	
road and street	5.6%	
car and r.r. shops	1.1%	
in stores	1.1%	
clay/glass industries	1.4%	
food/allied industries	0.8%	
general (not specific)	6.6%	11.0%
bldg. construction	6.4%	
petroleum refineries	4.6%	
public service	0.6%	
other	10.5%	5.3%
Other/Misc.	17.3%	6.3%

*Job classifications adopted from Albert Camarillo, *Chicanos in A Changing Society: From Mexican Pueblos to American Barrios in Santa Barbara and Southern California, 1848–1930,* Appendix 2, "Occupational Categories"
**Source is *Fifteenth Census of the U.S.: 1930,* Population, Vol. IV, Occupations, By States, pp. 1593–1596.

be located in the vicinity of Navigation Boulevard and Hill on a site of 10.30 acres.[30] But even as the War ended in 1945, this project was still in the planning stages.[31]

Pointing further to the unenviable conditions some in the colonia faced is a report submitted to the Harris County Grand Jury by a local civic group in 1944. According to the group's committee findings, entire families had to work when possible as wages paid to the head of the household were insufficient to support the family. "In the vicinity of Canal and Navigation Streets," the authors of the report noted, "the poor living conditions have brought about the most deplorable health conditions."

Moreover, they argued, crime inevitably flowed from such dire circumstances. In some of the crowded sections of the city where so many lived, "no recreation facilities exist; no playgrounds, no parks, no Boy's Clubs, nothing." There, juvenile delinquency was rampant.[32]

Resilience

While the Depression certainly ranked among the worst of times, life went on. To argue that the decade wrought disorientation and devastation distorts history and does a disservice to a community that proved resilient. As other people in other places and times have done, residents of the colonia took stock of adversity and kept going. One gets no sense of impending doom from reading the literature of the period. The Spanish-language press does not overdramatize the dire condition of the colonia, discussions of the Depression do not take up major portions of the minutes kept by social and recreational clubs, and, at least in the latter half of the thirties, civic groups concentrated on eliminating racial barriers such as segregation and on organizing for social improvement. Social institutions remained intact, families reproduced as before, and Mexicans did their part to see the country through the crisis. In the 1930s, indeed, a sizeable portion came to look to the United States as their home instead of condemning it for the poverty and misery which accompanied the 1930s.

All this is to say that the Mexicans in Houston continued a forward march. The Houston economy may not have been able to accommodate as many workers as it had previously, but Mexicans remained of importance to the city. As Table 3.1 shows, Mexicanos provided various types of labor to the industrial and manufacturing sectors of the city. In 1931, Mexicans still made up about 54% of the work force in the Oriental Textile Mill in the Houston Heights.[33] In the service sector, Mexicans were well represented, working in laundries, automobile repair shops, and as chauffeurs and deliverymen. While harder times followed as the decade unfolded, many of the industries in which Mexicans were entrenched survived. The Oriental Textile Mill still functioned through the war years, for example.

Furthermore, a small middle class continued taking shape. In 1930, about 6% of men were engaged in white collar occupations, and while the Depression may have undermined these gains, new businesses (funeral homes, theatres, restaurants, newspapers, etc.) took root. Many of those who founded LULAC Council #60 in 1934 stood fairly well financially, according to one of the charter members. In 1940, a Mexican Chamber of

Commerce was founded with its meeting place at 2701 Navigation; its membership was placed at 150 at the end of the year. The Chamber sought to promote the interests of the small but growing coterie of Mexican businessmen. As the president of the Chamber stated: "Mexican businessmen of Houston are engaged in practically all lines of business and are represented in all the professions. There are new opportunities for them here, and we expect to encourage development of new business enterprise."[34] This may have been a simplification, but the formation of the Mexican Chamber of Commerce is further testimony that the Mexican colonia experienced some degree of progression, not regression.

Then also, labor groups either continued active or surfaced in the 1930s, although the extent of their activities needs further scrutiny. I.L.A. Compress Local 1309, for instance, held regular meetings during the mid-1930s, inviting through the Spanish-language press "all who believe in organized labor" to attend its gatherings in its Union Hall at 76th St. and Avenue N.[35] Furthermore, Mexican American women members belonging to the International Ladies' Garment Workers' Union (ILGWU) participated in labor struggles, although their own contributions need to be isolated from those of the ILGWU proper.[36]

Deployment

Growth in the Houston colonia was not as much demographic as it was cultural. A set of factors prevented a population rise similar to the one which had occurred in the 1920s. The nativist reaction against continued Mexican immigration into the United States forestalled numerical growth, as did the spectre of the economic downturn and the repatriation efforts being undertaken throughout the country. Houston's own urban economy did not lure migrant farm workers from other parts of the state. The "Big Swing," which annually took cotton pickers from the southern parts of the state into Central and West Texas in the 1930s and 1940s, visibly circumvented Houston.[37] From 15,000 in 1930, the Mexican population had increased by only 5,000 in 1940—an intercensal increase of only 33.0%, the lowest such annual gain in Houston's Mexican American history.[38] These numbers are slightly deceiving, however, for in comparison to other counties, Harris County by 1930 had the seventh largest Mexican American population in the state. Save for Béxar and Nueces Counties, ever a mecca of Mexican settlements, all other counties with a greater Mexican population were located along the Rio Grande border and had histories of Mexican settlement dating back to the nineteenth century.[39]

Cultural growth, on the other hand, was another story, as a Mexican American way of life (to be discussed in Chapters IV and V) was deployed throughout the several barrios, albeit within their confines. El Segundo Barrio's own expansion was primarily internal. As Anglos in the neighborhood departed, Mexicans replaced them, though a slight push towards the Magnolia Park barrio did take place. Within the Segundo Barrio were located pockets of smaller barrios, some such as "El Alacrán" earning reputations for crime and misery. "El Alacrán," part of the aforementioned neighborhood known as Shrimpf Alley, was situated east of downtown Houston where the present-day Clayton Homes are located. Contemporaries of the period recall a notorious neighborhood infested with many an *alacrán* (scorpion), poverty worse than that which existed in other parts of the colonia, and numerous types of vices.[40] By the War years, the area from the Segundo Barrio to Magnolia Park was already being referred to as the "East End."[41]

A casualty of this internal growth after 1930s and the War years was the old downtown business district, for as the barrios expanded within, new commercial establishments were set up. By the late 1930s, for example, Magnolia Park was such a self-contained barrio that people could find within it whatever the downtown commercial section offered. To be sure, however, other forces played a role in the decline of the business center in the central district. There was, of course, the Depression. Also, downtown Houston's own expansion affected the Mexican business establishments. As the city tried to accommodate growth, it switched to one-way thoroughfares. Up until the era of WWII, people had stopped to patronize Mexican businesses as they rode or drove into town and as they left for their homes. But with one-way streets, it became difficult for businesses to attract the outgoing traffic of automobiles or busses.[42] The history of Houston compiled by the Writers Program of the Work Projects Administration in 1942 did not mention this downtown district. Instead, it was more impressed with the commercial district of Magnolia Park, although it only mentioned that one in passing.[43]

Social Institutions

Progress also occurred in the several socializing institutions carrying work in the barrios. Churches continued ministering to their flocks, enjoying expansion even as they faced the burden of tending to poverty-stricken people. Membership at Guadalupe Church in the Segundo Barrio climbed and enrollment of Guadalupe School reached its highest mark by the latter 1930s.[44] Guadalupe Church even begot an offspring—St. Stephen Church in the Sixth Ward[45]—as it had with Immaculate Heart of the Mary during the 1920s. Providence Home, a two-story building for the young ladies of the Catechists of Divine Providence, was built in 1935.[46]

As Guadalupe Church celebrated its twenty-fifth anniversary in 1937,[47] other barrio churches continued their own kind of expansion. In the Sixth Ward, the old St. Stephen Church (and Center) was demolished and replaced with a new brick church edifice which was dedicated on March 2, 1941.[48] In Magnolia Park, Immaculate Heart of Mary Church saw the rectory improved, a convent for the sisters built, and more buildings added to the parochial school.[49] The church's grounds became the setting of kermesses, jamaicas, and *noches mexicanas* during the summers and, sometimes, the host of the fiestas patrias in the Magnolia barrio.[50]

The Protestant denominations continued their own evangelical pace. In addition to those churches established in the 1920s, new ones appeared. The directory of 1930 lists at least three new churches in the Second Ward: Primera Iglésia Bautista Mexicana, 2720 Bering, Iglésia Pentecostal, 2706 Fox, and Iglésia Cristiana Pentecostal, 2332 Ann.[51] In 1940, more than ten Protestant churches ministering to Mexican Americans throughout the Houston barrios could be found in the directory.

School Days

Houston's educational system extended its hand to Mexican Americans in various ways. Of course, it made inroads into Americanizing the young; from what little of the record exists, enrollment in the predominantly Mexican schools seems to have increased. A census made in May 1939 lists the student population as follows: Rusk, 787; de Zavala, 623; Jones, 666; Dow, 1207; Hawthorne, 396.[52] PTA's were active, though to what degree remains uncertain.[53] Also, the school system permitted Mexicanos access to its facilities. Rusk school, for one, served as a favorite place for holding meetings and planning strategy sessions. The Mexican consul at times used its schoolrooms and auditorium to address the community and its grounds were used for fund raising festivities which might benefit the destitute in Mexico.[54] Further, Mexican clubs used the Rusk School Auditorium to present plays which had little connection to the functions of American education.[55]

But positive steps towards education were coupled with negative aspects: schools districts were intentionally gerrymandered to keep the

Mexicans segregated; lessons of Texas history, especially, deprecated the Spanish and Mexican role in the state's pre-Independence period; and teachers punished students for speaking Spanish on the school grounds.[56] Thus, the same system that succeeded in teaching many the proper skills for survival also taught hard lessons about being Mexican in Houston.

NOTES

[1]Feagin, "The Socioeconomic Base of Urban Growth," pp. 15–20.

[2]Houston *Chronicle,* December 20, 1931, p. 16; September 11, 1932, p. 14.

[3]R. Reynolds McKay, "Texas Mexican Repatriation During the Great Depression" (Ph.D. Dissertation, University of Oklahoma, 1982), pp. 249–250.

[4]Houston *Chronicle,* February 10, 1933, p. 12.

[5]"History of Council #60," HMRC, John J. Herrera Collection.

[6]Ibid. On racial practices in the Texas countryside, see Montejano, *Anglos and Mexicans in the Making of Texas,* p. 265.

[7]Marilyn D. Rhinehart and Thomas H. Kreneck, " 'In the Shadow of Uncertainty': Texas Mexicans and Repatriation in Houston During the Great Depression," p. 10, (unpublished paper).

[8]McKay, "Texas Mexican Repatriation," pp. 323–324.

[9]Ibid., p. 324; "Club Chapultepec, YWCA," HMRC, Melesio Gómez Family Collection.

[10]Houston *Chronicle,* May 3, 1932, p. 3; February 10, 1933, p. 12.

[11]McKay, "Texas Mexican Repatriation," pp. 324–325.

[12]Houston *Chronicle,* February 10, 1933, p. 12.

[13]Ibid., February 10, 1933, p. 12; Rhinehart and Kreneck, " 'In the Shadow of Uncertainty'," p. 11.

[14]Rhinehart and Kreneck, " 'In the Shadow of Uncertainty'," p. 5.

[15]Ibid., p. 14.

[16]Houston *Chronicle,* December 20, 1931, p. 16.

[17]McKay, "Texas Mexican Repatriation," pp. 323, 249–250.

[18]Rhinehart and Kreneck, " 'In the Shadow of Uncertainty'," pp. 3–5; Newsclippings (Houston *Post*), HMRC, John J. Herrera Collection.

[19]Houston *Chronicle,* September 11, 1932, p. 14; December 3, 1935, p. 2.

[20]Rhinehart and Kreneck, " 'In the Shadow of Uncertainty'," p. 7.

[21]Houston *Chronicle,* January 7, 1933, p. 8.

[22]Ibid., May 7, 1930, p. 8; May 11, 1930, p. 4; May 17, 1933; p. 2; May 22, 1933, p. 6; April 18, 1935, p. 17; March 8, 1940, p. 14A.

[23]Tsanoff, *Neighborhood Doorways,* p. 21.

[24]Tsanoff, *Neighborhood Doorways,* pp. 26, 28–29; Houston *Chronicle,* September 15, 1933, p. 23; November 13, 1935, p. 2; and April 11, 1945, p. 1B; *El Puerto,* Houston, Texas, Septiembre 13, 1935, p. 1.

[25]Houston *Chronicle,* September 21, 1930, p. 13; *Papel Chicano,* Houston, Texas, August 22 to September 11, 1970, p. 12.

[26]Ibid., March 6, 1930, p. 16.

[27]Ibid., October 6, 1940, p. 14D.

[28]Ibid.

[29]Housing Authority of the City of Houston, *Houston's Public Housing Program,* pp. 13–14.

[30]Ibid., pp. 7–8; Houston *Chronicle,* February 1, 1940, p. 7A.

[31]Houston *Chronicle,* May 9, 1945, p. 1A.

[32]"To the Honorable Grand Jury of Harris County, Texas," HMRC, Mexican American Small Collection.

[33]*Congressional Record,* 71st Congress, 3rd Session (1931), 74 (Part 4): 4386.

[34]Houston *Chronicle,* September 17, 1940, p. 2A; November 28, 1940, p. 10A.

[35]*El Puerto,* Julio 5, 1935, p. 1; Julio 12, 1935, p. 1; Agosto 2, 1935, p. 1; Noviembre 8, 1935, p. 1.

[36]ILGWU Local 214, Houston Box, Texas Labor Archives, University of Texas at Arlington, Arlington, Texas.

[37]Pauline Kibbe, *Latin Americans of Texas,* p. 184 (map).

[38]Rodríguez, "Patterns of Race and Ethnic Disparity and Conflict," p. 5 and Table 3.

[39]H. T. Manuel, "The Mexican Population of Texas," *The Southwestern Social Science Quarterly,* XV (June 1934–March 1935), 38.

[40]"Immigration of the Domingo Serrano Family . . . ," HMRC, Houston Mexican American Family History Collection; HMRC, Oral History Collection, interview with Mrs. Félix H. Morales, February 5 and February 19, 1979.

[41]Carl M. Rosenquist and Walter Gordon Browder, *Family Mobility in Houston, Texas, 1922–1938,* pp. 11–12, 48.

[42]HMRC, Oral History Collection, interview with Alfredo Sarabia, February 16, 1979.

[43]Work Projects Administration, *Houston: A History and Guide,* pp. 171–172.

[44]Valdez, *The History of the Missionary Catechists of Divine Providence,* p. 43.

[45]Ibid., pp. 24–28; Houston *Chronicle,* September 11, 1932, p. 14; October 9, 1932, p. 9.

[46]Valdez, *The History of the Missionary Catechists of Divine Providence,* p. 39; Houston *Chronicle,* October 11, 1935, p. 31.

[47]Houston *Post,* December 12, 1937, n.p.

[48]Houston *Chronicle,* April 20, 1940, p. 6A; April 26, 1940, p. 1D; Robert Giles, *Changing Times: The Story of the Diocese of Galveston Houston in Commemoration of Its Founding,* pp. 100–101.

[49]"Detalles Generales Del Poblado de Magnolia y Su Incorporación a la Ciudad de Houston," HMRC, Mexican American Small Collection.

[50]*El Puerto,* Julio 5, 1935, p. 1; Julio 12, 1935, p. 1; Agosto 2, 1935, p. 1; Septiembre 16, 1935, p. 1; Septiembre 13, 1935, p. 1.

[51]*Houston City Directory of 1930.*

[52]*Houston and Harris County Facts: Yesterday, Today, Tomorrow,* pp. 216–217.

[53]*El Puerto,* Agosto 30, 1935, p. 5; Septiembre 13, 1935, p. 1.

[54]"Acta #21 and Acta #45," HMRC, Félix Morales Collection ("Union Fraternal"); "Circular," 5 de marzo 1941, in ibid.

[55]Houston *Chronicle,* February 22, 1930, p. 3; February 23, 1930, p. 14.

[56]HMRC Oral History Collection, interview with Judge Alfred J. Hernández, January 15, 1979; "Chapultepec, YWCA" manuscript, HMRC, Melesio Gómez Family Collection.

CHAPTER IV
INTELLECTUAL AND CULTURAL
CONTINUITY AND CHANGE,
1930–1945

Within the milieu of the 1930s and the war years, there persisted with tenacity a Mexican ethos. Socialization vied with retrenchment in the several barrios as Mexicans sought to ward off racism and discrimination in Houston by falling back on the old and familiar. In the barrios, also, inhabitants found an essential reaffirmation for their cultural preferences. Furthermore, certain elements in the community consciously cultivated their Mexicanness. These included both the middle class refugees who had transplanted their survival skills to Houston as well as ordinary people who sustained themselves in low-paying, and often unstable and temporary occupations.

But during the 1930s, members of the Tejano community in Houston also began losing ties to the motherland and turning their loyalties to the United States. Immigrants themselves adopted a different mood. As the tailor Isidro García elaborated:

> When Lázaro Cárdenas was elected president of Mexico [1934–1940] and said that Mexicans with roots in the United States should become U.S. citizens and express loyalty to that country, we began to change our attitudes [toward naturalization].[1]

But changing loyalties were expressed more resolutely in Houston by those raised or born in the United States. What was present was a phenomenon to be found in other parts of the state during the same epoch, namely, a constant process of intellectual and cultural continuity and change expressive of both "lo mexicano" and "lo americano." The latter half of this chapter touches on transitional expressions and Chapter V discusses the emergence of the "Mexican American mind."

"Lo Mexicano"

Several forces bolstered the "Mexican mentality." Continued immigration from Mexico, however slight, nourished a familiar culture. Since educational, religious, and social institutions did not reach everyone, old ways lived on unperturbed. The presence of so many clubs and organizations which emphasized "lo mexicano," furthermore, kept the spirit aflame. Spanish-language newspapers and Spanish-language films helped keep Mexican thought intact.

By various means, moreover, Mexican Houstonians learned of the strong nationalist currents then prevalent in Mexico. Artists, literary figures, and scholars in Mexico supported revolutionary ideals by instilling the masses with the virtues of the new social order. Muralists like Diego Rivera, for example, took up the cause of the Indians and peasants while writers produced revisionist works which refurbished Indian culture. Such a revolutionary sense of purpose and pride was augmented by the reforms initiated by President Lázaro Cárdenas. During his administration, major programs of land distribution were enacted, socialist ideals were taught in schools, clergymen were coerced into showing more interest in the socio-economic well being of the people, and government encouraged labor unionism. This revolutionary ardor of the 1930s hardly escaped the colonia.

Barrio inhabitants, furthermore, were not completely forsaken by "la patria," a fact brought home in the concern the Mexican government expressed for those "en el estranjero" (in foreign soil). Efforts to assist them during the Depression, for one thing, showed Mexicanos of the care of the motherland. But there were still other gestures from Mexico which acted to maintain the faith among those with persistent cultural loyalties. The Mexican government, for example, in June 1934 sent supportive words to the colonia as Mexicanos in Houston sought to build a park (it became known as Hidalgo Park, or "Mexican Park") on a 10-acre tract of land set aside by the city on Harbor Boulevard, between Seventieth and Sunset Streets. To Dr. A. G. González, head of the project raising funds through dinners and dances, President Abelardo L. Rodríguez sent a letter praising the movement. Such a gesture on the part of the old country could not help but encourage feelings still intact.[2]

The activities of the Mexican consul in Houston, which seemed to have increased during the era, were open confirmation that a good portion of the people in the colonia had not yet taken the extreme step of naturalization. The Mexican consuls, indeed, were integrated into the life of the colonia; though it was their duty to intervene in behalf of Mexican nationals, they also worked in behalf of the entire community as strong cultural, linguistic, and familial ties bound both the foreign born and Americans of Mexican descent. Periodically, the consul in Houston was compelled to act with vigor and audacity as spokesperson for his government. This was especially the case during incidents of homicide against Mexicans. The consul participated in several such cases, but the one which attracted the most attention in the 1930s appears to have been the death in April 1937 of one Elpidio Cortez, a citizen of Mexico.

Responding to a call involving a domestic disturbance, Houston peace officers arrived at the home of Elpidio Cortez. According to the police, the Mexican was intoxicated and allegedly was beating his wife. When they approached Cortez, he struck at one of the lawmen, whereupon a scuffle ensued. Fighting to subdue him, one of the policemen hit Cortez with a blackjack repeatedly. The two men then escorted Cortez to the police car and took him to the station. There, they stopped the car and upon opening the back door, Cortez tried to jump out, fell, and struck his head against the pavement. Although unconscious, Cortez was taken up to be booked, then left on the floor of the city jail while officials booked other prisoners. An ambulance finally arrived, but Cortez was dead before reaching the hospital.

Mrs. Cortez immediately announced her decision to ask the Mexican consul for an investigation, and the Mexican government took an active interest in the trial held in the summer of 1937. A special assistant prosecutor, a Mexican American attorney from San Antonio who as a United States citizen and member of the state bar association had worked for the consulate before, represented the Mexican government as the state sought to show that the officers had committed murder without malice. The prosecution, led by staff members of the District Attorney's office, argued that Cortez had died of injuries from the blackjacks. The defendants in turn persisted in their argument that Cortez had died from a head injury suffered when he lunged out of the officers' car at the police station (the autopsy had failed to settle the question of whether Cortez died from a blow of a policeman's blackjack or an injury suffered from falling on his head). The jury found the two not guilty.

According to an editorial from the Houston *Post,* the Mexican government was assured that everything possible within the law was done to determine whether the arresting officers were responsible for the death of Cortez. Turning to the defendants, it noted, "The trial served notice on all officers of the law that they will be held strictly accountable for their acts when there is a question of legality involved. In the future the officers involved will be more careful in handling prisoners charged with minor offenses."[3] History would show that the Elpidio Cortez case did not serve as a deterrent against arbitrary law enforcement in Houston's barrios.

Periodicos

Spanish-language newspapers of the 1930s did their part to bolster "lo mexicano." Gone was the *Gaceta Mexicana,* a victim of the Depression, but persisting was *El Tecolote* of Rodolfo Ávila de la Vega. As already indicated, runs of *El Tecolote* are non-extant and only clippings remain to be studied; from them one can only catch a glimpse of the editor's posture vis-à-vis the Mexican colonia. Ostensibly, de la Vega belonged to the refugees of class and social standing. As he himself put it, his exile was both voluntary and forced, and he apparently expected to return to Mexico some day. In Mexico, he had already acquired respectable editorial experience, having served as editor of the *Revista de Aviación Tothli,* and the language he utilized in the columns of his Houston enterprise was that of a learned person, with a powerful command of the Spanish language.

It may be conjectured that his newspaper was an expression of the "Mexicanism" of the refugees. On the occasion of his induction as an honorary member of Club "México Bello," he was praised by the Mexican consul for his work in Mexico and for that which he had continued in Houston.[4] A contemporary of the 1930s recalled later that *El Tecolote* was anti-Mexican American, and that it carried few news items of a positive nature about Mexicanos who had made Houston their permanent home.[5] Nevertheless, de la Vega did give extensive coverage to colonia activities of every kind.

Vying with *El Tecolote* in the 1930s was *El Puerto: Semanario Independiente de Magnolia Park,* edited by A. D. "Sal" Salazar, with offices at 2016 Lamar Avenue. For those preferring to keep abreast of events in Mexico, *El Puerto* carried plenty of news; in some of the issues, approximately 75% of the stories dealt with the old country. The paper's customary reference to *"este país"* (this country) meant Mexico, not the United States. Often, *El Puerto* lent its columns to members of the Mexican consulate who desired to communicate with the colonia on matters relevant to the foreign born. Consulate officers chided, for example, the many associations in the city for being purely recreative organizations; the office felt it a duty to instruct the organizations that they should be protective and constant in their efforts to establish schools, libraries, and cultural functions which would be of use in uplifting the intellectual standing of the Mexican colonia "en el estranjero."[6] Further, *El Puerto* allowed Mexican American lawyers to use its space to make the immigrants aware of the immigration laws or the laws of Texas.[7] Occasionally, it printed creative literature, i.e., short stories and poetry. Among such items was a poem entitled *"Versos de la Inundación de Houston en Diciembre de 1935"* ("Verses on the Flooding of Houston in December 1935").[8] There were, however, articles published which revealed concessions to coverage of Mexican American events. Much of this attention dealt with the activities of local clubs, primarily in Magnolia Park, to whose audience *El Puerto* catered.

Cultural Affairs

The Mexican community continued enjoying those entertainment forms reminiscent of their native land and at times tried to duplicate them in Houston. As in the 1920s, professional entertainers and artists visited the city, some appealing to "middle class" tastes. When María Conesa, a Spanish dancer and singer known in Mexico as (*"La Gatita de Oro,"* or "The Golden Kitten") visited Houston in May 1935, for example, it excited numerous "persons prominent in Houston's Mexican colony," as the Houston *Chronicle* put it. Rodolfo Ávila de la Vega of *El Tecolote* took charge of the arrangements for her concert and a committee was selling tickets in the lobby of the exclusive Rice Hotel.[9] It was also de la Vega, who through his newspaper, sought to resurrect a bit of Mexico in Houston in 1940 by sponsoring a program honoring the celebration in Mexico for President-Elect Manuel Ávila Camacho. In the program, a soloist for the Latin Society Club of Houston sang the National Mexican Anthem over radio KTRH before the Mexican Mason Lodge Cosmos 39.[10]

It is difficult to determine if different performers, either visitors or locals, appealed to a cross-section of the community or whether they played to meet the preferences of different social classes. Formal occasions generally called for *orquesta* music. But did groups wishing music for their dances choose orchestras because they belonged to the middle class, or did elements of different classes feel that orquestas were the music of formality? Whatever the answer, the orquesta in Houston was a popular ensemble in the 1930s, the best known being *"La Orquesta Típica de Magnolia,"* conducted by Albino Torres, an immigrant who had received his training in Mexico City. Torres played at numerous dances sponsored by the more prominent clubs of the city, such as Club "México Bello," or on the occasion of the fiestas patrias.[11]

Certainly, Lydia Mendoza, who would win international acclaim in later years, had as her following the blue collar workingman to which she played in Houston during the early Depression years. Born in 1916 in the Houston Heights, she passed through Houston in the early 1930s with her family as they headed back to Mexico under repatriation pressures from Michigan. The family took temporary residence in Magnolia Park, and under the sponsorship of social and mutualist groups, performed before working-class audiences at places such as El Salón Juárez, 7320 Navigation, and El Salón Hidalgo.[12]

Attractive to different segments of the Houston colonia were Mexican film and stage idols. In 1945, an enthusiastic audience at City Auditorium cheered, squealed, and whistled a Mexican vaudeville show featuring Pedro Infante, the famous movie star of Mexico. Elements of Americanism were displayed by young dancers who preceded Infante, however, in their mixture of jitterbug steps with traditional Mexican routines.[13]

Most appealing to the different social elements within the colonia were the traditional fiestas patrias celebrations. Although the elaborate ceremonies of the 1920s—the downtown parades of gayly decorated floats and new cars, for example—declined somewhat during the Depression, improvement on other aspects of both the Cinco de Mayo and the Diez y Seis de Septiembre were made. By the 1930s, indeed, a *comité patriótico* (patriotic committee) brought together the increased number of societies in the city behind a common heritage. As had been occurring since the development of the different barrios, however, separate occasions were observed, usually one downtown at the City Auditorium and another in Magnolia Park. Invariably, the consul or his representatives delivered the "Grito" at the Diez y Seises, taking the opportunity to remind the colonia of their Mexican heritage. In 1935, for instance, the chancellor of the Mexican consulate admonished Mexicans with children born in the United States to teach them something of the "sacrifices of the heroes of Mexican independence in order that the liberty-loving spirit and enthusiasm might be imparted to generations yet to come."[14] The fiestas patrias, therefore, were occasions where culture might be rejuvenated lest Mexicans slide too much towards acculturation.

Also, Spanish-language theatres attracted all members of the colonia regardless of social standing or ambition. The Teatro Azteca continued showing films but competition included the *"Nuevo Palacio* Theatre." Those in Magnolia Park attended the *"Teatro Juárez"* at 7320 Navigation. Sensitive to the growing Americanization occurring among the young, these theatres also played English language films, starring such notables of the period as the western cowboy hero Tim McCoy and the cartoon character "Popeye."[15]

Clubes Mexicanos

Social and recreative clubs proliferated in Houston throughout the 1930s: the Mexican orientation of many indicates the continued nexus of the colonia with the mother country. Many were throwbacks to the philosophy of Club "México Bello" of the 1920s. But each had a special appeal to its members by its location in the different barrios, by a particular project it sought to carry out, by the name of the group, or by whatever other attractions lure different individuals to different clubs having a common purpose.

Club "México Bello" continued having mixed success throughout most of the Depression decade. As since its inception, a primary goal was that of presenting a sound, positive image of the Mexican before white society—that done, Anglos would accept Mexicanos for the cultured beings that they were. A favorite story recalled by old members and repeated in the Club's "History" relates how, by example, Club "México Bello" integrated the several hotel dance halls and other elegant ballrooms of Houston in the early 1930s. For their annual Black and White ball, the account goes, the Club's officers went to the skeptical owner of the Aragon ballroom (in downtown Houston, 1010 Rusk), who, wary of Mexicans desecrating the salon, asked them for a steep deposit and other assurances. Once having gained his cautious approval for using the Aragon, the membership impressed the proprietor so deeply by their dress and comportment that he freely confessed afterwards: "We Anglos have much to learn from Mexicans." With that singular demonstration of behavior (the Club's "History" reads) were torn down racial barriers and thenceforth, Mexicans had access to the rest of Houston's elegant ballrooms in the best hotels or those privately owned. Continued demonstrations of impeccable social manners and conduct erased the old sterotypes. "They could see that we were different than just the 'Mexican greasers,' " recalled Primitivo L. Niño, an early member of the club. After the dances, it was just "Latin Americans."[16]

Of course, Club "México Bello" had other goals besides projecting a good image before white society. Its main purpose remained that of keeping Mexicanismo alive, and to that end, the club limited its recruitment to those still nostalgic for the old land, regardless of their social standing. By the mid 1930s, it claimed a membership of about 300. Invited speakers addressed the club on a relevant topic; the consul or his representative, especially, captivated them with praises of the grandeur of Mexico and applauded their commitment to sustaining *"lo mexicano en el estranjero."*

And in trying to sustain "lo mexicano," the club took great care in presenting nothing less than "Mexico" at its cultured best. To the Black and White balls were invited "the most outstanding elements of our colony and the most distinguished of Anglo Americans."[17] During formal ceremonies, such as ones held for the induction of new officers, the best orchestras by the leading musicians in the city played. A typical program during such occasions involved the presentation of the most beautiful current songs in Mexico.

Additionally, Club "México Bello" participated in the festivities of the various Mexican holidays (its officers were frequently part of the *comité patriótico*) and commemorated such special dates as the "Día de la Raza." As a recreational organization, it sought to furnish an outlet for the social, athletic, and cultural activities of the young. Moreover, it took steps (contrary to the allegations made by some of its detractors, the club countered) to work for the betterment of the entire colonia. In this capacity, it organized fundraising suppers to help needy children at Christmas time. Its meetings at the clubhouse, 1209 Shearn, were open to other social and recreative clubs, including the mutualistas and the local council of the League of United Latin American Citizens.[18]

Difficult times afflicted Club "México Bello" during the latter half of the 1930s. In the midst of the Depression, some of the members failed to pay their dues. Still, the club continued carrying on its work, along with a women's auxiliary and a girls' youth group, in a less visible manner.[19] But other groups, among them *Club Recreativo Internacional* (established in 1935) filled the hiatus, standing, as *El Puerto* described it, "como una prueba patente de su cariño a la Patria y de su estimación por México" ("as patent proof of its affection for 'la patria' and its

67

great estimation for Mexico"). Club Internacional consisted of young adults who carried on the familiar motto of *"Unión, Fraternidad y Progreso."* Membership included "Mexican citizens, as well as a few *extranjeros* [foreigners] especially Argentinians, South Americans, and *Mexican Texans."* Naturally, the club had close ties to the consul and observed the traditions of Mexico. In July 1945, for instance, Club Recreativo Internacional commemorated the anniversary of the death of Benito Juárez.[20]

Other social and recreative clubs pointed to the dogged vitality of the Mexican community in the 1930s and during World War II—even if some may have been in response to the Depression. Clubs with names resurrective of the Mexican past included *Club Recreativo Anáhuac, Club Recreativo Xochimilco,* and *Club Terpsicore.*[21] New cultural groups included *"El Círculo Cultural Mexicano,"* founded circa 1930, which met at Rusk Settlement to study and discuss Mexican and Latin American cultural problems; it presented one-act plays written by some of its members.[22] A glee club, known as *"Los Amigos* Glee Club," existed during the early thirties.[23]

Self-Help Groups

Protective organizations born in the 1920s provided needed functions as the Depression deepened. Some, like the Sociedad Benito Juárez, sputtered. Like the members of Club "México Bello," those of the Sociedad Benito Juárez faced difficulty paying dues on a regular basis. In 1932, the Sociedad lost the hall which it had established in 1928, though it continued to limp along under the circumstances.[24]

Other groups were a bit more fortunate. Campo Laurel #2333, founded back in 1908, experienced unusual success between 1933 and 1945. It rented two floors in the Milam Building to accommodate full houses during its meetings and festivities.[25] Moreover, several other self-help groups were founded during the era. One was *El Campamento Navidad* 3698 W.O.W. formed in 1932.[26] That same year was established the *Sociedad Mutualista Obrera Mexicana* (SMOM), following the accidental killing of a man whose family lacked the finances for a proper burial. Concerned men collected nickles and dimes to provide for the deceased, but the emergency alerted them to the need for a mutualista in the Second Ward (the Sociedad Benito Juárez was in Magnolia).[27] Primarily, the SMOM aided widows and children and provided burial assistance to its foreign and native-born members. During the war years, the SMOM office was at 207 St. Charles, though it had a branch near the Liberty Road cresote works.[28] In 1936, a women's auxiliary to the SMOM was established, primarily as a burial association. It was connected with Morales Funeral Home, a business owned by Mrs. Félix Morales, one of its founders. Fees were five cents a week.[29]

Also conceived during the era of the Depression was the *Sociedad "Unión Fraternal."* Like the SMOM, it emerged to fill the needs of poverty stricken people unable to afford burial benefits. Organized in 1940 or 1941 by Mr. and Mrs. Félix Morales of Morales Funeral Home, Unión Fraternal provided a means by which Mexican families, unable to afford the price of lots in the cemetery, could avoid burying their loved ones in potter's field. For a $5.00 fee, members could reserve proper grave space on some ten acres of land the Morales purchased off Aldine Road. For the most part, the Unión Fraternal packaged itself as an organization for those with cultural ties to Mexico. Its motto was *"Patria y Altruismo"* (Country and Altruism), its standard had as its emblem the national symbol of the old country (the eagle and the serpent), and meetings were conducted in the Spanish language. Indeed, a reason for its founding was the fact that hospitals in Houston had barred the admission of those born in Mexico. The Unión Fraternal worked along with the Mexican consul and its activities included fund-raising drives for the needy back in Mexico.[30]

But the Unión Fraternal did not restrict itself to the needs of the foreign born. Mr. and Mrs. Morales, after all, were American citizens and spoke English fluently. Further, Houston by then had too many Mexican American residents wanting services in terms more appealing to their own bicultural lifestyle. The Unión Fraternal could serve both a Mexican and a Mexican American clientele with ease. And indeed, it evolved into somewhat of a civic organization, looking out after Mexicanos regardless of place of birth. By the 1940s, the Unión Fraternal was immersed in several causes, among them protesting the continued segregation of children in the public schools.[31]

Cultural Retention and Assimilation

The double role that Unión Fraternal balanced was one that other clubs had been playing for some time before the war years. Despite all the travail that accompanied Mexicans growing up in Houston, the exposure to American concepts and values, however discriminatory, enticed many into adopting American culture. Young people, especially, identified with the ways of their parents, but by now spoke English and did not find it difficult to balance a cultural duality.

Among the manifestations of this growing transformation were new Mexican American clubs springing up in Houston. For every group that emerged in the city with an emphasis on "lo mexicano," there appeared another that reflected the new biculturation. To be sure, the scant evidence available on these clubs makes it difficult to distinguish between "Mexican" and "Mexican American" organizations: their names were usually some reference to Mexico's past, the membership could easily have gone in the Mexican or Mexican American direction, and generally, meetings were conducted in Spanish. Nonetheless, clues are available indicating the Mexican American orientation of some of these groups. Among those whose activities stressed the Houston setting instead of the Mexican link were *El Club Orquidea, Club Masculino Faro, Club Femenino Dalia, Sociedad Latino Americano*, the *Club Pan Americano* of the Y.W.C.A., and the *Club Moderno y Recreativo*. The latter club had as one of its goals finding a place where young girls could participate in recreative activities without being "watched and criticized by the public." Perhaps this was an effort to preserve the type of modesty expected in Mexico and now by Mexican Americans in Houston.[32]

Representative of biculturation was the *Club Femenino Chapultepec*, a social and recreative club founded in 1931 (it continued until the mid-1940s) and made up of young girls from the several Houston barrios born or raised in the United States. While the members involved themselves in various traditional Mexican activities such as the fiestas patrias, they were very much in contact with mainstream institutions. Some were high school graduates, spoke English, and worked in the Houston Anglo business community. Indeed, Club Chapultepec was associated with the Business and Professional Department of the YWCA. Part of its purpose was to teach Mexican girls to become better citizens and in this context, members sold government bonds during World War II, helped the community to distribute the Sugar Stamps, and assisted in other activities to help Houston.[33]

Club Chapultepec felt comfortable enough with its Mexican Americanism that in 1937 it transgressed the usual activities of social and recreative clubs by submitting a report to appropriate agencies on the status of Mexican Americans in Houston. In part, the mild indictment of white society was prompted by the concern the girls had about "what the future [in Texas] will be for them [the membership] and their children." Being a United States born Mexican, the report stated, yielded few perquisites.

70

Mexicanos faced discrimination in housing, in the playgrounds, in the job market, and before the law (Mexican lawyers had practically no chance of winning their cases before a discriminatory judicial system). Mexicanos lived with a constant barrage of reminders which branded them as inferior and vile—Anglos relished reviewing the Texas War for Independence when Texas whipped them and the Mexican nation. Exposed to such attitudes and names such as "greasers," the letter from the Chapultepec Club noted, many Mexicanos refused to take out citizenship papers since it hardly changed their social condition. But more significantly, "Mexicans in a desire to get ahead have at times denied their nationality calling themselves French, Italian, and Spanish." In mentioning the last change, Club Chapultepec was alluding to many other Mexicans in Houston whose psycho-historical development put distance between the experience of the 1930s and that of the immigrants. While some in Houston looked with pride on their Mexicanness and attempted to impress whites with Mexico at its best, there were those now willing to subordinate it in favor of a bicultural identity more applicable to the circumstances in their adopted land.[34]

La Federación de Sociedades Mexicanas y Latino Americanas

Existing alongside the numerous social, recreative, and fraternal societies in Houston was an organization founded in the late 1930s with the intent of going before white society to agitate for the well being of the Mexican and "Latin American" citizens of the city. Said organization worked closely with the Mexican consul in Houston, yet took notice of the new generation of Houstonians who were either native born or naturalized citizens of the United. In this new cognizance, it displayed the growing awareness of the Mexican-oriented groups that "lo mexicano" did not solely embrace the foreign born or those who had fled the peril of the Mexican Revolution in the 1910s and 1920s. It was, seemingly, an entity that answered the needs of a community undergoing change; the office of the consul as a defender of the entire colonia was becoming outmoded given the shifting consciousness of the immigrants and their children. The new organization, therefore, signified the different, yet common, needs of those subscribing to "lo mexicano" and those acceding to "lo americano," and as such, bridged the gap between the two generations. Actually, it was to be a duplication of similar efforts elsewhere in the United States, such as El Paso, Texas, and in Los Angeles, California.[35]

Its beginnings went back to July 1938 when the Mexican consul in Galveston issued a call for a *Convención Regional de Organizaciones Mexicanas de las Jurisdicciones Consulares de Galveston, Beaumont, y Houston.* The purpose of the convention was to study the problems which affected "Mexican citizens and American citizens of Mexican origin residing in Texas." Delegates were asked to bring suggestions with them which might offer solutions to problems common to the Mexican communities.

In response to the call, the consul in Houston, Sr. Luis L. Duplán, himself appealed to all clubs, lodges, associations, and *comisiones honoríficas* in his consular jurisdiction to send delegates to the meeting scheduled for Galveston. While consuls in the United States were not to get involved in the politics and internal affairs of the host country, such agitation for self-protection fell within their duties to "protect the interests and rights of Mexican nationals."[36]

One of the things accomplished at the meeting was the formation of an Organizing and Coordinating Committee which moved with dispatch during the summer. First, the Committee worked to form regional confederations comprised of different civic, social, or recreative groups within each consular district in Texas.[37] Then in September 1938, the Committee called for a convocation of the Mexican consuls, comisiones honoríficas, regional confederations of Mexican organizations in the state, brigades of the *Cruz Azul Mexicana*, societies of all types formed by "Latin Americans" and Mexicans, Latin American civic organizations taking an interest in *"nuestra raza,"* journalists from Spanish-language newspapers, and anyone else interested in improving the lot of *"la gente mexicana"* in the state. All were to meet for a convention in Port Arthur, November 27, 1938.

The prime figures in the movement were aware that several organizations had historically worked in behalf of the moral, economic, and cultural betterment for Mexicans (*hermanos de raza*). Despite all those efforts, they felt, much was left to be accomplished for there existed no real advocate at the higher level to articulate such efforts being waged independently. With the help of the consuls, it was thought, these several independent elements might be brought under one umbrella organization. Following the example of President Lázaro Cárdenas, noted the Publicity Committee (*comité de propaganda*) in September 1938, "more than ever, the consuls feel obligated to work for the well-being of our colonia *'en el extranjero,'* without exclusively dedicating themselves, as they did previously, to holding banquets and bestowing honors on people not always deserving them.'' Disparate groups were to become one under the *Confederación de Organizaciones Mexicanas* in Texas. Once united, the solutions to problems faced by Mexicans could be pursued effectively.[38]

In striving for such an umbrella organization, the movers of what eventually became the *"Confederación de Organizaciones Mexicanas y Latino Americanas del Estado de Texas"* (COMLA) displayed something novel for Texas. First, they saw the need to look upon the Mexican American community as composed of both Mexicans and Americans of Mexican origin. Second, they seemed to diminish the importance of another large organization in existence already, namely the League of United Latin American Citizens (LULAC), which had as its subjects of concern the ''Latin Americans'' of Texas (native born or naturalized Mexicans) since its founding in 1929.

Specifically, COMLA had numerous purposes and only a sampling of its goals is listed herein. Socially, it sought to work so that Mexicans living in the country respected the laws of the land, to cooperate with the diplomatic and consular representatives of Mexico in the United States in defending the interests of Mexicans living in the United States, to help with the organized repatriation of Mexicans, and to work for the reconstruction of Mexico. Culturally, it tried to establish libraries, lecture halls, and cultural centers; found programs whereby Mexican children from the United States could learn more about Mexico; and initiate efforts to have disparaging portrayals of Mexico deleted from United States text books. Economically, it attempted to win better wages for Texas-Mexican workers; end employment discrimination; and inculcate the habit of thrift on Mexican Americans as a means of financial independence.[39]

For some time after its founding, COMLA did well. In 1940, its third annual state convention, attracting some 150 members, was held in Houston. The convention's theme attested to the organization's orientation. As Mexican consul Luis L. Duplán put it:

> The Mexicans are seeking recognition to which they are entitled under the constitution and the laws of the land. In some parts of Texas they are being discriminated against. We are going to try and solve this problem and better conditions for Mexicans and *Latin Americans* in Texas.[40]

Segregation persisted as a major preoccupation for COMLA and it became the dominant theme of the fourth annual state convention in Galveston. According to Señor Duplán, the convention would serve as a forum wherein the issue of segregation against Mexicans, both foreign and native born, would be discussed. Solutions to the problem would be sought. Particularly studied would be available legal means to get officials to correct the anomaly of racial separation.[41]

In Houston proper, efforts to join COMLA had been pursued in September 1938, i.e., at the same time that the larger organization was being assembled by its prime movers. According to the newspaper *El Puerto*, "a solemn, unforgettable occasion took place on the night of the sixth, in which delegates from the majority of the Sociedades Mexicanas of the city came together to achieve something which for years had been needed for our *connacionales*—unity." Finally, after numerous efforts, the paper said, unification of the different societies and clubs of Mexicans and the sons of Mexicans in Houston had been consummated under the aegis of one association.[42]

In Houston, the organization went under the name of *"La Federación de Sociedades Mexicanas y Latino Americanas"* (FSMLA).[43] In accordance with the structure envisioned by the founders of COMLA, the FSMLA embraced those societies and clubs and other organizations functioning within the jurisdiction of the Mexican consul of Houston, although, of course, not every group belonged. Its *Mesa Directiva* (executive board), chosen at the first meeting of September 6, included well-standing members of the Houston community, representing both Mexico and the Mexicans of Houston. Among them, of course, was the consul Luis L. Duplán, and Sr. Manuel Crespo (a local mortician) and the legal advisors, attorneys Daniel Fraser and John Duhig, who also belonged to the local LULAC council.[44]

For the next few years, the FSMLA did its best to work toward acquiring guarantees for both Mexicans and Mexican Americans.[45] As already indicated, it hosted the third annual convention of the parent group (COMLA) in 1940, but with Consul Duplán as one of its guiding hands, FSMLA also paid heed to such things as social and health problems in Houston. At Rusk School, for example, it sponsored a variety of exhibitions instructing members of the community on ways to avoid or control such diseases as syphilis, cancer, and tuberculosis. Other programs directed at the working class included explanations of Social Security. Said presentations were given in Spanish, either by city officials who spoke the language or, in the case of health discussions, by foreign students from Latin America studying medicine in Galveston.

Moreover, the FSMLA in Houston worked closely with the Mexican consuls throughout the state particularly regarding segregation. Jointly, they succeeded in March 1941 in getting (at least temporarily) Wharton

County (southwest of Houston), to remove signs from stores, restaurants, and other public places which read: "Mexicans not Allowed."[46] Also, both kept Mexico near at heart. In April 1941, FSMLA called on its member societies for assistance in an effort to raise funds for the unfortunate victims of an earthquake in the state of Colima, México. Specifically, it asked the societies in the colonia to form a *Comisión o Junta Pro-Damnificados de Colima* (Colima Benefit Commission), for the purpose of carrying out the work of money raising. FSMLA's appeal to a cross-section of the colonia may be seen in the language it employed in addressing the various groups during the emergency. Cleverly, it directed its request to the "patriotismo y buena voluntad que siempre han distinguido al mexicano de afuera" ("patriotism and good will which have always distinguished Mexicanos outside Mexico").[47]

Further, the FSMLA took serious steps towards dealing with conditions in the Houston colonia. When juvenile delinquency surfaced as an issue to be dealt with by Houston during the war years, the FSMLA called upon its various member groups to put together recommendations for curbing the problem and prepare them for submission to the Grand Jury of Harris County. The directive was dutifully fulfilled.[48] In another occasion during World War II, it assigned a special fact-finding committee to study the problem affecting so many Mexicanos in the city. The final report called for greater cooperation with city officials and the formation of numerous committees to deal with such issues as juvenile delinquency, education, and the need for civic involvement.[49]

While the FSMLA pursued an ambitious agenda, a final evaluation of its work awaits a more detailed study. In actuality, the FSMLA faced numerous problems from the beginning. Most important, it apparently was never able to live up to its goal of bringing all of the groups and societies in Houston under its dominion. The fact-finding committee above mentioned specifically noted the absence of a strong organization uniting Mexicans and Mexican Americans. More specifically, in 1941 the FSMLA consisted of only twelve groups of the many that existed in Houston.[50] Moreover, noted the Sociedad Unión Fraternal in a statement prepared for presentation at Galveston during the annual meeting of the COMLA in 1941:

> During the life of the Federation, several committees have been formed, none of which have reported any practical work. Everyone knows that the only thing that the Federación has done is convert itself into a Comité Patriótico. It has distanced itself completely from the sacred

purposes for which it was founded, giving as reason that it cannot attend to the grievances of Mexican citizens because its members are too involved in the preparation of this or that civic fiesta. When the Federación de Sociedades Mexicanas y Latino-Americanas becomes a sovereign body, with its own criteria and its own ideas, only then can it fulfill the intended mission for which it was founded.

With all due respect, we ask that the FEDERACIÓN REGIONAL DE HOUSTON TEXAS, BE REORGANIZED INTO A FORM WHICH GUARANTEES THE INDIVIDUAL RIGHTS WHICH ALL MEXICANS HAVE COMING TO THEM BY CITIZENSHIP OR BY RACE, and if this is not possible, then that the FEDERACIÓN REGIONAL DE HOUSTON, TEXAS, be dissolved.[51]

With such problems, the FSMLA was not able to rally the colonia together for some of its programs. The consul, Sr. Duplán, castigated the community for the lack of attendance during such dates: "It seems that the colonia takes no interest in the solutions of its own problems." It was essential, he noted, that the colonia show Anglo Americans that Mexicans cared about conditions in the community. To continue passively receiving favors without demonstrating interest, the consul admonished, naturally caused Anglos to consider Mexicanos as a "group of individuals incapable of self-management, thus creating the erroneous impression that we need to be subjected to the tutelage of the Anglo-Saxons."[52]

Despite its several deficiencies, the FSMLA still lived as World War II ended. Up to that time, it represented a point in the development of Houston's Mexican colonia during which threads of old intellectual and cultural tenets persisted but were undergoing transformation. Furthermore, the FSMLA represented one of the historical linkages between earlier types of Mexican organizations and newer Mexican American forms. Its presence points to the continuous process of cultural change among Houston's Mexican American people. When the Mexican community became more of a Mexican American community, the FSMLA's purpose would become passé, but during its life's span it had bridged the gap between the Immigrant and Mexican American Generation.

NOTES

[1]*El Sol*, March 21, 1969, P. 1.
[2]Houston *Chronicle*, June 19, 1934, p. 11.
[3]Houston *Post*, April 21, 1937, p. 1 (Section 1); April 22, 1937, p. 1 (Section 1); June 2, 1937, p. 2 (Section 1); June 3, 1937, p. 1 (Section 1); Newspaper clippings in HMRC, Juvencio Rodríguez Collection.

[4]*El Tecolote*, September 12, 1934, from newspaper clippings in HMRC, Chairez Family Collection.

[5]HMRC, Oral History Collection, interview with Mrs. Felix H. Morales.

[6]*El Puerto*, Julio 22, 1938, p. 2; Agosto 26, 1938, p. 2.

[7]Ibid., Julio 22, 1938, p. 2; Agosto 12, 1938, p. 1; Agosto 26, 1938, p. 1; September 9, 1938, p. 1; September 30, 1938, p. 1.

[8]Ibid., Diciembre 20, 1935.

[9]Houston *Chronicle*, May 21, 1935, p. 14.

[10]Ibid., November 10, 1940, p. 4E.

[11]Rosales, "Mexicans in Houston: The Struggle to Survive," p. 237; *El Tecolote*, Mayo 1930, Año VI, No. 276; Newspaper clippings, HMRC, Chairez Family Collection; Houston *Chronicle*, May 5, 1932, p. 16; November 24, 1935, p. 14; May 6, 1935, p. 7; September 16, 1935, p. 12.

[12]Carlos B. Gil, "Lydia Mendoza: Houstonian and First Lady of Mexican American Song," *The Houston Review*, III (Summer, 1981), 250–260.

[13]Houston *Chronicle*, May 9, 1945, p. 9B.

[14]*El Tecolote*, Houston Texas, May 1930; Houston *Chronicle*, May 4, 1930, p. 21; September 16, 1931, p. 24; May 5, 1932, p. 16; September 15, 1933, p. 23; May 6, 1935, p. 7; August 18, 1935, p. 4; September 16, 1935, p. 12; Houston *Press*, September 16, 1937, n.p.

[15]*El Puerto*, September 23, 1938, p. 1, 5; Houston *Chronicle*, January 23, 1945, p. 11.

[16]"Fiftieth Anniversary Program," HMRC, Club México Bello Collection; Houston *Post*, January 21, 1979, p. 8D; HMRC Oral History Collection, interview with Isidro García and Primitivo L. Niño, April 9, 1979.

[17]"Fiftieth Anniversary Program," HMRC, Club México Bello Collection.

[18]HMRC, Chairez Family Collection. See also, Houston *Chronicle*, April 5, 1935, p. 10; January 7, 1935, p. 7; Houston *Post*, June 26, 1934, p. 7; June 19, 1934, p. 4; HMRC, Oral History Collection, interview with Ramón Fernández, September 5, 1979.

[19]Fiftieth Anniversary Program, HMRC, Club México Bello Collection; HMRC Oral History Collection, interview with Isidro García and Primitivo L. Niño, April 9, 1979; *El Puerto*, Octubre 7, 1938, p. 5.

[20]Emphasis mine. HMRC, Melesio Gómez Family Collection; HMRC Oral History Collection, interview with Juvencio Rodríguez, August 14, 1980; *El Puerto*, Agosto 19, 1938, p. 1; Agosto 26, 1938, p. 1; Noviembre 8, 1935, p. 1; Houston *Chronicle*, July 15, 1945, p. 10C.

[21]*El Puerto*, Agosto 19, 1938, p. 1; Octubre 7, 1938, p. 5; Houston *Chronicle*, September 20, 1940, p. 10B.

[22]Houston *Chronicle*, February 22, 1930, p. 3; February 23, 1930, p. 14.

[23]Houston *Chronicle*, September 18, 1930, p. 14.

[24]Rosales, "Mexicans in Houston: The Struggle to Survive," pp. 236, 240.

[25]Campo Laurel, #2333 W.O.W., Marzo 2, 1908, typescript, HMRC, Mexican American Small Collection.

[26]*El Puerto*, Agosto 12, 1938, p. 3.

[27]HMRC Oral History Collection, interview with Refugio Gómez, March 24, 1980.

[28]Houston *Chronicle*, February 25, 1945, p. 3B; October 6, 1936, p. 12.

History of Mexican-Americans

[29]HMRC Oral History Collection, interview with Mrs. Félix H. Morales; *El Puerto*, Octubre 7, 1938, p. 1.

[30]HMRC Oral History Collection, interview with Mrs. Félix H. Morales; *El Puerto*, Octubre 7, 1938, p. 1; "Proyecto de Estatutos de la Sociedad 'Unión Fraternal'," Acta #21 and Acta #31, and "Poema Dedicado a la H. Sociedad 'Unión Fraternal'," all in HMRC, Félix Morales Collection. Also see *The Texas Catholic Herald*, September 27, 1968, p. 10.

[31]Acta #35, HMRC, Félix Morales Collection ("Unión Fraternal").

[32]Scrapbook, HMRC, Melesio Gómez Family Collection; *El Puerto*, Julio 12, 1935, p. 2; Agosto 2, 1935, p. 2; Octubre 4, 1935, p. 1; Diciembre 20, 1935, p. 1; Agosto 12, 1938, p. 1; September 6, 1935, p. 5; Houston *Chronicle*, May 4, 1930, p. 21.

[33]Thomas H. Kreneck, "The Letter from Chapultepec," *The Houston Review*, III (Summer, 1981), 268–69; *El Puerto*, Noviembre 8, 1935, p. 1; Noviembre 8, 1935, p. 1; Julio 15, 1938, p. 1; HMRC, Melesio Gómez Family Collection; HMRC Oral History Collection, interview with Carmen Cortez, December 16, 1983; "Chapultepec," manuscript, HMRC, Melesio Gómez Family Collection.

[34]This report, held in HMRC, Melesio Gómez Family Collection, is printed in full with commentary in Kreneck, "The Letter from Chapultepec."

[35]García, "Mexican Americans and the Politics of Citizenship: The Case of El Paso, 1936," pp. 195–198; Francisco E. Balderrama, *In Defense of La Raza: The Los Angeles Mexican Consulate and the Mexican Community, 1929–1936*, pp. 2, 22–23.

[36]*El Puerto*, Julio 15, 1938, p. 1; Balderrama, *In Defense of La Raza*, p. 6.

[37]*El Puerto*, September 23, 1938, p. 6; HMRC, Félix Morales Collection ("Union Fraternal").

[38]*El Puerto*, September 23, 1938, p. 1, 5, and 6.

[39]The long list that made up the COMLA's "Programa de Acción" is listed in ibid., Octubre, 7, 1938, p. 1.

[40]Houston *Chronicle*, August 30, 1940, p. 19B. Emphasis mine.

[41]"Circular Num. 7," HMRC, Félix Morales Collection ("Unión Fraternal"); "Convocatoria," Ibid.

[42]*El Puerto*, September 9, 1938, p. 1.

[43]Apparently, the organization went through changes of names before finally settling on "La Federación de Sociedades Mexicanas y Latino Americanas." At the beginning, it was named the "Confederación de Sociedades Mexicanas." *El Puerto*, September 9, 1938, p. 1; September 30, 1938, p. 1. Once in a while, members referred to it by its more descriptive name "La Federación Regional de Sociedades Mexicanas y Latino Americanas de Houston, Texas." See "Circular," 24 abril, 1941, HMRC, Félix Morales Collection ("Unión Fraternal").

[44]*El Puerto*, September 30, 1938, p. 1, 6; "Circular," 5 de Abril, 1941, HMRC, Félix Morales Collection ("Unión Fraternal").

[45]*El Puerto*, September 30, 1938, p. 1, 6.

[46]"Circular," 5 de marzo 1941, HMRC, Félix Morales Collection ("Unión Fraternal"). See further, Houston *Chronicle*, January 22, 1943, p. 16A; April 1, 1943, p. 5A.

[47]"Circular," 5 de marzo 1941, HMRC, Félix Morales Collection ("Unión Fraternal").

[48]"To the Honorable Grand Jury of Harris County," July 7, 1944, HMRC, Mexican

78

American Small Collection; and "Letter," May 30, 1945, HMRC, LULAC Council #60 Collection.

[49]"Honorables miembros de la Federación de Sociedades Mexicanas y Latino Americanas de Houston, Texas," HMRC, Félix Morales Collection ("Unión Fraternal").

[50]"Circular," 5 de abril 1941, HMRC, Félix Morales Collection ("Unión Fraternal").

[51]"Ponencia," HMRC, Félix Morales Collection ("Unión Fraternal"). Their emphasis. Also see, Houston *Chronicle,* September 12, 1943, p. 7B.

[52]"Circular," 5 de marzo, 1941, HMRC, Félix Morales Collection ("Unión Fraternal").

CHAPTER V
LOYAL CITIZENS OF THE UNITED STATES

Whether Mexicanos in Houston looked to Mexico or the United States for their cultural inspiration in the 1930s and the war years is difficult to determine precisely. From what can be ascertained from the current state of research, several strains of thought existed simultaneously. But the Depression decade was the era during which a good portion of the community manifested a philosophical outlook that reflected its acceptance of American culture. Intellectual and cultural change was evident in many things, including the need for an organization such as the FSMLA. But it was most clearly revealed in the founding of Council #60 of the League of United Latin American Citizens.

LULAC Council #60 was an offspring of the Mexican American Generation of the 1930s. Throughout South Texas, different ideas, values, and concepts were being disseminated by a corps of leaders within the Tejano community which sought to improve the socio-economic lot of their fellow Mexican Americans. This element represented those cohorts whose experiences mirrored their birth or upbringing in the United States. For the most part, they represented a new social class comprised of entrepreneurs as well as a small but significant number of professionals, doctors, and lawyers. They were in fact, the more fortunate in Texas-Mexican society whose living conditions and attitudes compared favorably with American standards. Their outlook was a further evolution of the visions held by those who comprised the Immigrant Generation.[1]

Such ways of thinking and feeling differed from those who had articulated the intellectual streams of the 1920s in Houston and elsewhere. Previous to the 1930s, the Mexican community in Texas was not too advanced in its degree of acculturation. For the most part, Mexicanos before then had not accepted the legitimacy of American social and political institutions. Born or raised in Mexico, most lacked command of the English language and even rejected the need to participate in the established institutions of the United States, many times because they were prohibited from doing so.[2]

By the Depression decade, however, native Mexican American groups seeking social and economic betterment for Tejanos could count on an emerging ethos springing from the American environment. The immigrants of the twentieth century had produced the first native-born generation—the 1930 census of Texas reported about 60% of the Mexican-stock people to be United States born[3]—and the formative years of the baby crop of the 1920s and 1930s were ones influenced by an upbringing amid institutions which, while snubbing Texas-Mexicans, nonetheless sought to mold them into Americans. Tejanos themselves displayed suspicion of mainstream institutions, yet at least endorsed their legitimacy since these institutions were the only ones they knew. Spanish remained the dominant tongue in the colonia, yet the schools yearly educated little ones in the language of their native land. Mexican culture proved durable, but allegiance for the younger generation was to the United States and Texas.

What the rising middle class did to counter discrimination and prejudice was to found new types of organizations in the communities of south and central Texas which tapped this incipient Mexican American element. Such organizations differed from their historical predecessors (like Houston's Mutualista "Benito Juárez" which endeavored to provide assistance for its members) in several ways, but namely they collectively challenged discriminatory public policies and practices and they focused their concerns toward the needs of "U.S. Citizens of Mexican ancestry." The earliest such organization was the *Orden Hijos de América,* established in Corpus Christi in 1921.[4] For several reasons, among them the fact that so many Texas-Mexicans were of foreign birth and not yet socially integrated, the OHA did not flourish. The times, therefore, favored another civil rights organization (which the OHA spurred), the League of United Latin American Citizens, founded in 1929. By then, a Mexican American generation could act as the base of LULAC strength.

Most certainly, LULAC articulated the new feeling. LULACers held up the virtues of the country responsible for oppressing Mexicanos, but they were bent on eliminating racial prejudice, struggling for legal equality, aiming for better equal educational facilities, and gaining a voice in local, state, and national politics. Theirs was a liberal attack on a society that restrained their rights as citizens, not a radical challenge to the country's political, social, and economic structure. Thus, LULAC opposed extreme methods of protest, such as strikes and marches. The capitalist system might be exploitative, but LULACers called for equality within it, not overthrowing it. Contrary to the mutual aid groups, LULAC sought cultural integration wherein Mexicans would adopt Americanisms, albeit they would retain their parents' cultural life. Whereas the other organizations were generally protective in design, LULAC desired to make Mexicans active citizens.[5] Further revealing of its evolutionary posture, its primary concern was with the Mexicans of American citizenship; while LULAC paid attention to the needs of their cousins born in Mexico (LULACers in Houston were active in the FSMLA), the foreign born had their defenders in the Mexican consul (at times, LULAC leaders did work closely with the consuls in cases involving Mexican nationals). Thus membership in LULAC was restricted to Mexican Americans, native born or naturalized (the mutualistas had been open to everyone).

The Mexican American mentality and the ideals of LULAC found expression in Houston through the formation of LULAC Council #60, chartered in November 1934. That a chapter was founded in Houston later than in other parts of Texas is not out of the ordinary; the earliest councils were in San Antonio and South Texas, towns which had a longer history of settlements and in which there had developed (in many cases since the nineteenth century) a class of entrepreneurs and professionals that serviced the Mexican community with grocery stores, barber shops, furniture stores, drug stores, and the like.[6] By the early 1930s, however, the Houston colonia was a community whose time for a LULAC council had come. It was receptive to the LULAC propaganda coming from South Texas, generated by the LULAC *News* and probably by personal proselytizing by leading LULACers. In May 1932, for example, M. C. Gonzales, the prominent lawyer from San Antonio who had helped found both the Orden Hijos de América and LULAC, was in Houston on a legal matter. Working as attorney in behalf of the Mexican consul general at San Antonio, Gonzales and the Mexican consul in Houston had presented evidence to a grand jury concerning the death of a Mexican by a Houston city detective (the officer had been suspended from the police department in the meantime).[7] It may have been quite in keeping with his sense of duty for Gonzales to try to get a council established in Houston during that visit, for as an editorial in the LULAC *News* entitled "Our Obligations and Community Progress" (March, 1933), stated ". . . the responsibility for the future of our people in this country rests squarely upon the shoulders of every leader of Latin extraction."[8]

Accommodation and Self-Help

Whether Gonzales or other LULACers from outside Houston were active in mustering support for the establishment of Council #60 is immaterial (it would not be the last time that Gonzales would come to Houston to deal with LULAC matters), for the circumstances of the 1930s made the birth of a council almost inevitable. That is, in Houston also, there existed counterparts who concurred with the ideas permeating other communities in Texas. Thus, when discussion for a LULAC chapter seriously got under way in 1934, the result was Council #60's founding in Magnolia Park. According to the Houston *Chronicle*:

> The object of the club is to study the laws of local government, and to induce the Latin people of Houston to understand the government, to partake of voting privileges, and thus to become better citizens. It is a civil organization composed of native born or naturalized poll-tax paying citizens of Latin extraction.[9]

Council #60's founders were an array of men with a modest standing in the community. "Most, or all of us, had fairly good jobs," remembered John J. Herrera, an early stalwart. Among them were Herrera, an aspiring attorney, Dr. Ángel González, Félix H. Morales, owner of Morales Funeral Home, Manuel Crespo, the mortician, John H. Duhig, a lawyer, Manuel M. Ortíz, Félix Tijerina, a restauranteur, and Juvencio Rodríguez, a grocery worker (graduate of the Houston high schools in 1925), and the tailor Isidro García (of "México Bello").[10] However, much of the rank and file was comprised of blue collar workers, including longshoremen who belonged to the union.[11] Membership was heavily weighted with people from Magnolia, and the council quickly took on the image of a club exclusive of other sections of Houston. The fragmentation which surfaced early on in Houston's Mexican American history, therefore, made its mark on LULAC's first years of existence.

During the first half of 1935, membership in Magnolia Council #60 continued growing. From its original meeting place at an old filling station on the corner of 74th and Navigation Boulevard, the Council moved to International Longshoremen's Association (I.L.A.) Union Hall, Seventy-Sixth and Avenue N, then to the more spacious "Benito Juárez" Hall on 7310 Navigation Boulevard.[12]

Within six months after its founding, Council #60 craftily won over the League's leadership by convincing it to hold its meeting of the South Texas division of the League at the Houston City Auditorium. Throughout the conference, thoughts expressive of the Mexican American mind were evident in the symbolic gestures and protocol of the proceedings: the pledging of allegiance and the formal presentation of an American flag sent to the League by Vice President John Nance Garner (an honorary member). But they were unmistakeable in the rhetoric of the convention. When Mayor Oscar Holcombe addressed the group, he stated unabashedly: "If inequalities and injustices are practiced towards you—and sometimes they are, I know—it is your own fault. You should come among us on an equal footing, pay your poll tax, exercise your suffrage, take an active part in your government." In language glaringly transparent of the League's new concepts, Ermilo R. Lozano, president general of the League responded:

> Mayor Holcombe is right in what he says, but I want to say to him that we shall take up, as a league, the challenge he laid down to us. Mr. Mayor, we are not Mexican citizens. We are American citizens. We know and recognize no other country. We have been accused of being liabilities to a community. If we exercise our American citizenship properly those accusations will cease. To you American citizens of Latin extraction I say, pay your poll tax and be independent financially. Be good, true and loyal American citizens. [13]

Even as the mayor distorted the reality of the times—segregation, discrimination, and economic exploitation—Lozano could say little else. Concededly, he made a diplomatic concession by not challenging Holcombe on his own turf, but LULACers were not disinclined to cast blame on Mexican Americans for their problems. Further, the system about which Holcombe spoke was to them unparalleled in the world. It would yield the necessary room that would lead to social improvement, LULAC believed, if only Mexicans made compromises with immigrant culture and traditions and accepted American habits, beliefs, and dispositions as part of a bicultural character. Once concessions were made to mainstream influences, society would accept Mexicans as equals to other Americans.

With the lift it got from the May 1935 meeting, Council #60 went about its goals of establishing committees to get people to make poll tax payments, of discussing ways and means of bringing about improved education and social betterment, and of naturalizing or at least trying to get the foreign born to take out first papers for naturalization. [14] Also, it acted to create a women's auxiliary, a movement that led to the establishment of Ladies LULAC Council No. 14. [15] Together, these councils worked to achieve what they deemed realistic for the epoch—persuading the Texas-Mexican community to accept the ways of the host country and adopt a "Mexican American" identity.

As circumstances had it, disagreement soon surfaced among members from the different barrios concerning the best location for Council #60's headquarters. Those from "Houston" (that is, from outside Magnolia), felt Magnolia to be too far for weekly meetings. Further, they wished to attract members from the Northside. Much of the summer of 1935 was thus spent contesting the true membership of Council #60: those from Magnolia maintaining they made up the council, those from Houston arguing otherwise. At one point, the Houston group (which included Herrera, Morales, Dr. González, and Juvencio Rodríguez) voted in the majority to move the meetings to the Milam Building at the corner of Milam and Texas Avenues. There Council #60 held some of its meetings for a while, until the flap drew the president general of LULAC, Mr. James Tafolla, and Mr. M. C. Gonzales, to come to Houston from their homes in San Antonio. Gonzales, the League's legal advisor, ruled that the meetings at the Milam Building were illegal and ordered everyone back to Magnolia Park.[16]

The Latin American Club

The "Houston" group, which included John H. Duhig, John J. Herrera, Juvencio Rodríguez, Félix H. Morales, Dr. González, and Félix Tijerina, among others, refused to return to "Magnolia Council #60" (as it was technically called). They believed in the LULAC creed, but they were prohibited from using the LULAC name. So, they kept up their LULAC dues and bided their time.[17]

In October 1935, the defectors organized themselves into a bona fide club, calling it the "Latin American Club of Harris County" (LAC) with its meeting place at 915 Milam Building. Its purpose was similar to that of the larger organization it sought to emulate; as LAC's constitution put it, LAC was "to protect Latin American Citizens of this country. To educate them, teach them the importance of United States Citizenship, and to study the Laws of local, state and National Government. To induce the Latin American people to understand the government and partake in voting privileges extended to them in the Constitution of the United States and all other privileges extended to them in said Constitution." In dramatic contrast to Club "México Bello" founded eleven years previous, the official language of the club was to be English and the official colors were to be red, white, and blue. Meetings would begin with a pledge to the United States flag.[18]

Further differentiating it from the Mexican-oriented clubs of the twenties and thirties was its detachment from the foreign born. LAC involved itself in matters involving people from Mexico, but to the leaders of the 1930s, the interest of those born in this country took priority. "The Mexicans had to complain to the Mexican consul," explained Alfred J. Hernández, who joined LULAC in 1938 and later became a LULAC National Director. "An alien could not go before the city council and make demands. He could not say he was a citizen, 'I have my poll tax, I have my rights.' "[19] In the Elpidio Cortez case, for example, LAC took a subdued role, lending moral support and monitoring the trial. In another front, LAC took no stand on the controversy arising with Mexico over that country's expropriation of American oil interests there in 1938. "The stand of Secretary of State Cordell Hull will be our stand," noted LAC president John Duhig. "While we hope for the friendliest possible relations between the two countries, we are American citizens, not Mexican citizens. We will regard developments in the oil situation just like any other foreign news."[20]

During the years immediate to its founding, LAC coexisted with LULAC Council #60, but it was far more active than the men from Magnolia; indeed, for a while, Council #60 even became dormant. In its efforts to bring about improvement for Houston's Mexicans, LAC plunged into numerous social, political, and welfare activities. It organized meetings around matters of education, Americanization, the value of the English language, the virtues of the capitalist system, worked in behalf of workers' conditions and better pay,[21] and tried to implement programs to benefit city youths. In the latter case, it formed a Boy Scout troop for Mexican Americans, and also endorsed recreation bonds and urged citizens to vote for them in August 1935, as said bonds would be used to improve recreational facilities in the several barrios.[22] Further, it organized youth groups such as the *"Club Recreativo Tenochtitlán."* This club worked on projects in efforts to get the city's Parks and Recreation Department to improve school playgrounds.[23]

LAC also made health one of its concerns and undertook projects to ameliorate conditions for the community. It assisted with programs undertaken under the aegis of the Red Cross and the Community Chest and participated in city and county health movements designed to stamp out contagious diseases. During the early Depression years, reports said, many Mexican workers contracted tuberculosis and the disease made heavy inroads into their families. LAC, therefore, pursued steps to aid in the fight against the disease. In May 1938, it sponsored along with other groups, "Latin American Health Week." The week's activities held in the several Mexican schools of the city involved lectures and free moving pictures on tuberculosis and other phases of health conditions.[24]

On the civic front, LAC's major campaign was for poll tax (*"impuestos de votación"*) payment. These drives were ambitious ones (in January 1938, LAC set as its goal the number for poll tax payments at 10,000 Latin Americans), which, according to newspaper accounts, met encouraging success. As well, the Club undertook such matters of civic interest as hosting demonstrations of new voting machines.[25]

In apparent recognition of LAC's work, the national LULAC held its ninth annual convention in Houston in 1937. Delegates from Texas, New Mexico, and California were in attendance and Félix J. Cerda of Houston was a candidate for president-general of the League. Once more, the speakers' rhetoric confirmed the sentiments of the LULACers. The loyalty of Mexicans to Texas history was conspicuous by its repetition, both by the Mexican American delegates and the Anglo guests of honor. Scores of Mexicans were loyal to General Sam Houston and Texas during the Texas Revolution, emphasized the mayor. At San Jacinto, Mexican-Texans fought against a dictator, noted another orator. Frank J. Galván, incumbent president general of the League, reminded his listeners that it was Juan N. Seguín who had given the Alamo dead a military funeral.[26] These were belated tributes which could well have been delivered during the state's centennial—for the Houston LULAC had just missed getting the national convention to meet in the Bayou City the previous year.

While the addresses of the convention attested to the thinking of the Mexican American Generation, other episodes confirm the new consciousness. Mexican Americans downplayed "lo mexicano"; still they faced rejection. So many American institutions might be extolled, but Mexican Americans nonetheless felt discomfort in the pejorative attitudes Anglo society displayed toward them as people of mixed-blood (*mestizos*). The new generation sought conformity, but it also sensed insecurity in the racial slurs which denigrated them to less than whiteness.

Indicative of their sensitivity toward color was their response during a 1936 incident in which the newly established Social Security Board called upon Mexicans in the United States applying for social security to designate themselves as a race other than "white" (typical examples were Mexican, Chinese, Japanese, Indian, Filipino, etc.). LAC immediately rose to the occasion as did fledgling Council #60 and other LULAC councils in the rest of the state.[27] In a drive spearheaded by Juvencio Rodríguez in Houston, LAC brought together the different organizations that existed at that time in the city and immediate areas and commenced a letter writing campaign to rescind the designation. As one of LAC's letters to Joe H. Eagle, Congressman-Eighth District, stated: "We are NOT a 'yellow' race, and we protest being classified as such, and ask that this classification be corrected to eliminate such classification for the Latin-American Race." Eagle's own letter to the Social Security Board, which tried to put the protestors' minds at ease, is worth quoting at length:

> The more than 60,000 citizens of Houston of Mexican descent unitedly protest that classification [of placing Mexicans in a class "other than white"]. They insist that they belong to the white race having descended from Spanish. They urge, in agreement with hundreds of thousands in Texas belonging to the same racial group, that this discrimination is humiliating to their pride and unjust to their proper status, and they beg and urge that such classification as excludes them from designation as white race be promptly amended.

In the end, the Social Security Board in Washington sent apologies to LAC and assured them that Mexicans would be classified as whites by the board.[28] But the indignation raised by the episode cannot be dismissed lightly, and it is subject to at least two interpretations. On the one hand, it underscored the defensiveness and ambivalence of the Mexican organizations toward their identification. The outrage at being defined as colored signified a break with the Indianness of a Benito Juárez and their refusal to accept the racial connotation and its social meaning in the country they loved. In actuality, the Social Security benefits would have been the same regardless of the color designation. On the other hand, LAC took umbrage with the designation because the membership foresaw the ramifications of reclassification for de jure segregation. Astutely anticipating the effects of classification, members moved swiftly to nullify the perceived subterfuge.

Further manifesting LAC members' sensitivity to their citizenship as white Americans was a flap over a racist remark made by a member of city government in 1938. Since its inception, LAC had asserted itself as a liberal group carrying its activities within the spirit of peaceful aggression as advocated by the League, and indeed LAC proved more confrontational than any other previous group in Houston. In its drive for equality it showed gallantry by standing up to epithets and open disparagement of Mexican Americans.

The affair arose from a request for payment of wages lost by thirty-seven Water Department employees including seventeen Mexicans, for having taken off to celebrate San Jacinto Day (April 21). To that demand, City Council commissioner S. A. Starkey allegedly had quipped: "What! Pay Mexicans for the day they were beaten [at the Battle of San Jacinto]." LAC, joined by the Magnolia Council #60, protested heatedly before the City Council that the remark was derogatory and that Tejanos fighting on the American side at San Jacinto laid the foundation for the birth of the independence of Texas. Among those thirty-seven petitioning for the lost wages, wrote John J. Herrera to the Houston *Press,* were himself, a direct descendant of one of the signers of the Texas Declaration of Independence (March 2, 1836), a World War I veteran wounded in action, and two men who could trace their ancestry to ten generations back on Texas soil. All were American citizens and possessed a poll tax.[29]

LAC threatened to press the issue beyond remonstration. Before the City Council, John Duhig, president of the Club, chided Starkey:

> We are not going to be led by the nose by politicians, who, once they are elected go their way, draw big salaries, pay no income tax, and forget the Latin American citizen, who has done his duty in placing him in office, for we know those but who have shown us by their deeds that they have no respect and consideration for our people, and for those we will not cast our vote.

LAC claimed to have had 1,500 poll taxes to battle the commissioner and proposed putting up a candidate of its own in the field against Starkey if he had no other opposition. In his defense, Starkey noted that he had been misquoted on the issue, but offered no apology. To appease LAC, the mayor instructed the water department to pay the workers for the day off.[30]

While LAC's work had been more aggressive than Council #60's, the two groups' ideologies had always been reconcilable, so plans to unite the two seemed not an impossibility. In 1939, the famous *Esquadrón Volante* (Flying Squadron) of LULAC leaders from San Antonio (the *Esquadrón* got its name from the many sweeps it made into different areas of the state to organize new clubs and recruit new members) arrived in Houston to discuss the reorganization of the Houston LULAC Councils. LAC was just one club with its voice limited to Harris County, the argument was made by the San Antonio people, but it could well become part of a national organization. With not much more persuasion, therefore, the Latin American Club of Harris County merged with Council #60.[31]

The Venture Into Politics

Towards the latter part of the 1930s, LULACers showed increased interest in politics, both at the local and state levels. While involved in a wide variety of anti-discrimination activities, LULAC from its birth had been a non-political organization which steered clear of partisan politics. But satellite organizations were apparently founded for the purpose of getting the Houston community integrated into the politics of the era, for Council #60 members doubled as officers and movers of these newer clubs. Indeed, these other groups were distinguishable from LULAC only by their names and their emphasis on politics.

The "Texas American Citizens" of Magnolia Park, for example, could hardly have been accused of having an un-American name. Its purpose was to acquaint Mexican American citizens with the qualifications of aspiring political officeseekers. At one of its meetings in 1938, the club brought before the barrio some eight Anglo politicians, among them Ernest Thompson, candidate for governor of the state. Many of the candidates spoke for themselves while LULAC members such as John H. Duhig and Félix Tijerina spoke in behalf of others. Each contender promised to work for the betterment of the Mexican people.[32]

The "Latin Sons of Texas," similarly, was behind the guidance of LULACers like Juvencio Rodríguez and duplicated the LULAC requirement that members should be "native Texans or naturalized citizens of Latin blood" (Victor de Zavala, grandson of Lorenzo de Zavala, was an honorary member). Like Council #60, the group encouraged Mexican Americans to participate in politics and to buy their poll tax. But in direct contradistinction to LULAC, it took political stands. In November 1940, it endorsed a slate of candidates, the first endorsement ever by a Mexican American organization in Houston, according to the Houston *Chronicle*.[33] By 1940, also, other organizations were politically active in Houston, holding rallies for Anglo candidates. Among them were the Pan American Club and the Cooperative Club of Latin American Citizens, both in Magnolia Park.[34]

Council #60: New Struggles, 1941–1945

Even before the Japanese attacked Pearl Harbor, the United States began preparation for war. Houston became part of President Franklin D. Roosevelt's program for building up an "arsenal for the democracies." Then, as the United States joined the Allies against the Axis, Houston became an even more significant contributor to the war effort. Millions of dollars in state-provided capital flowed into private and joint private-public oil-related enterprises in the Gulf Coast area, especially the petrochemical industry. Aviation fuel and synthetic rubber in particular were important products in the war effort and Houston reaped a significant windfall by meeting the emergency.[35]

Oil refineries needed workers and hired them at good wages, but they maintained a policy of discrimination against minorities, not giving jobs to Mexican Americans higher than ditch-diggers or janitors. Council #60 worked closely with the Fair Employment Practice Committee to expose these inequities. Shipyard companies, which made liberty ships and pursuit boats (PT boats), followed practices similar to the refineries,[36] and on a regular basis, Council #60 received complaints about hiring discrimination there and the releasing of personnel on the basis of nationality; i.e., Mexican Americans went before Anglo Americans. It was made aware, also, of other businesses that rejected Mexican help. One large canning company in the city went so far as to post a sign on its spacious lawn which read "We Do Not Hire Mexicans Here."

In protesting discrimination at the workplace, Council #60 avoided an overzealous stance; after all, it did believe in the institutions which it attacked and in the war against the Nazis. Instead of blasting racist practices, Council #60's most vociferous spokesman, John J. Herrera, appealed to Anglos' common belief in the meaning of America. "It is the selfish practices of a vicious minority that boomerangs on our entire country," he wrote to the Houston *Press* in 1941. "Let's put up a complete and united front and show the world that the greatest democracy composed of a melting pot of races and nationalities will and can survive." In another letter to one of the shipyard companies, he scolded the personnel superintendent: "It is unbelievable to me that members of my racial extraction, who fought as Americans at Pearl Harbor, Luzon, and Bataan could be treated so unfairly on the home front. The elimination of racial discriminations is essential in our defense industries in order to use every available man for our ultimate victory."[37] These were actions in consonance with LULAC's liberal criticism of the institutions it admired.

In addition to tackling problems in the war-connected industries, Council #60 continued battling long-standing prejudice. As late as 1944, not a single Mexican American had served in a Harris County grand jury. But working closely with attorney Percy Foreman and other interested groups, Council #60 was able to make LULACer Fernando Salas, the old organizer and leader of *"La Asamblea Mexicana,"* the first person of Mexican descent to serve in that capacity.[38] Also, it continued its campaign against inequality in the schools, believing that segregation and its attendant problems (e.g., inferior equipment) blocked the drive towards Americanization. In early 1944, therefore, Council #60 formed the "Anti-Segregated Mexican School Committee" for the purpose of fighting this "threat of discrimination to our great Democracy."[39] At the state level, it worked alongside other groups in support of the establishment of the Good Neighbor Commission in 1943.[40]

World War II: At Home and Abroad

There was no question by the era of World War II that many Mexicans in Houston had accepted the consciousness espoused most clearly by the LULACers. As the war got into high gear, it became obvious that "la patria" was now the United States. The American flag, service to the country, and honor to its war heroes were the symbols around which most Mexican American Houstonians rallied. With the declaration of war against the Axis, patriotism and allegiance were displayed with unprecedented ardor. The newspapers of the period abound with stories about men from Magnolia, El Segundo Barrio, and the Northside fighting courageously, some being decorated for their valor, while others are reported listed as a prisoner of war, wounded in action, coming home on convalescent furlough, or proclaimed as killed in action. Tragically, Houston's first war victim was a Mexican American, Mr. Joe Padilla, a naval fireman from the Northside.[41]

For its part, LULAC took several initiatives. In April 1942, it began a practice that would last for some forty years: laying a wreath and reading a few words at the San Jacinto Memorial Park on San Jacinto Day (April 21). On that occasion, LULACer John J. Herrera (a seventh-generation Texan whose ancestors included several Texas Revolutionary luminaries) delivered a speech which LULACers throughout the state would have endorsed:

> From San Jacinto and the Alamo to Pearl Harbor, Bataan and Corregidor, the Latin Americans have fought side by side to their brother Anglo Americans, and the armed forces of our country, the Army, the Navy and the Marines are loaded with determined young Latin Americans whose only thought and attitude is to "Set the Rising Sun" and to "Beat the Axis."[42]

These words, with appropriate adjustments, would be read by Herrera at the San Jacinto Memorial until 1983.

Furthermore, Council #60, under president John J. Herrera, succeeded in 1943 in getting the U.S. Maritime Commission to approve the naming of Liberty ships after Mexican and Latin American statesmen. These ships were built at the Houston Shipbuilding Corporation, a yard which employed hundreds of Mexican Americans. In April of that year, the SS Benito Juárez was launched amid the festivities of Pan American week, with Senator Dennis Chavez delivering the main speech. The SS José Navarro was launched from the same yard several months later. It was named after José Antonio Navarro, signer of the Texas Declaration of Independence.[43]

LULAC also took a lead in recognizing the feats of the war heroes. In 1944, for one thing, it initiated an attempt to put together a history of war memories, namely a leather bound book to serve as a permanent archive of all Latin American men and women of Mexican descent who served in the armed forces during the War.[44] At war's end, Council #60 could look at several Latin American heroes whose example was undeniable proof of Mexicanos' willingness to fight for their country. It paid homage to the Medal of Honor winners from Texas—Cleto Rodríguez of San Antonio, Luciano Adams of Port Author, and the most prominent of all, Macario García of nearby Sugarland; on more than one occasion, García was feted by the Council as the epitome of Mexican American bravery.[45] For the LULACers, Macario García was as true an American as had been the Texas-Mexicans that had died at the Alamo or fought with Sam Houston at the Battle of San Jacinto. In 1981, the old 69th Street on Magnolia Park would be named after him.[46]

A Note on the Early LULACers

Chicano activists during the 1960s and early 1970s looked disdainfully upon the League of United Latin American Citizens, now past its half-century of existence. The League, it was said, was too sold on mainstream institutions to mount effectively a challenge similar to the one in which Chicanos were participating. More recently, scholars have begun to understand LULAC's efforts in behalf of civil rights. Historians now recognize that LULAC represented a middle class and that their social standing shaped their particular form of protest. As more is learned about Mexican American history, furthermore, it becomes evident that certain modes of thinking and acting reflect an adjustment to times. Forms of protest are not consistent. Historical subjects express their discontent in ways which might effect change and still preserve their lives and dignity (slaves in ante-bellum South revealed their hatred of the system by break-ing tools and slowing down on the job instead of rebelling and insuring their own death). As has been noted repeatedly, Houston is minus a his-tory of massive protest, and in the 1930s, no one else was demonstrating, picketing, or boycotting. LULAC's tactic of writing letters to those en-gaged in the discriminatory treatment of Mexicanos, dispatching delega-tions to investigate cases of racial prejudice, and appealing to society's sense of justice in order to get people on grand juries, for instance, con-formed to a time period during which militant protest was intolerable. Ironically, the men who staunchly believed American society to be the best in the world were run out of places on numerous occasions and warned to take their Communist organization (LULAC) along with them.

LULACers have also come under attack for advocating assimilation. This they did, but never at the expense of renouncing "lo mexicano." Politically, the LULACers were Americans, but they took pride in their cultural past. Most were selective about their political and social life and were comfortable being bicultural. They sought to adhere to democratic ideals while maintaining their prerogative of observing their parents' old tenets. Even as members of LULAC Council #60 invoked the ideals of the Texas Revolution, the meaning of the flag, the purpose of their League, and the symbols of country, service, heroism, and honor, they spoke Spanish fluently. The majority did not Anglicize their names. Many LULAC people did double duty as members of clubs such as "México Bello" and the FSMLA. In the naming of organizations for the young, they harked back to the Aztec past to find names such as "Club Recre-ativo Tenochtitlán." In the search for names for the cargo ships built at the Houston Shipbuilding Corporation, the most appropriate names were those of men of Mexico—Benito Juárez and Miguel Hidalgo—heroes who would have been more in tune with the ideals of Mexico-oriented clubs. American ways were to be learned and cherished, but not at the expense of cultural traditions.[47]

NOTES

[1]The discussion on the Mexican American Generation borrows heavily from Rich-ard A. García, "The Mexican American Mind: A Product of the 1930s," in Mario T. García (ed.), *History, Culture, and Society,* and from Marío T. García, "La Frontera: The Border As Symbol and Reality in Mexican-American Thought." See further Rosales, "Shifting Ethnic Consciousness Among Mexicans in Houston."

[2]San Miguel, "The Struggle Against Separate and Unequal Schools," p. 344.

[3]Arthur F. Corwin (ed.), *Immigrants—and Immigrants: Perspectives on Mexican Labor Migration to the United States,* p. 116.

[4]Barrera, "The Historical Evolution of Chicano Ethnic Goals," pp. 10–12.

[5]San Miguel, "The Struggle Against Separate and Unequal Schools," p. 345.

[6]García, "The Mexican American Mind," p. 70.

[7]Houston *Chronicle,* May 12, 1932, p. 16; García, "The Mexican American Mind," p. 80.

[8]*LULAC News,* March 1933, p. 5.

[9]Houston *Chronicle,* March 13, 1935, p. 12; April 9, 1935, p. 25.

[10]"History of Council #60," HMRC, John J. Herrera Collection.

[11]HMRC, Oral History Collection, interview with Juvencio Rodríguez.

[12]"History of Council #60," HMRC, John J. Herrera Collection; Houston *Chronicle,* April 9, 1935, p. 25; May 21, 1935, p. 17.

[13]Houston *Chronicle,* May 13, 1935, p. 3.

[14]Ibid., June 9, 1935, p. 20 ("Building and Business" Section); June 13, 1935, p. 5; June 26, 1935, p. 19; July 3, 1935, p. 14.

[15]HMRC, Oral History Collection, interview with Mrs. Félix H. Morales; *El Puerto,* August 9, 1935, p. 2; August 23, 1935, p. 2; August 30, 1935, p. 2; September 6, 1935, p. 1; October 18, 1935, p. 1.

[16]Houston *Chronicle,* June 26, 1935, p. 19; "History of Council #60," HMRC, John J. Herrera Collection; HMRC, Oral History Collection, interviews with John J. Herrera, May 22, 1981, and with Juvencio Rodríguez.

[17]"History of Council #60," HMRC, John J. Herrera Collection; HMRC, Oral History Collection, interviews with John J. Herrera and Juvencio Rodríguez.

[18]"Constitution of the Latin American Club," HMRC, Juvencio Rodríguez Collection.

[19]HMRC, Oral History Collection, interview with Judge Alfred J. Hernández.

[20]HMRC, Juvencio Rodríguez Collection.

[21]Ibid.

[22]Houston *Chronicle,* August 22, 1935, p. 10; HMRC, Juvencio Rodríguez Collection.

[23]HMRC, Oral History Collection, interview with Judge Alfred J. Hernández.

[24]HMRC, Juvencio Rodríguez Collection.

[25]Ibid.

[26]Houston *Chronicle,* June 5, 1937, p. 2; June 6, 1937, p. 5.

[27]A related episode is discussed in Arnoldo De León, *San Angeleños: Mexican Americans in San Angelo, Texas,* p. 52. A different case involving the issue of color classification is studied in García, "Mexican Americans and the Politics of Citizenship."

[28]"Resumé of Juvencio Rodríguez," HMRC, Juvencio Rodríguez Collection.

[29]Houston *Chronicle,* May 11, 1938, p. 1; and HMRC, Juvencio Rodríguez Collection.

[30]Houston *Press,* May 12, 1938, p. 12; Houston *Chronicle,* May 11, 1938, p. 1; and HMRC, Juvencio Rodríguez Collection.

[31]HMRC, Oral History Collection, interview with John J. Herrera; "History of Council #60," HMRC, John J. Herrera Collection; García, "The Mexican American Mind," p. 83.

[32]*El Puerto,* Houston, Texas, Julio 15, 1938, p. 3.

[33]Houston *Chronicle*, August 10, 1940, p. 6B; November 1, 1940, p. 15A; November 24, 1940, p. 14D; HMRC, Juvencio Rodríguez Collection.

[34]Houston *Chronicle*, October 18, 1940, p. 4A; July 14, 1940, p. 5B.

[35]Feagin, "The Socio-Economic Base of Urban Growth," p. 19.

[36]HMRC Oral History Collection, interview with John J. Herrera.

[37]"Letter" to the Editor of the Mail Bag, June 9, 1941; "Letter" to Mr. E. L. Hausler, August 14, 1942; and "Letter" to Dr. Carlos E. Castañeda, August 11, 1944, all in HMRC, John J. Herrera Collection.

[38]"Letter," Percy Foreman to John J. Herrera, May 13, 1944; and "Letter" to Dr. Carlos E. Castañeda, August 11, 1944, in HMRC, John J. Herrera Collection; Houston *Press*, August 7, 1944, p. 5.

[39]"Letter" to Whom it May Concern, January 15, 1944, HMRC, LULAC Council #60 Collection.

[40]"Letter" to Sr. Lic Ezequiel Padilla, 2 de agosto, 1943, HMRC, John J. Herrera Collection.

[41]Houston *Chronicle*, March 31, 1942, p. 14A; Houston *Press*, March 30, 1942, p. 5; "Sociedad Unión Fraternal, 1941–1944," HMRC, Mexican American Collection.

[42]"Speech Delivered April 21, 1942, Before a Crowd Gathered at the San Jacinto Memorial Park—Houston, Texas," HMRC, John J. Herrera Collection. On the attitudes which the LULACers of the 1930s held towards the Texas War for Independence, see Arnoldo De León, "Tejanos and the Texas War for Independence: Historiography's Judgment," *New Mexico Historical Review*, 61 (April, 1986), p. 140.

[43]Houston *Chronicle*, March 7, 1943, p. 4A; April 11, 1943, p. 1A, 4B; April 15, 1943, p. 15A, 8B; September 13, 1943, p. 3B.

[44]"Letter" to Dr. Carlos E. Castañeda, HMRC, John J. Herrera Collection.

[45]Houston *Chronicle*, September 7, 1945, p. 13A; December 10, 1945, p. 1A.

[46]Houston *Post*, April 23, 1981, p. 24A; Houston *Chronicle*, December 25, 1972, p. 1 (Section 1); Newsclippings, HMRC, Mexican American Small Collection.

[47]García, "The Mexican American Mind," p. 88; San Miguel, "The Struggle Against Separate and Unequal Schools," p. 346.

CHAPTER VI
THE POST-WAR COMMUNITY, 1945–1960:
TOWARDS A NEW ETHNICITY

Just as the Depression decade has been identified as a crucial period in the evolution of Mexican American communities, similarly has the post-war era of the late 1940s and the 1950s been tagged a "watershed" in the cultural transformation of colonias in Texas. World War II exposed virtually the entire spectrum of Texas Mexican society to unfamiliar dimensions of American life and culture. Mexicans and Anglos were thrown together by the crisis of the moment and the call for patriotism even abated racial feelings temporarily as all rallied together against a common enemy. Texas Mexicans, meantime, profited by military service or work in the wartime economy. But the war's effect did not stop with the Japanese surrender. The post-war era introduced the United States to the contemporary era of mass industrialization, modern urbanization, and consumer culture.

The post-war era also brought with it a new turn. Reactionism surfaced. After four years of total commitment to defeat totalitarianism, Americans were ready to enjoy victory with some calm and predictability in their lives. Conservatism returned and complacency set in; the New Deal liberalism fell into disfavor. Amid this atmosphere, interest in the welfare of the disadvantaged almost dissipated. In Texas, where the Mexican American population lived on a median income of $980 per year,[1] hope of assistance from government agencies was not even considered. Government pursued a laissez faire policy toward the downtrodden.

The fears of communism which abounded in this age fostered hysteria and abetted the reactionism. Old traditions were to be protected; in

Texas race relations, for example, the movement in favor of institutionalized Jim Crowism was strong enough that the 1956–1957 state legislature passed several segregationist bills,[2] which, though directed at blacks, nonetheless could easily be interpreted to extend to Mexicans. Those representing a line of thinking left of center risked ostracism and condemnation. Anti-alien feelings also ran amuck; such attitudes allowed the Border Patrol a free reign to round up foreign-born Mexicans in campaigns which often involved the civil rights violations of Mexican Americans.

Demands for conformity and consensus went hand in hand with the conservatism and reaction of the Cold War period. Schools placed emphasis on the proper patterns of behavior and discouraged thinking which deviated from the tenor of the times. Television executives, literary figures, and fashion designers were among the many influential actors who promoted the trend toward conformity. The severe pressure to comply with the new rules did not exclude Texas-Mexicans. As this chapter will show, the upward mobility, urbanization, and acculturation which the Mexican American community of Houston experienced from circa 1945–1960 was part of a process in which Mexicanos yielded to mainstream culture while they maintained an attachment to the culture of their parents.[3]

Expansion

Mexicans entering Houston were part of the aforementioned trend toward urbanization that followed World War II. Up until the war, most Mexicanos in the state lived in rural areas where they comprised a mainly agricultural work force. By 1940, however, almost half of Texas-Mexicans resided in urban areas, and World War II accelerated the pace of urbanization to the point that by the latter 1950s, Texas Mexicans constituted for the most part an urbanized community.[4]

In the score of years after 1940, the Houston Mexican population more than tripled. From the small 20,000 enumerated by the 1940 census, the colonia grew to 40,000 in 1950, then to 75,000 in 1960 within the Houston Standard Metropolitan Statistical Area (SMSA—by the 1950s, Harris County was considered the SMSA for Houston).[5] The increase coincided with a rising national demand in the post-war era for oil and oil products such as asphalt, jet fuel, plastics, and other petrochemicals. Continued support from the federal government guaranteed the Texas-Houston oil industry stability and investment capital from outside the state bolstered the prosperity. During the era, growing numbers of truck, pipeline, and shipping companies sprouted up around greater Houston's oil and petrochemical complexes as businesses in steel, aluminum, metal fabrication, oil tools, and construction escalated.[6] The city's population kept pace with economic expansion so that the 1960 census placed the number of people in the SMSA at 1,243,000.[7]

That those entering Houston were coming in from rural areas, or at least smaller communities in Texas, is corroborated in the fact that by the 1950s, those living in Houston were American citizens. Tabulations derived from the 1950 census indicate that as high as five of every six Spanish surnamed American in Harris County were native-born, half of the rest were naturalized citizens, and less than nine percent of the remainder came from Mexico.[8] Further calculations from the 1960 census reveal that only 9,590 (or about 13%) of the Mexican population in Harris County were of foreign stock.[9] Of course, illegals have ever ducked the census counters, and their presence and that of those legally in the city buttressed "lo mexicano." But, the percentage of those native born still remained high enough to make the Houston colonia an American one.

Geographically, the colonia experienced intense change during the post-War period. The original barrios in the west and north sides continued to grow, increasing both their densities of Mexican American population and expanding outwardly. El Segundo Barrio pushed southwest of Commerce Street and penetrated part of the old Third Ward. Magnolia Park was the scene of usual demographic enlargement and while still separated from the Segundo Barrio by a space of low density, the population concentration there, along with that one in the Segundo Barrio, permitted the use of the appropriate sobriquet given to the region as the "East End." By 1950, however, newer pockets of Mexican American enclaves located away from the pre-War colonia were identified by the Census Bureau. Still, the bulk of the Mexican population in Houston was placed by census agents in both 1950 and 1960 as being in the inner city. But this proximity did not avert fragmentation, for people continued to differentiate themselves from their counterparts in the other barrios.

Socioeconomic Fragmentation

La Gente Pobre

The forces of change—urbanization, industrialization, consumerism—which so reshaped American society in the post-War era also served to mold and accentuate class and cultural differences within the Houston Mexican community. Many of those living in Houston during the epoch remained poverty-stricken. As Table 6.1 shows, the primary types of occupations available to obreros as of the end of the period were as operatives, laborers, and lesser types of semi-skilled or skilled workers. Not surprisingly, many lived amid conditions akin to those characteristic of slum areas.[10] The lot for many in the colonia was one of overcrowding in substandard housing.[11]

Table 6.1
Occupational Distribution for
Employed White Persons of Spanish Surname
in Houston, 1960*

	Males	Females
Professional, Technical, and Kindred Works	4.8%	6.4%
Managers, Off'ls, & Propr's Exc. Farm	4.4%	2.5%
Clerical and Kindred Workers	6.5%	24.8%
Sales Workers	3.7%	7.9%
Craftsmen, Foremen, and Kindred Workers	19.3%	1.2%
Operatives and Kindred Workers	24.8%	20.6%
Private Household Workers	0.2%	5.8%
Service Workers, Exc. Private Household	7.3%	18.0%
Farms and Farm Managers	0.6%	0.1%
Farm Laborers and Foremen	1.5%	0.4%
Laborers, Except Farm and Mine	19.3%	1.5%
Occupation Not Reported	9.4%	10.7%
N	16,321	5,421

*Source: U.S. Census of Population: 1960, *Persons of Spanish Surname,* Final Report PC(2)–1B, Table 12.

Conditions were so appalling in some quarters of the colonia that little hesitation was made to call the barrios in "Heavenly Houston" some of the worst slums of any large city. Along Navigation Boulevard within three quarters of a mile of the courthouse, the Houston *Chronicle* reported in 1945, could be found rows of privies amidst homes with patched-up fronts, roofs, and walls. Such blighted areas, the paper continued, bred "diseases of all kinds which not only afflicted those living in the sections but are carried to all parts of the community."[12] In the area of the Second Ward, the Houston Housing Authority (HHA) elaborated in 1947, "tuberculosis, diarrhea, typhus and other diseases spread city-wide. Hand in hand with these conditions are the costs to the city and its citizens of fighting these diseases, and providing city services to this blighted area."[13] Toward the latter 1950s, conditions hardly improved. The decades' old nemesis of tuberculosis lingered. It remained a "main problem of the Latin American. Houston's facilities for caring for its victims are inadequate. Every man, woman, and child in the city is threatened by the untreated case of active tuberculosis."[14]

A solution to the problem of poor housing and its attendant consequences was reached through the efforts of the Housing Authority in the early 1950s. William L. Clayton, a cotton magnate and former United States undersecretary of state, and his wife Susan, who had long been interested in housing projects as a means of slum clearance, bought a large tract around Schrimpf Alley ("El Alacrán" barrio) and offered the land to the HHA for a low-cost development for Mexican residents. In March of 1952, Susan V. Clayton Homes was dedicated.[15]

As of the late 1950s, some 2,500 Mexican American families lived in the housing project. According to the Houston *Chronicle,* the facility ranked somewhere between the splendor of "Easy Street" and the sordidness of slum areas. Clayton Homes offered comfortable apartments and the project charged rent on a scale adjusted to income. Still, Clayton Homes was not fully utilized by the poor, due, the *Chronicle* explained, to its isolated location. The complex was bounded by two railroad tracks, factories, and a bayou. The closest school was more than a mile away and students had to negotiate hazardous traffic conditions. About the same distance separated the project from the nearest grocery store.[16]

Public schools, of course, did their part to ameliorate poverty by seeking to educate barrio young, generally with incongruent results: education reminded Mexican American students of their inferiority and second-class status while simultaneously introducing them to the mysteries of knowledge and Americanizing them. The condition of many of the "Mexican schools" acted as daily reminders of the bane of segregation and the lesser regard authorities held towards educating the Mexicans. Schools in predominantly Mexican neighborhoods were generally old, run down, and short on playgrounds space.

They were also riddled with danger. In the mid-1950s, the school district condemned Rusk Elementary school and closed it to make way for the Eastex Freeway. Most of the students were sent—across a chain of traffic hazards—to Jones Elementary at 914 Elysian. There, the same freeway that caused the closing of Rusk swept by the front entrance only a few feet from the classrooms and students using the upper floor rooms looked out upon the overpass. To rectify this danger, the school board in 1956 voted to build a new Rusk school at Paige and Garrow, near Settegast Park.[17] Said school, which was not finished until 1960 at 2805

Garrow, relieved elementaries like Lubbock and Jones schools, and served the children of the Clayton Homes. Although now having a longer walk than they did to Jones, students from the Clayton Homes at least faced less dangerous traffic hazards on the routes and had the benefit of signal lights when crossing dangerous intersections.[18]

Aside from inadequate facilities, predominatly Mexican schools were staffed by beginning and inexperienced teachers. As of 1957, less than twenty-five Mexican American educators were employed in the Houston schools and no major efforts were being undertaken to recruit more. In the first grade, Mexican American children were thrown into an unfamiliar environment, unable to communicate with their mentors. Teachers were generally outsiders who petitioned for transfers as soon as they acquired the necessary experience to teach elsewhere.[19]

The Amorphous Many

Poverty inevitably resulted in poor attendance records and high dropout rates. As of 1950, the median number of years of schooling completed by Mexican-Americans twenty-five years old and over was 5.2, compared with 11.4 for Anglos and 7.6 for blacks. In the next decennial, a slight increase occurred: Mexicans had 6.4 median years of school completed, as opposed to 12.1 for Anglos and 8.8 for blacks.[20]

These statistics have several implications. First, and most obvious, change was virtually miniscule. Those falling by the wayside probably descended from households of the unskilled and lower-level skilled laborers and workers detailed in Table 6.1. They testified to the impact of the worst effects of barrio life—substandard housing, poor health, and poverty which compelled them to go to work mid-way through their adolescent years. Many of these found socioeconomic advancement and cultural assimilation elusive. This means that within the Houston community there persisted strong elements of Mexicanismo, which, reinforced by Mexican immigration (though slight during the period), sustained Mexican tastes and influenced the identity of those becoming Americanized.

But the slight improvement revealed by the figures on median years of school completed is also significant for the clues it provides concerning inevitable changes transpiring. As Table 6.2 shows, Mexican Americans in Houston did achieve a degree of educational advancement during the 1950s. An increased percentage of residents twenty-five years old and older in 1960 completed grades past the eighth grade and the percentage reporting no school completed declined. These numbers are not used herein to show the improvement (however modest) of Mexicans in light of the bleak conditions they faced in the city's schools. Rather they are employed to reiterate the point of Mexican American resilience in Houston.

Table 6.2
Years of School Completed
Mexican Americans, 25 Years Old and Older
in Houston, 1950 and 1960*

	1950	1960
· Elementary:		
1 to 4 years	28.2%	22.3%
5 and 6 Years	17.0%	17.7%
7 years	6.6%	6.7%
8 years	6.6%	8.8%
High School:		
1 to 3 years	9.6%	11.6%
4 years	6.4%	9.4%
College:		
1 to 3 years	2.2%	4.4%
4 years or more	1.6%	3.0%
No School Years Completed:	17.7%	15.8%
School Years Not Reported:	4.1%	——
N	16,175	30,626

*Source: U.S. Census of Population: 1950, *Special Reports Persons of Spanish Surname*, Census Report P–E No. 3C, Reprint of Volume IV, Part 3, Chapter C, Table 8, p. 3C–54; U.S. Census of Population: 1960, *Persons of Spanish Surname*, Final Report PC(2)–1B, Table 10.

First, they confirm the fact that despite severe conditions, life in the Houston community remained stable. Parents dispatched their children off to school and kept them there as long as possible. People struggled to make a living, but provided the necessary ambient within homelife for children to grow up with a sense of normality. Despite the high cost of living in the post-War years, Mexicanos coped. As one immigrant who had been in the country since the late 1920s explained to his brother in 1947:

> Con lo que nos pagan a nosotros los trabajadores en E.U. vivimos muy bien, compramos nuestra comida, y nuestra ropa, y calzado, y nos sobra un peso para alzarlo, o traerlo en el bolsillo.

With what they pay us workers in the U.S. we live well, buying our groceries, our clothing, and shoes, and a dollar is still left over for savings or for carrying in our purse.[21]

Further, though so many lived amidst conditions which promoted crime and delinquency, barrio residents did not allow their surroundings to overcome them. While commentators conceded that crime was more prominent in the barrios than in the Anglo areas of the city, they nonetheless qualified their conclusions by noting that the percentage of crimes committed by Mexican Americans (about 9%) was only slightly higher than the percentage of the Houston population they comprised (about 5%). As one journalist noted in 1958, Mexicanos were overly represented in some crimes, but not murder. "Houston, off and on, has been considered the murder capital. Here, the Latin American cannot be held responsible. Last year the Houston police charged 110 persons with murder, only nine were Latin American," the reporter wrote.[22] Which is to say that there existed an amorphous mass of people, most of them from the bottom rung, whose socioeconomic and ideological stance cannot be quantified. In all societies, there are those who struggle against adversity, who despite material conditions, endure. Slum conditions, health hazards, crime, and other banes of man do not demoralize homelife universally. That there were those in Houston who made educational and other gains despite their disadvantage is testimony to the general normalcy pervading the barrios. Disadvantage does not produce defeat.

Those of Middling Status

The data from Table 6.2 point to another equally important aspect of the Houston Mexican community. Namely, they attest to the continued exposure of Mexicans to the United States way of life and to the further growth of elements within the Houston community making for a class of middling status or aspiring to become part of that. This is made clearer by the numbers in Table 6.1. Taking the classifications of professionals, managers, proprietors, sales and clerical workers, then adding to these a part of those belonging in the craftsmen category, it is apparent that between 25% to 35% of workers in Houston by 1960 (the 1950 census did not provide a similar breakdown for Houston) comprised a marginal element making for a middle class. These figures agree with, if not exceed, those calculated by Professor Manuel Peña in his profile of Texas-Mexican social classes for the same era.[23]

104

Indeed, commentators during the 1950s saw such a socioeconomic improvement. It was partly apparent in home buying. With racial attitudes tempered by the experience of the War and Supreme Court decisions outlawing segregation, real estate agents were not as reluctant as they had once been in selling to Mexicanos. During the era, therefore, more Mexican Americans were able to buy homes outside the traditional barrios. The move was towards the Freeway subdivisions along the recently-opened Gulf Freeway and the new developments in southwest and west Houston. By 1960, Mexicans lived in all areas of the city.[24]

The presence of such a class speaks again to the continued acculturation of part of the Mexican community in Houston in the post-War era. These segments looked towards Anglo American sentiments and attitudes with appreciation and emulation. There existed, it might be presumed, those within the community who, though poor, were already armed with a degree of acculturation; this included a command of the English language which equipped them for their struggle towards achieving a better lot than the one they faced. Women, as one example, increased their representation in the work force (23% of Spanish surname women fourteen years and over worked in 1950s, this increased to 28% by 1960), thereby taking on the habits and attitudes of other Houston women.[25] Put another way, a substantial portion of the Houston community by the 1950s valued conformity, though not necessarily rejection of their Mexican heritage.

Zoot-Suiters and Pachucos, 1943–1950s

The stage of development of the Mexican American generation of the 1950s, of course, had its roots in the transformation which occurred two decades previously. As argued, by the 1930s, the Houston community was experiencing internal diversity. With nationalist, class, and ethnic variety existing, the barrios spurred different, at times competing ideological perspectives reflecting change within the community. This heterogeneity was apparent in the different ideology of the organizations already discussed, and it is seen further in the expression toward zoot-suiterism and *pachuquismo* which prevailed in Houston during the period from about 1943 until the mid-1950s, as well as in the reaction to the phenomenon of pachuquismo by the rest of the Houston Mexican colonia.

Though adolescents from the barrios had organized themselves into youth gangs for some time, the issue of gang warfare did not become a public matter until the case of the "Long-Hair" gang made ward gang fights a topic of sensational discussion. Briefly recapped, the gang allegedly killed, in Magnolia Park, the forty-year-old father of one of the gang members who sought to expose the "Long-Hairs" to police unless they left his son alone. The case was made all the more sensational as two of the six accused were juveniles, one was a woman, and the alleged "brains" of the gang was a youth whose legs had been severed above the knees in a railroad accident several years back.[26] Further accentuating the sensationalism of the episode was the coincidental eruption of the so-called "Zoot-Suit Riots" in Los Angeles, California. The newspapers in Houston carried the California stories alongside coverage of the trial of the "Long-Hair" gang members in June 1943, thus popularizing the term "Zoot-Suit" as applicable to Mexican American gang members.[27] Californians visiting the Houston area used the term freely, so that "Zoot-Suit" rapidly became an externally bestowed label for juvenile gangsters in Houston.[28]

In seeking to explain the phenomenon of "zoot-suiters," or *"pachucos"* as they were known in the barrios, scholars have had to grapple with tentative explanations. Youngsters, of course, have ever been defiant and ready to prove their bravado—Mexican Americans have been no different. Professor Mauricio Mazón, in his intelligent study of the Zoot-Suit Riots in Los Angeles, attributes the rise in gang warfare in part to a general increase in juvenile delinquency during the war years throughout the entire United States.[29]

In Houston, such an explanation has relevance. According to a report issued by the Houston Crime Prevention Bureau in July 1943, juvenile delinquency increased alarmingly from the previous year. The number of girls between ten and eighteen and boys between ten and seventeen handled by the Bureau almost doubled—among those arrested were forty "Victory Girls" (women who made themselves available to military men) and the number of runaway boys and girls also rose. The head of the Crime Prevention Bureau attributed the increase in delinquency to war conditions as "many mothers who never held jobs before are working in war plants and many boys and girls are living away from home." The large concentration of men in uniform in the Houston area further contributed to the condition.[30] And indeed, the upsurge in junior gang activities among Mexicans was reported early on as part of the city's increase in juvenile deliquency. Conceding the existence of said gangs for a number of years, the press pointed out the wave of activities by gangs in 1943 as being "new" or "bolder" in character.[31]

Whatever the causes for the rise in juvenile delinquency, pachuco crime intensified within the Mexican American barrios between circa

1943 and the mid-1950s. That activity unfolded in two waves, it appears: the first during the war years, then the other around the time of the Korean Conflict in the early 1950s. The reality of pachuquismo, like other aspects of the colonia, revealed the structural diversity of the Mexican community, first because of the "standing" of the pachucos in the historical evolution of the community, and secondly because they held a somewhat ambivalent niche in the eyes of their fellow Mexicanos.

What exactly the pachucos represented during the 1940s and 1950s is still being debated by both their defenders and detractors.[32] In the case of Houston, they stood as another of the several cultural and ideological strains within the colonia. In numerous ways, they were distinct—in the language which they spoke (*caló*), in the garb with which they draped themselves, and in their aloof behavior. But, they were also caught up in the trend toward Americanization. The very fashions which they employed were singularly American; often they shopped at the better stores for the right shoes and clothing, or, said the police, gang members would break into cleaning and pressing shops to obtain enough clothes to dress up the whole gang in sport clothes or zoot-suits.[33] Their names as revealed in the press were at times Anglicized: Joe, Pete, Jesse, and Tommy either replaced their Mexican first-names or were used interchangeably with the names given to them by their parents. Some of the names of their gangs—"Black Shirts," "Snakes," "Long-Hairs," "Old San Antonio Gang," "Fifth Ward Gang"—were printed in the newspapers in English, although it is probable that in many cases these were translations from such self-designated titles as *"Camisas Negras," "Víboras,"* or *"Pelu-dos/Pelos Largos."*[34] Many of the gang members either were fluent in English or had a working knowledge of it—they interacted with authorities without the benefit of translators. Most had by now internalized the racial connotations of the word "Mexican." Indeed, one particular gang, allegedly led by a girl named "Black Ora," was provoked into beating a white girl and her escort when the Anglo teenage girl turned to an arguing group on a city bus and asked them: "Why don't you Mexicans go back to Mexico where you belong?" (The white couple stated that the attack was unprovoked, however).[35]

To mainstream society, however, the zoot-suiters and pachucos were nothing less than hoodlums, gangsters, young toughs, and other unsavory types who confirmed the worst of the Mexican character. The image of the zoot-suiter and pachuco conjured up images that fell outside the pale of decency and conformity. According to a newspaper report, they were "mostly second and third-generation American citizens who had failed to adopt our ways or even to learn our language—because no other racial group in Houston engages in organized hoodlumism."[36]

Zoot-suiters and pachucos stigmatized youths as an element that had gone awry. Most were young folks, usually between thirteen and twenty-two, among them a small percentage of young girls.[37] In an era calling for conformity, the pachucos defiantly violated societal norms. According to police authorities, gang members would get "hopped up" by smoking reefers (marijuana cigarettes). At best, this made them vicious and at worst, it gave them the urge to commit various crimes, even kill.[38]

Further, they skirted conformity with their outlandish uniforms: zoot suits during the 1940s, and in later years, other types of fancy clothes.[39] Long hair, slick, with the ends curled upward, set them apart. Tattoes marked their arms and hands to show which pachuco gang they belonged to: in the early 1950s, Magnolia gang members displayed a small round wheel between the thumb and finger on the right hand; the Second Ward youths had a heart with an arrow through it; and the Capitol Avenue group had a sombrero tattoed or drawn in ink on their hands.[40]

More ominously, the zoot-suiters and pachucos displayed a streak of criminal nature. Some carried pistols, razors, blackjacks, and daggers.[41] They terrorized citizens (both Anglos and Mexicanos), shot, slugged, and slashed their opponents in gang warfare.[42] Pachucos prowled the barrios under such names in the 1940s (in addition to ones already listed) as the "Magnolia Gang," the "Liberty Road Gang," the "Sixth Ward Gang," the "Canal Street Gang," the "Scorpions," the "I.G.N. Alley Gang," and in the 1950s, under geographically descriptive designations like the Magnolia Park, Second Ward, and Capitol Avenue gangs.[43] As the names of the some of the gangs indicate, they owed their allegiance to certain turfs within the larger barrios.[44]

If the above describes the way in which the larger community saw pachucismo, members of the colonia saw them with ambivalence. While most residents of the Mexican barrios probably did not understand the phenomenon any better than scholars do today, they probably condemned the more violent aspects of pachuquismo and perhaps even disavowed it as something which did not represent the reality of their experience. Indeed, the little evidence that exists points to a sort of defensiveness on their part—a response which once more exposed the ideological and cultural cleavage that stamped the colonia.

To deal with troubles of the War years, the Houston police in July 1944 created something called the "Latin American Squad." Comprised of a Mexican American policeman and Spanish speaking Anglo officers, the Squad targeted the elimination of the Mexican juvenile delinquency. It did this by patrolling the Mexican neighborhoods, raiding places where suspected troublemakers congregated, confiscating weapons, and generally pursuing every approach to dissolve the lawlessness. By the latter part of 1945, the police claimed that wartime delinquency was at an end.[45]

In actuality, initiatives from within the Mexican community designed to rehabilitate the youths helped in suppressing the gangs, albeit temporarily. From its inception, the colonia resented the creation of the "Latin American Squad," as its name and objectives seemed to bring "Latin Americans" in for treatment different than for other "Americans." By 1947, Mexicanos had ostensibly pressured the police to abolish the team.[46]

Also, the colonia seemed bent on eliminating those aspects of barrio youth that cast a negative light on Mexicanos. For such a reason, several drives were implemented to reform youths and shape them into "good Americans." Among the most prominent efforts undertaken to retrieve the venerable name of Latin Americans was the "Good Citizens League." As the "brainchild" of an integrated nucleus of both influential Anglo leaders and prominent figures of the Mexican community such as restauranteur Félix Tijerina, it sought to persuade gang youths to turn to sports instead of crime. Its approach involved trying to keep juveniles in schools, attempting to get employers to teach them useful trades, and providing an adult educational program to "make better citizens of those people."[47]

Also striving to help defuse zoot-suiterism was the FSMLA, which through its Juvenile Delinquency Committee, organized a number of clubs intended to get youngsters to move the scene of action from alleys to baseball fields, football gridirons, and basketball courts and transform the weapons from knives and clubs to footballs, baseballs, and basketballs. By October 1945, the committee had persuaded other organizations like the SMOM and the Xohomilco Recreation Club to donate space and time to the effort, and clubs had been established or were in the process of being organized in all the major barrios. According to the head of the FSMLA Juvenile Committee, a "strong effort was being made to get the youths to abandon their extra long haircuts, so that in the future the term 'longhair' will not have a place in the Latin American sections of Houston." Further efforts to convert the pachucos into respectability included trying to get the youngsters to change their style of clothing, that is, discarding their tight-ankle britches and extra long "zoot" coats for more conservative apparel.[48]

When during the second wave of pachuquismo in the early 1950s the police attempted to form a "Latin American Squad" patterned after the one created during the war, the initiative was met with denunciation. As in the earlier era, the protests revolved around the notion that Mexican Americans were being singled out for special condemnation. The majority of the Mexican people were blameless, and should not be stigmatized for the crimes of a lawles few, it was argued.[49] Among the loudest protestors were the LULACers, but this will be taken up in the following chapter.

Mexican Americanization

Conformity

The presence of ideological cleavages, exposed by the reaction to pachuquismo, are evident also in the conformity to American behavior which several elements within the Houston community sought. Acculturation followed from interaction between Mexicans and the dominant culture in the schools and workplace, but other forces during the post-war era enculturated Mexicanos further. There was, for one thing, the size of the Mexican population—though in 1950, Houston had the fifth largest Spanish surname population in Texas, Mexicans comprised only 5.8% of Houston's total population. Mexicanos in the other four cities comprised at least 33% of their respective city's total population and were therefore not as readily influenced by the dominant society as was the minority in Houston. Despite the growth that occurred between 1950 and 1960, Houston's own population grew at a rate that kept the Mexican population at a similar proportion.[50]

Further acting upon Mexicanos was their place of upbringing. Most Mexican Houstonians, as already indicated, were native born or naturalized and had known no other country save the United States. Moreover, their exposure was that of an urban environment. While many lived in their own enclaves, they were exposed more readily than their rural counterparts to consumer culture, an industrialized setting, and the values of movers and shakers in Houston. Those fortunate enough to belong to the middle class copied mainstream ways, but even the less fortunate vicariously identified with trendy fashions, voguish speech forms, and other patterns of conformity.

The young, of course, have always been more inclined to accepting the new (even inventing it) and young Mexicans in Houston were no exception. "Although the school children mainly attend schools in the Mexican districts," noted a staff writer for the Houston *Chronicle* in 1950, "they are as 'hep' to American movie stars, radio stars and the latest jitterbug steps."[51] Several youth groups were committed to upholding American cultural ways, and the Junior LULACers are herein held up as an example of youth acculturation during the post-war era.

Established as an outgrowth of LULAC Council #60 in 1948, Junior LULACers immediately made a civic and social contribution. They contributed toward curbing juvenile deliquency during the period of ward gang fights. They engaged in all civic activities such as helping the Red Cross, March of Dimes, United Fund, and Anti-TB League. Further, they assisted during the annual Christmas basket drives for underprivileged children and helped the parent council in any of their activities.[52]

During the 1950s, the Junior LULAC Council of Houston continued to "follow the LULAC Banner to Better Citizenship." The Juniors sponsored speakers who addressed them on such topics as "Youth and the Law" and "The Evils and Effects of Narcotics." They continued to assist in several drives, among them the "March Against Polio," and to help in worthy projects as annual Easter Egg Hunts. Committed as they were to upholding LULAC Americanism, they accompanied, on occasion, members of Council #60 attending the yearly laying of the floral wreath at the San Jacinto Battleground in memory of the Texas Mexicans who had fought in the Texas War for Independence. Regularly, they hosted fundraising "Be-Bop" affairs in the barrio during which those attending competed in the latest dance crazes.[53] This, of course, reflected the rock 'n roll generation whose idols were such figures as Elvis Presley, the Everly Brothers, Little Richard, among others. An example of the thorough acceptance of their music into barrio life is manifest in an excerpt from the following letter comprised from songs of the era by one of the Junior LULACers:

> I don't want "Mary Ann," "Lucille," a "Party Doll," or even "Maybelline" for "You Are My Love" and I'm "Crazy 'Bout You Baby." "Why Do I Love You" so? Is it that you have "Lucky Lips"? . . . or are pretty like a "Butterfly"? . . . or is it "Spring Fever"? Don't know, "Honey Child," but "I Believe" "There Oughta Be A Law" so you won't "Let Me Go Lover" because "Since I Met You Baby" my weeks no longer have a "Blue Monday."
> "Sincerely,"
> Your "Brown Eyed Handsome Man"[54]

Several other clubs manifesting Mexican Americanization either continued into the era from the 1930s or were born during the post-War

111

period.[55] A Pan-American Political Council was founded in 1948 for the purpose of informing itself, its members and other interested individuals or organizations "of the platform and qualifications of those seeking political preferment and will from time to time, invite candidates for public office to its meetings so that they may express their aims and views." With its motto of "Equality, Justice, and Freedom," it was essentially political, though it promised to refrain from sponsoring the candidacy of any particular office-seekers and so "avoid attaching itself to this or that political bandwagon." It seemed somewhat reminiscent of the pre-war "Latin Sons of Texas" and the "Texas American Citizens," and like those organizations, apparently did not thrive.[56] In 1948, also, was founded "Club Familias Unidas," which had as its goal promoting the progress and culture of young Mexican Americans through social events. This club enjoyed success throughout the 1950s.[57]

That by the latter 1950s the Mexican community of Houston felt more comfortable reading the English language (or that it had lost touch with Spanish) is made apparent by the format of a newspaper established in 1959. *El Puerto,* as it was called, candidly announced: "This journal will be published in English." It was, primarily, a social magazine, publishing news about civic, church and service organizations. Politically, it steered an independent course, though it did take part in political issues, defending political positions which might benefit the Mexican community, or attacking those which stood against the best interests of the colonia.[58]

Further testifying to the assimilative bent of the Houston colonia by the 1950s was the waning of some institutions once intended to help out Mexican nationals. The FSMLA, which had experienced difficulty since its inception, hardly survived the 1940s. Following the war, it was still struggling, more and more becoming an organization much like the one which the "Unión Fraternal" had criticized in 1941. By the 1950s, it was inactive, and presumably defunct.[59] The Mexican consulate moved away from its former activist position in behalf of the entire colonia. When in June 1944, for example, stories circulated that the Mexican consul had gone before the Harris County Grand Jury to inveigh against Mexican American discrimination, the consul himself issued a statement denying the protest.[60] As time passed, the consuls played roles more in keeping with diplomatic protocol, mainly looking out for the welfare of the foreign born. They continued working closely with the comites patrióticos to see that the many responsibilities attributed to the comité were carried out, among them the celebration of the fiestas patrias. In 1950, the consul confessed that his duties as representative of a foreign nation prohibited him from speaking for American born persons of Mexican extraction.[61] By the mid-1950s, the consul's office was more involved in overseeing the affairs of Mexico in the Houston areas and was primarily concerned with commercial exports and imports.[62] Of course, this reflected the continued decline in the number of foreign born Mexicans in Houston and the fact that Mexican Americans by now had their own civic organizations.

Lo Mexicano Retained

At the other end of the cultural spectrum persisted allegiance to things Mexican. In various ways, "lo mexicano" was driven home in the barrios, even to those, as a newspaper article put it in 1950, "who may never visit their motherland."[63] For the most part, this element included the aforementioned mass of working people only partly Americanized as well as the smaller upwardly mobile middle class.

Among the myriad of vehicles helping sustain old ways was the Spanish language, a medium of speech in the colonia. Parents passed it on to their children even as students picked up English in the classroom. But even on the school grounds, young people clung to their mother tongue. At De Zavala Elementary school, one parent complained in 1948, it was difficult for his son to pick up English as Spanish was the only thing spoken there.[64] Older folks naturally remained fluent and dominant in Spanish—it was this group which in the early 1950s still frequented, in the dying 1800 block of Congress, the old "librería" established by the Sarabia brothers in the 1920s where they purchased *La Policía* (*Mexican Police Gazette*), *El Universal* (Mexico City newspaper), *Todo* (the Mexican counterpart of *Life* magazine), as well as *cancioneros* (songbooks) with lyrics to the latest Mexican tunes.

The Catholic Church, sustained "lo mexicano" by carrying on part of its work in Spanish. Parish school instruction, masses, and confessions were done in English; simultaneously, concessions were made to parishioners as priests preached in Spanish and heard confessions in that tongue. The Church observed and celebrated traditional holy days like "El Día de la Virgen de Guadalupe" (the Virgin of Guadalupe was the patron saint of Mexico). In homes, Mexicanos displayed their allegiance to their Mexican religious past by maintaining small altars and pictures of Christ or the Virgin Mary. Both men and women carried small crosses or medals of patron saints around their necks.

Spanish-language movie theatres continued as conduits of Mexican culture. Flashed upon the screens of the Aztec and Ritz Theatres were such movie stars as María Félix, Pedro Armendáriz, the commedian Cantinflas, and the comic Tin Tán whose gimmick was the zoot-suiter of the period.[65] The songs of Mexican crooners were brought into the homes of barrio folks after 1950 with the establishment of Houston's first Spanish-language radio station, KLVL. Founded by the long-time Houston activists, Mr. and Mrs. Félix H. Morales, KLVL became known throughout the 1950s as "La Madre de los Mexicanos" ("The Mother of the Mexicans"). By 1960, it beamed its programs to some 250,000 Mexican Americans in the Gulf Coast region, using the air waves, in addition to the maintenance of culture, for disseminating educational, religious, and public information.[66]

Mexican clubs also presented themselves as vehicles for the preservation of Mexican culture or as altruistic organizations intended to assist those in need. Club "México Bello," founded in 1924, still displayed its love and allegiance to the old land. In 1945, for example, one of its members laid a floral wreath at the monument of "los Niños Heroes" at Chapultepec in Mexico City in behalf of the Club. "México Bello" still held its formal black and white ball and in 1957 initiated a yearly "Baile de Quinceañeras" to introduce young fifteen-year olds before society. In 1954, the Club Femenino "México Bello" was founded.[67]

Old organizations established in the 1930s as social or recreative societies persisted. Still strong were the SMOM and others affiliated with the W.O.W. Naturally, the comité patriótico, headed by the Mexican consul, continued its efforts towards holding the fiestas patrias celebrations, most especially the Cinco de Mayo and the Diez y Seis de Septiembre.[68] Throughout the 1950s, the fiestas patrias drew usual large crowds and enthusiasm.[69]

Ethnicity at mid-century

It is most difficult to calculate realistically what balance existed between "lo americano" and "lo mexicano" in the ethnicity which was underway by mid-century. As other scholars have noted: "the cultural absorption of Tejanos into American life proceeded at highly disparate rates."[70] This applied not only to classes, but to adjustments within classes. Thus, Mexican Americanization was never a static relationship, or a balancing of equally potent forces or influences. Even the subjects themselves, though bicultural, could not have explained precisely how they had syncretized the two cultures. But clearly, they lived in a world where they could voluntarily pick and choose from "lo americano" and "lo mexicano."

NOTES

[1]Carl Allsup, *The American G.I. Forum*, p. 21.

[2]Montejano, *Anglos and Mexicans in the Making of Texas*, pp. 276, 286.

[3]Saragoza, "The Significance of Recent Chicano-Related Historical Writing." My guide in interpreting the period between 1945 to 1960 is Peña, *The Texas-Mexican Conjunto*, Chapter 5. See further, Montejano, *Anglos and Mexicans in the Making of Texas*, pp. 268, 270, 280.

[4]Peña, *The Texas-Mexican Conjunto*, pp. 116, 126, Table 2.

[5]Mary Ellen Goodman and Don des Jarlais, "The Spanish Surname Population of Houston: A Demographic Sketch" (Houston: Rice University, 1968), p. 2.

[6]Feagin, "The Socioeconomic Base of Urban Growth," p. 21.

[7]Goodman and des Jarlais, "The Spanish Surname Population of Houston," p. 2.

[8]Joseph L. Zarefsky, "Spanish Americans in Houston and Harris County" (Houston: Research Bureau Community Council, 1953), p. 1.

[9]U.S. Census of Population: *1960, Persons of Spanish Surname*, Final Report PC(2)–1B, table 14, p. 191.

[10]Goodman and des Jarlais, "The Spanish Surname Population of Houston," pp. 5, 8.

[11]Zarefsky, "Spanish Americans in Houston and Harris County," pp. 8–12.

[12]Houston *Chronicle*, October 19, 1945, p. 5B.

[13]*The People of Houston vs. Slums, Annual Report*, p. 3.

[14]Houston *Chronicle*, December 11, 1958, p. 1A.

[15]Tsanoff, *Neighborhood Doorways*, p. 85; Houston *Chronicle*, January 15, 1950, p. 25A; June 20, 1950, p. 11C; Houston *Post*, July 27, 1961, p. 1 (Section 8).

[16]Houston *Chronicle*, December 4, 1958, pp. 1A, 7A.

[17]Houston *Chronicle*, December 3, 1958, pp. 1A and 19A; December 10, 1958, pp. 1A and 4A; December 6, 1958, p. 1A; Tsanoff, *Neighborhood Doorways*, p. 114.

[18]Houston *Chronicle*, December 6, 1958, p. 1A.

[19]Ibid., December 3, 1958, pp. 1A and 19A.

[20]Goodman and des Jarlais, "The Spanish Surname Population of Houston," p. 10.

[21]"Letter," May 25, 1947, HMRC, Victoriano Rodríguez Family Collection.

[22]Houston *Chronicle*, December 7, 1958, p. 1A. In 1957, calcuated the reported Marie Dauplaise, Mexicanos committed 9% of the 64 criminal assault cases, 10% of the 777 aggravated assault and assault to murder cases, 7% of the 1472 burglaries, 10.7% of the 2426 theft cases, 8.1% of the 637 carrying or displaying a deadly weapons cases, 6.5% of the 1891 prostitution cases, and 23.2% of the 276 narcotics violation cases. See further, Goodman and des Jarlais, "The Spanish Surname Population of Houston," p. 11–12.

[23]Peña, *The Texas-Mexican Conjunto*, pp. 122–133.

[24]Houston *Chronicle*, December 1, 1958, pp. 1A and 13A, December 4, 1958,

p. 1A, and December 10, 1958, p. 1A.
[25]Goodman and des Jarlais, "The Spanish Surname Population of Houston," p. 10.
[26]Houston *Chronicle*, March 27, 1943, p. 2A; April 9, 1943, p. 15A; Houston *Press*, April 2, 1943, p. 1; April 15, 1943, p. 3; April 26, 1943, p. 1; April 27, 1943, pp. 1 and 8; April 28, 1943, p. 1; April 29, 1943, p. 15; June 11, 1943, p. 13; June 10, 1943, p. 3.
[27]Houston *Press*, June 10, 1943, p. 3.
[28]Houston *Chronicle*, June 28, 1943, p. 14A; Letter, July 12, 1943, HMRC, Santa Fe Railroad Papers; Houston *Press*, May 9, 1944, p. 5; Houston *Chronicle*, March 10, 1950, p. 1C; February 8, 1954, p. 5A.
[29]Mauricio Mazón, *The Zoot-Suit Riots: The Psychology of Symbolic Annihilation*, p. 60.
[30]Houston *Press*, July 9, 1943, p. 17; July 15, 1944, p. 1.
[31]Houston *Chronicle*, January 11, 1943, p. 9A; January 25, 1943, p. 1A.
[32]Mazón, *The Zoot-Suit Riots*, pp. 113–122.
[33]Houston *Chronicle*, March 10, 1950, p. 1C.
[34]Ibid., January 11, 1943, p. 9A; January 25, 1943, p. 1A; Houston *Press*, September 16, 1944, p. 2.
[35]Houston *Press*, September 15, 1944, pp. 1 and 19; September 23, 1944, pp. 1 and 2; September 26, 1944, p. 5; Letter, March 11, 1950, HMRC, John J. Herrera Collection.
[36]Houston *Chronicle*, March 8, 1950, p. 1C.
[37]Houston *Press*, September 15, 1944, p. 1.
[38]Ibid., September 16, 1944, p. 1; Houston *Chronicle*, March 8, 1950, p. 1C; March 9, 1950, p. 32A.
[39]Houston *Chronicle*, March 10, 1950, p. 1C.
[40]Ibid., March 8, 1950, p. 1C.
[41]Ibid., March 10, 1950, p. 1C.
[42]Ibid., March 10, 1950, p. 1C; March 3, 1955, p. 1.
[43]Houston *Press*, July 24, 1944, p. 1; Houston *Chronicle*, May 8, 1948, p. 5; March 8, 1950, p. 1C.
[44]See further, Houston *Press*, July 6, 1944, p. 1; July 10, 1944, p. 1.
[45]Houston *Press*, July 12, 1944, p. 17; July 18, 1944, p. 18; September 16, 1944, p. 1 and 2; Houston *Chronicle*, July 17, 1945, p. 11A; December 2, 1945; March 8, 1950, p. 1C.
[46]Houston *Chronicle*, February 26, 1950, p. 1A; March 8, 1950, p. 1C; Letter, March 5, 1947, HMRC, LULAC Council #60 Collection.
[47]Houston *Chronicle*, July 27, 1945, p. 14B; October 14, 1945, p. 6A; "Circular," Febrero 18, 1946, Federación de Sociedades México Latino-Americanas, HMRC, LULAC Council #60 Collection.
[48]Houston *Chronicle*, July 28, 1945, p. 10; October 12, 1945, p. 15A; "Circular," Febrero 18, 1946, Federación de Sociedades México Latino-Americanas, HMRC, LULAC Council #60 Collection.
[49]Houston *Chronicle*, February 26, 1950, p. 1A; March 8, 1950, p. 1C; March 13, 1950, p. 14A.
[50]Goodman and des Jarlais, "Spanish Surname Population of Houston," p. 2; Robert H. Talbert, *Spanish-Name People in the Southwest and West*, p. 29.
[51]Houston *Chronicle*, January 1, 1950, pp. 14–15 (Rotogravure Magazine).

[52]"History of the Junior LULACS of Houston" and *LULAC News,* June 1954, both in HMRC, LULAC Council #60 Collection.

[53]*LULAC News,* June 1954, HMRC, LULAC Council Collection; Houston *Chronicle,* June 16, 1955, p. 5C; August 4, 1955, p. 7C; August 18, 1955, p. 7C.

[54]Letter, March 23, 1957, HMRC, LULAC Council #60 Collection.

[55]Lists of these clubs may be found in "The March of Dimes," letterhead, n. d., HMRC, LULAC Council #60 Collection, and "Houston Civic and Social Organizations," in ibid.

[56]"The Constitution of the Pan-American Political Council," HMRC, LULAC Council #60 Collection.

[57]"Historia Del Club Familias Unidas," HMRC, Mariano Rosales y Piña Collection.

[58]*El Puerto,* Houston, Texas, September 1959, p. 3.

[59]Houston *Chronicle,* September 6, 1945, p. 2B; "Circular," Federación de Sociedades México Latino-Americanas, Febrero 18 de 1946; "Minutes," February 23, 1950; "Federación de Sociedades México-Latino-Americanas"; Letters, July 3, 1958 and September 16, 1958, all in HMRC, LULAC Council #60.

[60]Houston *Press,* June 22, 1944, p. 15; June 23, 1944, p. 11.

[61]Houston *Chronicle,* March 17, 1950, p. 10A.

[62]Circular No. 4, noviembre 14, 1947, HMRC, LULAC Council #60; Houston *Chronicle,* February 20, 1955, p. 18 (Rotogravure Magazine).

[63]Houston *Chronicle,* January 1, 1950, pp. 14–15 (Rotogravure Magazine).

[64]Houston *Chronicle,* January 23, 1948, p. 21A.

[65]Ibid., January 18, 1948, p. 6C. January 1, 1950, pp. 14–15 (Rotogravure Magazine).

[66]Houston *Press,* May 27, 1960, and *The Catholic Herald,* September 27, 1968, p. 10, both in HMRC, Félix Morales Collection.

[67]"Historia del Club México Bello," HMRC, Club "México Bello" Collection; *El Puerto,* November 1959, p. 9.

[68]Circular No. 4, noviembre 14 de 1947, HMRC, LULAC Council #60 Collection; Houston *Chronicle,* May 8, 1948, p. 5; January 1, 1950, pp. 14–15 (Rotogravure Magazine); Houston *Post,* September 15, 1945, p. 6.

[69]Houston *Chronicle,* May 4, 1950, p. 13A; May 6, 1950, p. 4A; September 15, 1954, p. 14A.

[70]Peña, *The Texas-Mexican Conjunto,* p. 138.

General Santa Anna's surrender to the Texas rebels at the San Jacinto Battlefield, April 1836.

A representative Mexican immigrant family in Houston during the 1920s. G.T. Valerio Collection, HMRC, Houston Public Library.

Our Lady of Guadalupe Church, Houston, 1923. Villagómez
Family Collection, HMRC, Houston Public Library.

Mexican American workers for the Southern Pacific Railroad, 1924. A. P. Flores
Family Collection, HMRC, Houston Public Library.

Members of *La Sociedad Mutualista Benito Juárez* of Magnolia Park, 1921.
Chairez Family Collection, HMRC, Houston Public Library.

Delegates to the 1937 LULAC National Convention held in Houston. Isidro
García Collection, HMRC, Houston Public Library.

Eloy Pérez and The Latinaires, a well known Houston dance band, circa late 1940s. Eloy Pérez Family Collection, HMRC, Houston Public Library.

Membership of Houston LULAC Council #60, 1948. Alfred J. Hernández Collection, HMRC, Houston Public Library.

Formal portrait of Houston Ladies' LULAC Council #22, in 1957. Carmen Cortes Collection, HMRC, Houston Public Library.

Félix and Angelina Morales, circa 1950, at their Radio Station KLVL. Félix and Angelina Morales Family Collection, HMRC, Houston Public Library.

Macario García, recipient of the Congressional Medal of Honor, 1945. Houston *Press* Collection, HMRC, Houston Public Library.

Attorney John J. Herrera, national president of LULAC, 1952–1953, and community activist. John J. Herrera Collection, HMRC, Houston Public Library.

Félix Tijerina, Houston businessman, philanthropist, and LULAC national president, 1956–1960. Houston *Press* Collection, HMRC, Houston Public Library.

123

San Antonian Albert Peña thanking Houston's Civic Action Committee members
who participated in John F. Kennedy's presidential campaign. Alfonso Vázquez
Collection, HMRC, Houston Public Library.

President and Mrs. John F. Kennedy speaking to Houston
LULACs, November 21, 1963. John J. Herrera Collection,
HMRC, Houston Public Library.

Harris County PASO activists at the 1966 farm workers' strike
and Minimum Wage March to Austin. Alfonso Vázquez Collection, HMRC, Houston Public Library.

La Raza Unida Party members in Houston during the 1972 election. Alfonso
Vázquez Collection, HMRC, Houston Public Library.

CHAPTER VII
THE LULAC ERA, 1945–1960

If LULAC Council #60 was a weathervane of changing ideological currents during the 1930s, it became, through two national presidents from Houston, the voice for national LULAC philosophy in the 1950s. To be sure, the Houston leadership fit in snuggly as part of the Mexican American Generation. For the middle class leaders of the era, the American way of life was to be upheld, the educational system was to be modified (not restructured) in order to permit for increased Mexican American schooling, and the "Latin American" was to be brought into the fold of national cultural ways by a constant struggle against institutions which denied them equality. Also, the Mexicans' whiteness was to be defended—LULACers showed a remarkable preoccupation with color classification. "Latin Americans or so-called 'Mexicans'," insisted an editorial in the LULAC *News* (October, 1945), "are Caucasian or white."[1] As white people, they had rights as Caucasian Anglo Americans. Protests against segregation in Houston were presented in that guise. As a letter from LULAC Regional Governor John J. Herrera to a local warehouse plant argued in September 1948:

> I don't think that it is necessary for me to discuss the segregation laws of Texas with you in connection with this matter [of having Mexicans eat in the section of the company commissary designated for blacks], but Latin Americans of Mexican descent belong to the Caucasian race and are therefore white and any person or company which sections or orders the mixing of races in a cafe or commissary is violating the segregation laws of our State.[2]

Loyalty for Mexicans born in the country, furthermore, was to be shown unceasingly. Mexican Americans were working and helping to build a greater America, protecting that which was American, and living, thinking, and speaking what was true American, argued another column in a 1947 LULAC *News*. "We are true Americans in every sense of the word," the editorial read, "for as yet no American of Spanish or Mexican descent has been catapulted into notoriety because of treason to his country; of subversive activities; of detrimental oratory to the policies of the country; or of defaulting his duty to his country."[3] Such expressions of allegiance would be general themes adhered to by Houston LULACers in the post-War era as they strived for the social betterment of Mexicanos. Still, there was no betraying their dual identity as a people appreciative of America for its beneficence and of Mexico for nourishing them culturally.

The Cause Goes On: 1945–1950

In the period immediately following the War, LULAC Council #60 continued attending to problems of barrio concerns. Some of its members assisted with the drive to rehabilitate Mexican American youths in 1945. LULACers, of course, had a vested interest in suppressing the negativism brought on by the pachucos upon "Latin Americans"; to that end, they helped in the work of the "Good Citizens League" (Félix Tijerina, the restauranteur, was a prominent LULACer) and the other groups organized to eliminate the zoot-suit presence.[4] As the "Latin American Squad" had given Mexican Americans a bad press, the Council sighed relief when the squad was disbanded in the spring of 1947. Council #60 president Dr. John J. Ruiz sent the Chief of Police a polite note thanking him for showing "sound judgment" in terminating the organization.[5]

In point of fact, LULAC dealt with relatively minor and routine matters—the absence of major issues to tackle may have been due, of course, to the general readjustment in Houston and elsewhere to a peace time society. LULACers became active in the movement to bring public housing for the poverty-stricken in the barrios, both as representatives in the several committees appointed by the city to study the needs for the project, and as an organization pledging itself to the program of public housing to stop the spread of tuberculosis.[6] Newer commitments to finding Mexican Americans for Grand Jury duty and placing them on the Grand Jury remained an issue of importance,[7] and poll tax payments persisted as a major goal for the membership.[8]

Significantly, LULAC Council #60 organized a Pro Macario García defense committee in 1946 to help the Medal of Honor Winner clear himself of aggravated assault charges (when denied a cup of coffee in Richmond, Texas, García had responded angrily—the League and friends raised money to defray legal fees). It cooperated with Club "México Bello" in sponsoring a Boy Scouts troop—after all, LULAC placed much faith in future, bicultural leaders who would assist in the work of Americanizing the rest of the population.[9] The committee supported, through letters to the Federal Communications Commission, Félix H. Morales' application for a permit to operate KLVL radio; when established in 1950, KLVL granted Council #60 free time for a LULAC program. Other lesser activities during the last half of the 1940s included blood drives for Mexican American patients.[10] All these, of course, were standard matters which produced progress and social betterment, but begot few major breakthroughs. Writing in late 1948, Regional Governor John J. Herrera summarized the work of the previous years with mixed emotions: "Houston Council No. 60 has gone virtually unheralded and unsung, except for the 'loyal guard,' that earnest, unselfish group of civic minded Latin Americans who have kept the flame and spirit of Lulac alive."[11]

The Veneer of "Social Gatherings": 1950–1960

LULAC's activities went unheralded for several reasons. First, its members were the more assimilated residents of the Houston community—the *gente decente* (class people) of the colonia—and la gente pobre somehow saw a social barrier between the two. Secondly, the League openly embraced "lo americano" when it was self-evident that mainstream society shunned Mexicans. Also, LULAC's strategy for change entailed using the courts or going through mainstream channels (it disapproved of protest demonstrations and the like which to the masses might have been more visible manifestations of protest), and the changes it brought about were often not readily apparent to the public (Anglo society found subterfuges to get around legalities in most cases). Then, the fundraising dances and social activities through which LULAC financed its programs created a skewed image of the organization in the public's eye. As one critic of Council #60's stand on dealing with the problem of pachuquismo in 1950 stated: "They are more interested in picnics and dances than in helping clear up this problem."[12]

In the 1950s, LULAC engaged in numerous programs, which, though perpetuating before the masses a reputation of an organization given to "social gatherings" (the Council's more significant undertakings are discussed in greater detail below), reflected LULACers belief in the goals of the League (already into its twenty-fifth year of existence by the mid-1950s) and the types of projects which the conservative era of the fifties permitted among minority groups. Indeed, the decade was a time of heightened activity by Ladies LULAC Council #22, which, after a hiatus during the War years, was reorganized and incorporated in October 1948.[13] Emerging among Ladies LULAC Council's most popular and successful projects of the era was the *"Rey Feo"* ("Ugly King") *Fiesta,* a fundraiser that pitted the several social and recreative clubs in Houston in a contest to raise the most money through dances, *tamaladas* (tamale sales), picnics, raffles and the like. The representative for the winning club was crowned "Rey Feo."[14]

Several worthy causes won the altruism of the Ladies Council. In the mid-1950s, it established a Milk Fund (under the auspices of the Houston Tuberculosis Clinic, the Council purchased milk tickets for needy families whose parents were victims of tuberculosis), the Eye Glass Fund to provide glasses for underprivileged school children, the Christmas Toy Fund to donate toys to the poor, and the Baby Garments Fund (diapers, shirts, dresses and other such necessities were donated to local hospitals for distribution to babies of needy families confined to the hospital or visiting the clinic). In the way of social services, Council #22 members worked with the Veterans Administration Hospital, with the Family and Child Welfare of the Community Council which worked with pre-delinquent children, and gave time, service, and funds to the Emergency Relief Committee for Cancer Patients Aid. It contributed money to the March of Dimes,[15] the Polio Drive, and emergencies, as in the case of the May 1955 Rio Grande Valley flood which rendered many homeless.[16]

The men's council worked with the same ardor. LULACers proceeded with projects which kept with the civic mindedness of the LULAC tradition. The desire to see high school graduates attend college produced the regular scholarship dances, and the preoccupation to see the young stay in school led them to look into school problems and into sponsoring "Back to School Drives." Through radio programs, they urged youths not to drop out of school and counseled juveniles about delinquency. Sponsoring Little League baseball teams was intended to help young people form a positive impression for themselves. Poll tax acquisition was encouraged through campaigns and rallies. Blood and tuberculosis drives, March of Dimes and Christmas Basket programs were adopted, and emergency relief was extended to the desperately sick. Discriminatory practices—in ambulance service, the schools, swimming pools, public halls—were investigated. Finally, adherence to their cultural heritage compelled them to assist with the holding of the fiestas patrias.[17]

In the 1950s, manifestly, Council #60 kept up activities which were not unlike those of other groups and clubs in Houston. But this was only part of the work being carried on during the era, for simultaneously, the Council agitated before mainstream society consistently and sometimes vociferously. The remainder of this chapter treats the more spirited efforts of Council #60 in the LULAC era. As will be seen, these efforts paralleled those being undertaken by the Mexican American leadership in other parts of the state, at least according to the current crop of works that touch upon the post-war G.I. Generation.[18]

John J. Herrera

During the 1950s, Council #60 indeed became one of the most important LULAC chapters in the country. Two of the most aggressive Council #60 spokesmen were elected national presidents during the decade: John J. Hererra, who served between 1952–1953, and Félix Tijerina whose term extended from 1956 to 1960. Throughout the fifties, therefore, the Houston council was embroiled in the most significant issues of the day. Council #60 emerged as a center of activity, coordinating policy with a distinguished cadre of Tejano activists, among them Alonso Perales, J.T. Canales, James Tafolla, George I. Sánchez, Carlos E. Castañeda, Gus C. García, and Hector P. García, plus younger cohorts (Ed Idar and Chris Alderete come to mind). These were the leaders of the so-called Mexican American Generation which had made its mark since the 1930s. No other Tejano generation has produced such a venerable crop of activists.

In the first half of the decade, Council #60's most articulate and persistent spokesmen was John J. (Johnny) Herrera, so that Herrera's actions and those of the Houston council often converged. Herrera's career before the 1950s was already punctuated with distinction. A former dish washer, ditch digger, cabman, and sundry other laboring types, he had been among the founders of the Latin American Club in the 1930s and had been among LAC's more active members throughout the Depression decade. He spoke with pride of his ancestry: he was a direct descendant of Francisco Ruiz, signer of the Texas Declaration of Independence of 1836, and Blas and Pedro Herrera who had contributed militarily against Santa Anna. During World War II, Johnny Herrera had continued working towards acquiring his law degree (he was admitted to the Bar in 1943) while simultaneously carrying on the struggle against discrimination in the shipyards and getting liberty ships named after Mexican heroes. In 1947, he ran seventh (among forty-two) in a special Senatorial race in Harris County to fill the unexpired term of a deceased representative; this was the first time any Mexican American had run for political office in the county. As a tribute to his achievements, the Council had elected him president in the late 1940s. In 1947, he became regional governor of LULAC in the Houston area, a position which he held until 1950 when he became National First Vice-President.[19]

The second wave of juvenile delinquency during the post-war era absorbed Council #60 and district governor Herrera in a controversy over the resurrection of the "Latin American Squad." For Herrera, forming the Squad was inadvisable and unwise. First, it would create diplomatic repercussions as Houston was a center of administrative activity for diplomats from Latin America, he said. More importantly, the Latin American Squad was a "form of discrimination against a minority group." Mexicanos in Houston resented it, he and the LULACers argued, as it singled them out as a problem where none existed, for in fact, they noted, the notion of organized gangs was an invention of the press. True, gangs prowled the barrios, Herrera wrote to the Houston *Chronicle,* but forming a Latin American Squad would penalize and stigmatize the hardworking, law-abiding majority. "We do not think that innocent Latin Americans should suffer just because we have a small minority of Hoodlums in Houston."[20]

The Mexicans in Houston, Council #60 argued further, were Americans being distinguished from other Americans. As Herrera put it, the newspapers were on a "witch hunt" against Mexican Americans, coloring crime news with a racial tint. "The inclusion of the word 'Latin American' in any crime story cannot be interpreted except as calculated to appeal to the baser instincts of our citizenry: racial prejudice and discrimination. No good can be meant to anyone when you point out the racial extraction of a person charged with a crime." The Latin American Squad, therefore, was a concept germinating from the exaggerated image of all Mexicans as hoodlums.[21] A better solution to the gangsterism, the LULACer recommended, was hiring five or six Mexican American officers, and assigning them to different divisions in the police department. These men would be bilingual and understand the problems and customs of the colonia.[22] In the end, the chief of police dropped the idea of a "Latin American Squad."[23]

LULAC measures to work against juvenile delinquency and pachuquismo involved working with the youngsters to correct their waywardness. As in the 1940s, this meant occupying them with sports, working closely with the police on specific cases, and holding periodic public sessions on what could be done about the problem.[24]

Another issue of significance for Houston LULACers was what the generation of the fifties called the "Wetback Problem." Since the 1940s, the national LULAC office had taken a stand against the Bracero program (a guest worker arrangement between Mexico and the United States, 1943–1964) and the use of illegal laborers from Mexico by agricultural interests. For the League, this type of workers constituted a source of cheap labor that lowered wage standards of resident laborers. "Wetback" (*mojado*) labor in particular displaced American workers as growers could afford to pay cheap wages, keeping the illegals in virtual peonage with the threat of denouncing them to the immigration authorities.[25]

Actually, the role of Houston LULACers' concerning the "Wetback" question was one of lending moral support to other councils, as undocumented workers were concentrated in rural areas, picking cotton primarily. But opposition to the use of illegals was everybody's problem; as one LULAC *News* headline read: "Wetback Round-up Needs Support of LULAC."[26] Expectedly, Council #60 rode the anti-alien sentiment. As John J. Herrera explained it at that time, "We Lulacs are accused of being agitators and of not wanting the poor alien Mexican to come into Texas and augment the poor existence that he is having in Mexico; however, we Lulacs feel that the steady flow of immigrant wet-back labor from Mexico into Texas will continue to make our problem of communication [with Anglo Americans] difficult; and as long as this influx of laborers is allowed to come into Texas, the problem shall continue to be a vital one for us all."[27]

Herrera, therefore, considered it his duty to support the anti-wetback movement, even if Houston's stake in the issue was somewhat peripheral. In July 1954, Herrera co-chaired a G.I. Forum convention in Houston, which had as its principal speaker Willard F. Kelly, retired assistant commissioner of immigration and naturalization. Known as "Mr. Border Patrol" during his active days, Kelly had masterminded airlifts, trainlifts, and buslifts in 1951 to move "wetbacks" into the interior of Mexico. There in Houston, he repeated his stand on the perils of the wetback nuisance, commending the 400 Forumeers in the audience on the approach they were taking toward solving the "wetback problem."[28] The Forumeers and Herrera, no doubt, appreciated Kelly's supportive words, for in having him speak, they found the essential praise to reinforce their beliefs in the justice of the anti-wetback cause. The position which those members of the Mexican American generation took in the 1950s would be seriously challenged by newer ideological currents a generation later.

As Kelly spoke, the Immigration and Naturalization Service prepared to launch a massive drive historically known as "Operation Wetback" (the project commenced on July 17, 1954). Its intent was to evict the thousands of "mojados" in the country. To what extent the campaign reached the Houston area is undeterminable at this point of research. The primary literature is almost mute concerning any sweeps made into the city. The major newspapers took practically no note of it and archival material is thin on the issue. The drives were concentrated on the border agricultural areas primarily, but that does not preclude sallies into Houston in search of illegals. Further study seems imperative on this point.

For Herrera, the question of undocumented laborers was only one of the several matters which occupied his interests in the 1950s. Most of his time was devoted, especially during his National Presidency, to issues needing his attention elsewhere beyond Houston. There were newer councils to be organized, joint meetings to be held with the G.I. Forum to coordinate policy, school segregation cases to be taken before the courts, and the LULAC word to be spread.[29] Upon yielding the LULAC high office, Herrera's commitment to Mexican American causes persisted. He acted as counsel in the landmark *Pete Hernández v. The State of Texas* (1954) in which the Supreme Court ruled that Mexican Americans were not be excluded from juries. He sought political office—three times between 1954 and 1958 he ran for the State Legislature, backed by a strong labor, Mexican American, and black coalition. He worked indefatigably for the Democratic Party during the fifties.[30] His career was hardly finished as the decade ended—Herrera's presence in Houston would be felt until the 1980s.

Félix Tijerina

In the latter part of the 1950s, the major issues which had preoccupied LULAC Council #60 during the early years of the decade were unheeded, either because they dissipated or they were supplanted by other goals with greater priority. Juvenile delinquency no longer seemed to be the problem it had been since the zoot-suit days of World War II, the "Wetback Problem" ceased to be an issue of critical concern, and some of the cases dealing with school segregation or non-representation in juries, which had been of such importance to men like Herrera, had been resolved in LULAC's favor by the courts (inevitably, they were ignored by Anglos, however). Lastly, the new leader in Houston, Félix Tijerina, led Council #60 towards new horizons.

Between 1956 and 1960, Félix Tijerina, as national president of LULAC, trumpeted the need for the educational advancement of Mexican Americans. This was no impulsive idea he embraced; it had its roots in LULAC's emphasis on education and on Tijerina's own upbringing. Tijerina had experienced first hand the life of a migrant as the son of an itinerant farm worker family. He spent time in trucks and camps, following the cotton and vegetable crops from the Rio Grande Valley to the Houston area. He had been forced to abandon ideas of schooling by his father's death; instead, at the age of nine he found himself working the fields in efforts to help support his widowed mother and his three sisters. The family moved to Houston in the early 1920s from Sugarland, just south of the city, and young Tijerina took up work as a street vendor, selling vegetables, then acquiring a job as a waiter in a Mexican cafe.

As fate had it, the young man's future was to be in the restaurant business; from the good fortune he achieved in his line of work would come the status and time to devote to worthwhile causes, including educating Mexicanos. After numerous years as a waiter, Tijerina opened up a restaurant of his own on the 1100 block of Main Street. It was successful enough in the early years to permit him to marry Janie Gonzales (the two became inseparable in the public's mind as owners of the Felix Restaurants), but the Depression took its toll forcing the Tijerinas to close down. Undaunted, Félix and Janie Tijerina reopened, after accumulating some cash from his truck-driving job and her work, at the 1200 block of Westheimer Avenue. Felix Restaurants have thrived in Houston ever since.

Even as Tijerina toiled to make a go of his restaurant, he joined numerous organizations and participated in several civic causes during the 1930s, among them those of LULAC. He had been among the founders of LAC and often could be found participating in matters of interest to Council #60. As already mentioned, he was a member of the group appointed to advise the Houston Housing Authority and he headed, at least briefly, the "Good Citizens League." He had sponsored or financially subsidized youth clubs. In the years after the war (he served in the Air Force during World War II) Tijerina rose through the LULAC ranks, developing contacts and establishing a place among Houston's mainstream society in the meantime; indeed his list of achievements as co-worker and even director of some of the city's "Anglo" organizations was impressively lengthy. By the mid-1950s, he was Regional Governor of LULAC. Tijerina represented an approach and philosophy which kept to LULAC tradition, though alongside Herrera's more anti-Anglo position, seemed more critical of Mexicanos. A self-taught and self-made man, he relished education and criticized those unwilling to take advantage of the abundant opportunities available to them in the United States. In an interview published in the Houston *Post* at the height of his financial career, the reporter noted: "His viewpoint on most matters is more 'Anglo'—or North American—than it is Latin."

For Tijerina, no excuse could be advanced for rejecting English. According to the *Post,* he would instruct Mexicanos: "You are American citizens and English is the national language." Failure to accept English posed pitfalls to first graders. It meant inability to keep up with the other children, unnecessary embarrassment, and inevitably, dropping out. The destiny for these casualties was farm work or menial labor instead of business or professional work.

In essence, Tijerina's campaign of Anglicization exceeded the cultural pluralism preferred by most LULACers. There are American born Mexicans who still think of themselves as "Mexicans" instead of "Americans," he informed the *Post.* "That is not right; if they are going to live here, they must become Americans, just like the English and Swedes and the French and Italians who have come to this country." Example started in one's home, of course, and Tijerina implemented his philosophy therein. "I want my children to learn Spanish when they grow a little older," he commented, "but I want them to know their English well first, so they won't speak it with an accent." Tijerina in the 1950s carried weight in the organization, for the LULAC *News* of September 1955 reprinted the *Post* story in toto for fellow LULACers to read.[31]

Upon rising to National President of LULAC (1956 to 1960), Tijerina moved to implement his dream of educating disadvantaged Mexican children, and despite his numerous LULAC achievements, it is with the "Little Schools of the 400" that he is most closely identified. As National Director of the League, Tijerina, with the help of supportive LULACers, began plans to form the LULAC Foundation, Inc., a non-profit entity intended to help lower language barriers which handicapped Mexican American children in schools.[32] By then, a volunteer project had been launched in nearby Ganado (southwest of Houston, in Jackson County) by seventeen-year old Isabel Verver. Specifically, the Ganado program consisted of teaching key words and phrases which preschool children would need to get along with their English-speaking classmates. Youngsters were taught the Pledge of Allegiance, how to speak to the teacher, and how to conduct themselves in an unfamiliar, English-speaking setting. The result had been so encouraging that Tijerina picked up the Ganado model and made plans to erect it throughout Texas and perhaps the entire United States.[33]

In 1957, with his own money, Tijerina launched two tuition-free "Little Schools of the 400" in Ganado and nearby Edna, both in Jackson county. As the name implies, the program sought to teach 400 words of basic English to Spanish speaking five-year olds. After a bit more than three months of instruction, the "graduates" enrolled in the towns' public schools; where more than half of the previous Mexican American first graders had failed the year before, all who attended Tijerina's pilot program performed well.[34] By the next year the experiment was so successful that Tijerina spread it to other schools and won the support of Texas Governor Price Daniel. In June 1958, the governor journeyed to Sugarland for the formal opening of the first state-funded "Little Schools of the 400." He presented the LULAC National President with a flag of the State of Texas and called him "the father of an educational program that is becoming national in scope."[35]

By the latter 1950s, Tijerina's concept of pre-school language training had become one of the most relevant concerns of LULAC. At its annual state convention held in Houston in February 1959, one of the prime objectives was planning strategy for the passage of H.B. 51 and S.B. 62; they would authorize a preschool instructional program for non-English speaking children. The bills would decree instructional units and financing as well as require the Central Education Agency to develop the program and set teachers' certification standards.[36] That spring, the state legislature passed a $1,300,000 bill to set up Tijerina-style schools throughout Texas.

The appropriation led to a grand crusade aimed, as *Time* magazine put it in profile of Tijerina, "at smashing the language barrier forever." So popular was the idea that Latin communities in New York City, Buffalo, and Elizabeth, New Jersey considered launching similar schools. Tijerina himself joined the crusade, selling the idea to Mexican parents, broadcasting his appeals on Spanish language radios throughout the state.[37]

In 1960, Tijerina called the LULAC presidency quits. His concept of the "Little Schools of the 400" lived on, though did not survive state-funding cuts for long. In a way, his brainchild may have been a bridge between the LULACers of the 1950s and the middle class liberals of the next decade. Both departed from the integrationist philosophy of the Mexican American Generation since they called for separate institutions designed to assist Mexican Americans—specifically, the "Little Schools of the 400" singled out Mexican Americans for remedial instruction and the concept was federalized during the Great Society era of the 1960s in the form of the "Head Start" program. While the LULAC supporters of the project may have inclined towards that departure, Tijerina in particular seems to have been too much of an advocate for integration to have had in mind making such a move. It seems more logical to think that he was willing to experiment with anything for the good of Mexicanos. To him, the "Little Schools of the 400" was a program intended to prepare little ones for fuller absorption into American life.

A Contrast of Styles

Houston may have been the spiritual headquarters for LULAC during much of the 1950s, but the approaches taken by Herrera and Tijerina towards helping *la raza* may well have emanated from opposite parts of the country. Though true believers in the LULAC cause, the two often clashed over matters of technique, priorities, and interests. That they held different viewpoints in the era when the Mexican American Generation reached its adult phase is a reminder of a basic fact. That is, LULAC as an organization was composed of different elements, yet through a common belief in its aims and purposes could reach consensus.

During the 1950s, when both men were in the prime of their careers, Herrera and Tijerina sniped at each other, sometimes with hostile ferocity. On one occasion in 1953, for example, when Herrera charged the police with brutality against Mexican American teenagers, Tijerina publicly criticized the attorney for complaining. Not only did Tijerina defend the police, but accused Herrera of self-aggrandizement. Everytime Mexican Americans got into trouble, Tijerina informed the press, Mr. Herrera cashed in on the publicity. "He is not the representative of the Mexicans here," he proclaimed.[38]

Herrera was equally caustic in describing his competitor. In 1956, he faulted Tijerina for supporting the Eisenhower-Nixon Republican ticket. While Tijerina explained that as the National President he could not endorse anyone for president, Herrera bitterly pointed out that the restauranteur had nonetheless been outspoken in his support for the Republicans, even when knowing that Vice President Richard Nixon was "reactionary and unsympathetic to minority group problems."[39]

The next year, Herrera denounced Tijerina savagely following a newspaper interview published in Monterrey, México. Explaining the status of Mexicans in Texas, Tijerina informed the periodical, in Spanish, that Mexicanos earned extremely low salaries, that their educational achievements were still poor, and that discrimination was not such a problem as generally considered. Herrera countered by accusing Tijerina of mendacity, noting that the educational achievements of Tejanitos had shown great improvement during the last few years, that workers earned legally-established minimum wages, and that discrimination was blatant around the Houston area. True, Herrera conceded, there were some places where Mexicans earned dismal wages, but those were exceptions, among them "Mr. Tijerina's restaurants which employ recently arrived Mexicans from Mexico, and because of their bad fortune, have to accept a salary of $20.00 a week." Sad to say, Herrera continued in his diatribe, Tijerina was LULAC National President, but that was a position the restauranteur had achieved "due to his money, and not for his ideological convictions." Texas-Mexicans did not need "semi-literate leaders," Herrera concluded.[40]

Soon after this episode, Herrera criticized Tijerina for not taking a stand with the National Association for the Advancement of Colored People (NAACP) against HB 231 which would allow school superintendents in Texas the right to place any pupil in any school in his district. Tijerina's position was, as one of his advisors put it, that "a stand taken by LULAC on such bills would tend to admit to our anglo-saxon friends that we considered ourselves separate and apart from the majority of American citizens and had no faith or confidence in our rights of equality of treatment in accordance with the law of the land."[41] Herrera not only reproached Tijerina for not seeing that such a Bill was designed to circumvent laws prohibiting segregation, but labled the case as still another example pointing to the National President's "ineptness." Tijerina, Herrera said, refused to take stands on controversial issues and had grown "too rich for our LULAC blood." For personal reasons, Herrera confessed, he would miss his first LULAC national convention in twenty years: "Frankly, I feel ashamed and embarrassed at the way Félix has conducted himself as our National President. Since I backed him up so strongly, when he was elected in El Paso, I feel at least partly responsible for what has happened [during the course of Tijerina's tenure]."[42]

The two men's rivalry continued until Tijerina's last years as national president. "The Little Schools of the 400," so dear to Tijerina, was an anomaly for Herrera. The restauranteur was an "appeaser," the attorney said in an anonymous interview to the Houston *Chronicle,* and the school "a big step backward." LULAC had been founded to protect the rights of Mexican Americans, such as fighting school segregation. "Now Tijerina turns around and starts a school which says, in effect, that the Latin American child should be segregated."[43]

Manifestly, contrasts are evident in the two leaders. Herrera had a penchant for confrontation. In the 1950s, he seemed more in tune with the cadre of politically alert Mexican American World War II veterans then launching vigorous protests against inequalities through organizations like the G.I. Forum (Herrera was a lifetime Honorary Member of the Forum). Tijerina, on the other hand, seemed to have taken accommodation to bounds past the ideal of a bicultural way of life. What made a difference? After all, both were of the same age, of humble birth and upbringing. The two had belonged to just about the same Mexican *sociedades* in Houston. They had made it as professionals through dogged determination and had risen to heights which earned them respect both in Anglo and Mexicano circles. Personality, of course, always motivates different behavior, but Herrera appears to have had less restrictions on the freedom to act more boldly. His legal training conditioned him for confrontation and his business did not suffer from attacks upon mainstream institutions; if anything, it profitted. By his own count, his law business included no more than 25% Anglo.[44]

Tijerina, on the other hand, had much to lose, for his restaurants' clientele was primarily Anglo. An argument can be made that much of what found itself into the newspapers was meant for Anglo consumption. His defense of the police in 1953 and his famous interview of 1955 with the Houston *Post,* where he expressed unabashed assimilation, must have been read by hundreds of his customers. His work among Mexican Americans was undeniable in the 1930s and 1940s, and notwithstanding Herrera's accusations of *"vendido"* during the 1950s, LULAC members elected Tijerina for a tenure of four terms, still a record for National Presidents.

Still, common threads tied Tijerina and Herrera as members of the Mexican American Generation. In fact, the things which provoked mutual criticism at times revolved around personality, not major philosophical differences. The men disagreed on approach, not ideological tenets. Conspicuously, neither looked to Mexico with the sentiments of those of another age. Indeed, both were steadfast in expressing their love for the United States. Tijerina talked about speaking English and establishing schools to Americanize youngsters; Herrera pridefully boasted of his membership in the Sons of the Republic of Texas and yearly went to the ceremonies at San Jacinto monument on April 21 to speak, as he said in one of his yearly speeches, of "the sacred cause of liberty which has always united the lovers of freedom, regardless of race."[45]

World War II meant the same thing to each. Tijerina volunteered for service, and let that speak for itself. Herrera had not served (deferred) but spoke with pride of fellow Mexicanos who had. He could always invoke that sort of patriotism in confronting the enemies of equality. In denouncing the "Latin American Squad" in 1950 he assured the editor of the Houston *Chronicle:*

> We of LULAC are not agitators, we are American Citizens all born in this country and we want to take our place and keep it as members of our American community. The Latin American colony of Houston has been as a whole, law-abiding and patriotic. During World War 2, we gave seventy-five lives to the cause of freedom and democracy, including the first Houston casualty of World War 2, who was a Latin American boy. The only winner of the Congressional Medal of Honor during World War 2 in Houston is of Mexican origin. How do you think all of these people feel when they read a blanket accusation or an attempted crusade [the establishment of the "Latin American Squad"] against their entire people.[46]

Education hit close to the heart of both. Herrera had amassed extensive experience as LULAC counsel in school desegregation cases, most significantly in *Delgado* v. *Bastrop ISD* in 1948. Tijerina exemplified, even embodied the Mexican American Generation's unflinching belief in the value of education as the key to progress. From the preparation provided by the "Little Schools of the 400" would come a fuller education and from that a means to a better life. Bilingual doctors, lawyers, professors were envisioned for a future generation.

In their attitudes toward fellow oppressed blacks, the two appeared to have assented, to a degree, to the segregationist policies of their times. Tijerina was more set in his anti-black feelings (discussed in Chapter 9) than Herrera. But even the more sympathetic civil rights lawyer, who saw the cause of the NAACP in the fight against HB 231 as the cause of LULAC, could protest against the segregation of Mexicans with blacks. Mexicans, after all, were white persons, and the segregation laws of Texas applied to black people, not Mexicanos.

Their stand against "wetback" labor similarly reflected the thinking of those in the fifties. While Tijerina did not have to face the question squarely, his stand on the matter could not have been much different than that of his fellow LULAC contemporaries. Like others of the Mexican

American Generation, Tijerina must have agonized over the irony of having to work against a people who wanted nothing less than what which his ancestors wished when they trekked to Texas. Tijerina did not say much on the matter, but Herrera conceded that his organization felt the pangs of resentment from the people it was supposed to represent. "The LULAC program which has, perhaps, caused the Lulacs to be criticized most [by Texas-Mexicans], is its stand against wet-back or immigrant labor from Mexico into Texas," he admitted in a speech.[47] Yet, the generation of the fifties took their licks because the native born was their primary concern. In a choice between foreign born brethren who in their struggle to survive depressed wages for Tejanos, the Mexican American Generation chose the well-being of their own.

Finally, neither Herrera nor Tijerina ever advocated radicalism or revolutionary change. At least a few reasons explain their beliefs in a peaceful approach toward reform. First, each spoke for a middle class and that standing conditioned them to pursue a moderate tack. Second, they were products of their generation and they stood vigil over troublemakers and those others who might smear the LULAC name. How could they denounce through militant action the very institutions LULAC cherished and defended? Further, protest in the 1950s was a dangerous undertaking even when done peacefully. The label of "Communist" was too freely flung about during the era, with LULAC reformers and their G.I. Forum allies often the target. Last, Houston did not provide the most conducive setting for overt protest; bloody strikes, massive demonstrations, destructive rioting, and inflammatory rallies were still unknown in the city at mid-century. Discontent, when expressed, was carried out through grassroots organizations, and LULAC and its leaders conformed to that pattern.

A Case Study

The roles played in Houston by Herrera and Tijerina present a glimpse of LULAC at work in the 1950s. Whether their approaches and philosophies represented the norm or the exception during the period remain to be studied elsewhere. While other regions of the state, such as those in south and west Texas, may have lacked men of the stature of the two, it seems logical that such cities as Corpus Christi, Laredo, El Paso, or San Antonio would offer the circumstances for a similar comparison.

The activities of the two men do say something about Mexican American leadership in the 1950s. First, they reveal that the thinking of the Mexican American Generation, first blanketing communities in the 1930s, was still prevalent as late as mid-century. Put another way, the Mexican American Generation continued on the steed and the ideology which they espoused during their youthful years carried on into the Cold War era. In efforts at ameliorating the status of the colonia, therefore, Herrera and Tijerina abided by tactics and principles that accorded with the times.

The conduct of the two men is also instructive as to Mexican American leadership. That is, the Mexican American Generation of the 1930s through the 1950s was itself diverse and not necessarily monolithic as sometimes supposed. In Houston, business interests and strong egos could produce conflicts in approach. That such a cleavage could exist is a reminder that historically, cultural change in Texas-Mexican communities has not been uniform. In fact, Mexican American culture would become more fragmented as time wore on.

NOTES

[1]*LULAC News,* October, 1945, p. 5.
[2]Letter, September 8, 1948, HMRC, John J. Herrera Collection.
[3]*LULAC News,* June, 1947, p. 15.
[4]Houston *Chronicle,* December 2, 1945, p. 24A; *LULAC News,* May 1946, pp. 20 and 42.
[5]Letter, March 5, 1947, HMRC, LULAC Council #60 Collection.
[6]Houston *Chronicle,* August 2, 1945, p. 3A January 23, 1948, p. 11A.
[7]*LULAC News,* May, 1946, p. 20.
[8]Houston *Chronicle,* January 9, 1948, p. 13A.
[9]"Speech," February 13, 1971, HMRC, John J. Herrera Collection; *El Sol,* December 29, 1972, p. 1; *LULAC News,* May, 1946, p. 17.
[10]Letter, September 7, 1946, HMRC, LULAC Council #60 Collection; Minutes, April 27, 1950, ibid.
[11]*LULAC News,* October, 1948, p. 3.
[12]Houston *Chronicle,* March 12, 1950, p. 22A.
[13]*LULAC News,* June, 1954, p. 15.
[14]Houston *Chronicle,* August 20, 1950, p. 19A; *LULAC News,* January 1956, p. 5.
[15]*LULAC News,* April, 1954, p. 6; June, 1954, p. 15.
[16]Ibid., May, 1955, p.21.
[17]Various documents in HMRC, LULAC Council #60 Collection.
[18]See for example, Guadalupe San Miguel, Jr., *"Let All of Them Take Heed"*: *Mexican Americans and the Campaign for Educational Equality in Texas, 1910–1981;* and Montejano, *Anglos and Mexicans in the Making of Texas.*
[19]*LULAC News,* May, 1947, p. 16, *LULAC News,* May, 1950, p. 3; *LULAC News, 25th Anniversary Issue,* p. 21; and "Resumé" of John J. Herrera, HMRC, John J. Herrera Collection.

[20]Houston *Chronicle*, February 27, 1950, p. 9A; March 7, 1950, p. 6A March 9, 1950, p. 15B; Minutes, February 16, 1950 and February 28, 1950, HMRC, LULAC Council #60 Collection; Letter, March 11, 1950, to Houston *Chronicle*, HMRC, John J. Herrera Collection. The letter of March 11 was published in *Chronicle*, on March 15, 1950, p. 14B, in an edited version.

[21]Letter, March 11, 1950, to Houston *Chronicle*, HMRC, John J. Herrera Collection; Minutes, February 16, 1950, HMRC, LULAC Council #60 Collection; Houston *Chronicle*, March 17, 1950, p. 1A.

[22]Letter, March 11, 1950, to Houston *Chronicle*, HMRC, John J. Herrera Collection; Houston *Chronicle*, February 27, 1950, p. 9A.

[23]Houston, *Chronicle*, March 7, 1950, p. 6A.

[24]Ibid., March 17, 1950, p. 1A; Houston *Press*, March 11, 1953, p. 2; March 13, 1953, p. 11; March 10, 1953, p. 1; and Houston *Post*, MArch 10, 1953, p. 1 (Section 1).

[25]*LULAC News, 25th Anniversary Issue*, p. 25; "Statement to the Press" (1951), HMRC, John J. Herrera Collection.

[26]*LULAC News*, July 1954, p. 4.

[27]Speech, "LULAC and the Latin-American in Texas," HMRC, John J. Herrera Collection.

[28]Houston *Chronicle*, July 15, 1954, p. 9A; July 17, 1954, p. 4A.

[29]*LULAC News, 25th Anniversary Issue*, p. 71.

[30]"Resumé" of John J. Herrera, HMRC, John J. Herrera Collection; Letter to Luciano Santoscoy, May 15, 1954, ibid.; Houston *Chronicle*, July 9, 1954, p. 7D.

[31]Houston *Post*, August 8, 1955, p. 1; *LULAC News*, September 1955, p. 3–4, *LULAC News, 25th Anniversary Issue*, p. 49, and newspaper articles in HMRC, Félix Tijerina Collection.

[32]Houston *Chronicle*, October 6, 1957, p. 12A. For a full discussion of the "Little Schools of the 400," see San Miguel, *"Let All of Them Take Heed,"* Chapter 6.

[33]Ibid., October 6, 1957, p. 16A.

[34]*Time* magazine, August 17, 1959, p. 56.

[35]Houston *Press*, June 24, 1958, p. 4.

[36]Houston *Press*, February 10, 1959, p. 2; *El Puerto*, Houston, Texas, October 1959, p. 14.

[37]*Time* magazine, August 17, 1959, p. 56.

[38]Houston *Chronicle*, March 11, 1953, p. 1A; Houston *Post*, March 12, 1953, p. 2.

[39]Newspaper clippings, HMRC, John J. Herrera Collection.

[40]"Resultan Ridículas Las Declaraciones del Sr. Félix Tijerina," HMRC, John J. Herrera Collection.

[41]Letter, May 27, 1957, HMRC, LULAC Council #60 Collection. See further, Houston *Chronicle*, December 8, 1958, p. 4A.

[42]Letter, June 14, 1957, HMRC, John J. Herrera Collection.

[43]Houston *Chronicle*, December 8, 1958, p. 4A.

[44]"Resumé" of John J. Herrera, HMRC, John J. Herrera Collection.

[45]*LULAC News*, May, 1947, p. 11 and June, 1955, p. 14; "Speech at San Jacinto Monument," April 21, 1954, HMRC, John J. Herrera Collection.

[46]Letter to the Editor, March 11, 1950, HMRC, John J. Herrera Collection.

[47]"LULAC and the Latin-American in Texas," HMRC, John J. Herrera Collection.

PART III:
MANY MEXICANOS, 1960 to 1980s

CHAPTER VIII
MEXICANS IN SPACE CITY, USA, 1960–1975

By the 1960s and mid-1970s, the Mexican community in Houston belonged as much to the greater Houston metropolitan landscape as did oil refineries, skyscrapers, freeways, and some of the new fixtures which became identifiable with Houston during the era. Among the latter were the Astrodome, an enclosed air-conditioned sports stadium proclaimed at its opening in 1965 as the "Eighth Wonder of the World," and the Manned Spacecraft Center of the National Aeronautics and Space Administration (NASA) which earned Houston the sobriquet of "Space City, USA." The several barrios had accompanied Houston's own march towards grandness—most especially during the post-1945 era when three-fourths of the city was built. From about 600,000 people in 1950, Houston's population increased to approximately 938,000 in 1960 and a decade later, the city boasted a figure of 1.2 million people. Comparatively, Mexican Americans comprised 7% of Houston's population in 1960; by 1970, their numbers stood at 150,000 and Mexicanos (less undocumented residents from Mexico overlooked by the census) accounted for 12% of the city's population.[1]

As the size of the colonia swelled, Mexican Americans became more and more visible in the minds of fellow Houstonians. Their growing numbers attracted a cross section of proselytizers. Politicians campaigned for their vote, entrepreneurs desired their business, employers needed more workers, religious groups sought believers among them, and so on. Mexican Americans themselves used that visibility and turned to their numerical strength to attempt change in their historical condition.

It was during this period that most Houstonians came to accept Mexican Americans as part of the city's own diverse cultural makeup. True,

147

the inequities of the barrios, the segregation, the concentration of most Mexicanos into blue-collar occupations were apparent to the greater Houston society. But no longer were Mexican Americans broadly perceived as "quaint" and colorful people. References to labels like "Little Mexico" disappeared. By the 1960s and 1970s, mainstream society generally understood that the majority were bicultural, now commanding purchasing power, fluency of language, political savvy to wage electoral battles, and keen insights into the nuances of societal complexities.

The changing perceptions did not occur out of a new benevolence. Rather, numerous historical forces compelled white society to reconsider old attitudes toward minority groups. Urbanization, for one thing, continued apace and altered recognitions grounded on rural values. By the 1950s, the federal census showed for the first time an urban population in Texas. This farm to city relocation continued to the point that by the 1970s, about eight of ten Texans lived in urban sites. San Antonio and the Dallas-Fort Worth area accompanied Houston towards megalopolis status; by the decade of the seventies, about half of the state lived in these three metropolitan centers.

Suburbanization, also, worked to alter entrenched views about the backwardness of Texas Mexicans. The move to the suburbs picked up in rapid pace for several reasons, among them the construction of freeway linkages to smaller surrounding towns, the affordability of the automobile, and the desire to get away from the problems of the inner city (Sugarland and Tomball, for example, became the place of residence for many in Houston's work force). With many citizens living comfortably away in the quiet of the suburbs, tolerance seemed more permissible, especially from a vantage point where minority groups were less visible, or where minorities in those suburbs resembled their neighbors in social class and values.

Industrialization, furthermore, prompted mainstream society to question the relevancy of the old racial stereotypes. Following World War II, Texas became a magnet for military installations, defense industries, and for the expansion of the petro-chemical facilities. The impact of these new enterprises was tremendous. By the 1970s, the Texas economy was diversified and mature. No longer did Texas hold the dubious status of the pre-War years of having a colonial economy which exported its raw products to other states.[2]

The civil unrest of the 1960s and 1970s also made mainstream society retreat from the attitudes of the previous decade. Held back by the norms of the 1950s, a movement for social change suddenly erupted in turmoil. Liberal groups took on the cause of the dispossessed. More leftist elements sought to create radical change. Youths now struck for a freer lifestyle. The norms so much admired in the 1950s were changed irreversibly by the movements of the 1960s.[3]

Minority groups were not left too far behind in forcing society to modernize views. Black Texans, for one, contributed to the early civil rights movement with sit-ins in the bigger cities such as Houston and Dallas. Though the more extreme expressions of discontent (e.g. burning of ghettoes) never did afflict Texas, racial troubles did occur. In Houston itself, a confrontation between police and students at Texas Southern University in 1967 led to the indictment of five student activists for the murder of a policeman. In 1970, another conflict between police and black activists in Houston produced the killing of a leader whose group the police considered revolutionary.[4] Antagonistic episodes in Houston also occurred with Mexican Americans; they are discussed in the next two chapters.

Proclamations of cultural pride from minorities themselves gave whites a new understanding of "people of color." The black civil rights movement set off a surge of ethnic consciousness throughout the American population. Blacks showed renewed interest in their African past, American Indians a concern for tribalism, and Mexican Americans displayed an awareness of their Aztec and Mayan past. This fervor produced a new mood in favor of a more positive recognition of minority peoples.

Culture

Geographically, the outlay of the Houston community resembled the shape of the pre-WW II colonia, though the new patterns of population dispersal surfacing in the 1950s intensified after 1960. Mexicanos still lived in the old neighborhoods which they had entered during the early twentieth century, but they were also spread throughout the city. They had either created new barrios or vanished into integrated neighborhoods. The result was further diversity for an already heterogeneous people.

By far, the greatest concentration of Mexicanos during the era of the sixties and seventies was in Houston's inner city: such a density resembled the modern pattern of settlement for minority groups throughout the United States. This segment of Houston embraced the old barrios, namely the Northside, the First and Sixth Ward areas, and the East End (El Segundo Barrio and Magnolia), as well as newer pockets of Mexican presence in areas like Denver Harbor (due north of the Houston Ship Channel, three and a half miles east of the Houston Central Business

District). Whereas less than half of the white Anglo population lived in the central city by the 1970s, about two-thirds of Mexicanos made their home in the barrios therein (slightly more than 80.0% of blacks resided in the inner city).[5]

Moreover, these several inner city barrios were growing and not declining. With the Mexicano population in Houston doubling between 1960 and 1970, the poorest of families found the most shelter there. Simultaneously, Anglo residents of the barrios—mostly older folks reluctant to move out because of their long residence in the area—picked up and fled for other parts of Houston, either attracted by the lure of suburban living or pushed out by the influx of Mexican Americans. The area between El Segundo Barrio and Magnolia filled in during the process of expansion.[6]

Still, this area in the inner city had never been geographically homogeneous. As earlier indicated, railroad yards, Buffalo Bayou, the downtown area, warehouses, and other physical structures had separated the several barrios since the 1910s. During the 1960s, newer physical or functional boundaries such as freeways, industrial zones, or major commercial strips related more to the city at large than to the community cut through the barrios, further distinguishing them from one another.[7] Each barrio existed independently of each other and was indeed internally cohesive. Historically, people had identified with their own barrios, and the modern partitions isolated them even further.[8]

During this era, Mexican Americans in Houston played a more forceful role in getting mainstream society to recognize their presence. As ever, such efforts were undertaken by bicultural men and women wanting recognition on terms defined by the *colonia*. Such a bicultural way of life was not too difficult to maintain in Houston, even if the urban scene did distinguish them somewhat from their rural cousins. The compactness of the inner city allowed for cultural values and traditions rooted in the Mexican past to be transmitted to younger generations. The community itself preferred the notion of bilingualism and a way of life combining "lo mexicano" and "lo americano." As always, different variables within the barrios acted to mold individuals of diverse identities.

Churches contributed to cultural maintenance by offering services to their respective congregations in ways that jibed with barrio life; that is, some services were in Spanish, others in English. Protestant churches made headway as the several Catholic churches, so active since the 1910s and 1920s, kept expanding to keep up with the tremendous growth of the post-War era. Our Lady of Guadalupe in the Segundo Barrio added a more modern twelve-room school in 1949 and, in subsequent years,

THE BARRIOS OF HOUSTON

El Barrio Magnolia
El Barrio de Second Ward

El Barrio de Baytown

El Barrio de La Porte y la Red Bluff

El Barrio de Deer Park

El Barrio de Pasadena

El Barrio de Denver Harbor

El Barrio de South Houston

El Barrio Northside

El Barrio de Hobby

El Barrio de la Shepherd

El Barrio Almeda

El Barrio de Memorial

El Barrio de St. Joseph's y la Washington

El Barrio de Bellaire

El Barrio del Astrodome

Copyright 1979, The Houston Post, Reprinted by permission.

acquired adjoining land, improving on it to provide playground space for students.[9] Immaculate Heart of Mary, in Magnolia Park, built a new eight-room parochial school in 1946 and in 1950 dedicated the present-day church at 7539 Avenue K. Throughout the 1950s and 1960s, new construction kept adding to the church complex: in 1952, a new rectory, in 1959, a new convent for the nuns who taught in the parochial school, in 1960 a cafetorium to serve as a place for meetings, parish functions, and school presentations, and later the Confraternity of Christian Doctrine building which served as a CCD office, school library, and credit union.[10]

Clubs and organizations, present since the 1920s, had proliferated to such an extent by the 1960s that they provided for every type of need demanded by diverse elements within the barrios. A directory compiled by the Magnolia Business Center, Inc. in 1970, affirmed the heterogeneity of the Mexican American community and the presence of different degrees of acculturation. It listed everything from Hispanic mothers' clubs, to labor unions, to barbers associations. Functioning in Houston as of that date were at least three American Legion Posts, nine LULAC councils, and six chapters of the Woodmen of the World (including Campo Laurel 2333, founded in 1908). About half of the "Spanish Speaking Organizations" in the long list had English names.[11]

Absent from this list were most of the old recreative clubs of the thirties and forties, but conspicuously present were some old pre-World War II *sociedades* and *asocaciones.* Prominent among these were the Sociedad Mutualista Benito Juárez, the Sociedad Mutualista Obrera Mexicana, Campo Laurel 2333, and the venerable Club Recreativo Cultural "México Bello." The latter club, by the 1970s past its fiftieth year of existence, had decided to revise the club's statutes as they seemed inapplicable to the changing times. Instead of trying to perpetuate "lo mejor del carácter mexicano" as it had done previously, it now sought to instill young people with ethnic pride in their Mexican heritage. Its Black and White dance, however, continued to be an annual occasion and the quinceañeras, begun in the 1950s, attracted great participation from various other Mexican American organizations in Houston. In the mid-1960s, its membership included several doctors or dentists, businessmen, and salesmen.[12]

The many organizations in Houston during the 1960s and 1970s manifested the gamut of Mexican American social diversity. In addition to those organizations listed above, there were such clubs as Sembradores de Amistad, a professional, middle class organization comprised of people who lived outside the barrio but who believed that education was the most important issue facing Mexican Americans. So, they strove to help students obtain scholarships, either through direct aid or by providing information on alternative sources of financial aid. The Instituto de Cultura Hispánica, another elite group, was dedicated to preserving Spanish culture and language.[13]

Various newspapers, much different from the old *El Tecolote* and *La Gaceta Mexicana* of the 1920s and the Depression decade, surfaced in the barrios in the 1960s and 1970s. They were either in English, or were bilingual, and touched on the social matters of the community or reflected the varying political currents which surfaced during the 1960s and 1970s. In 1965 appeared *El Sol*, concentrating on social issues and promising not to "be the tool of any political, social, or radical group," although it gave extensive coverage to the political movements occurring in South Texas in 1966.[14] *El Observatorio Latino* published community oriented news during the 1960s and 1970s[15] as did the *Semanario El México* (pronounced Meshica) which went to press in December 1974, publishing in Spanish.[16] *Compass* began publishing in 1967 and represented the mood of the emerging militant youth movements of the era.[17] *Papel Chicano,* established in the early 1970s was outspoken in its anti-establishment stand and voiced the aspirations of the Mexican American Youth Organization (MAYO) and Raza Unida Party (RUP) to be discussed in the next two chapters.[18]

The fiestas patrias celebrations remained, but (like the Club "México Bello") by the 1960s had become occasions more for reminding barrio residents of the Mexican link as opposed to recreating the grandeur of "la patria querida." Indeed, it was the very meaning of the commemorations which in September 1973 produced a clash between what the Mexican American community thought the fiestas patrias to be, and what the Mexican consul understood them traditionally to symbolize. One the one hand was the Fiestas Patrias, a local, state-chartered non-profit organization composed of volunteers of Mexican American organizations, and on the other, the Comité Patriótico Mexicano (CMP), a group of Mexican nationals and Mexican American sympathizers under the guidance of the Mexican consulate. For Fiestas Patrias leaders, the commemorations represented a well-established community project, expanded upon during the 1960s when a comité patriótico ceased to function. For the Mexican American organization, the event was now being encroached upon by the consul, who under orders from the Mexican government, sought to promote tourism. For the latter, of course, fiestas patrias celebrations were for paying tribute to the mother country, and comité patrióticos had always worked closely with the consulate, just as had been the case in

153

Houston historically. A Comité Patriótico Mexicano had been re-established in the city in 1973, and it was its role to work with the consuls. But Fiestas Patrias leaders refused to subordinate themselves to the consulate. As they saw it, the function of the Diez y Seis celebration was to promote Mexican American heritage and culture and not necessarily Mexico.

At stake, of course, were monies to be solicited from businesses and large corporations for financing the occasions, crowds to be pleased, park sites to be set aside by the city, the granting of the Distinguished Mexican American Award, as well as the success of the fiestas which Mexican American leaders hoped to develop into a Houston Mardi Gras. In the end, a sense of confusion and division prevailed. Some businesses and industries found themselves being solicited twice for ads and many Mexican American organizations divided their attention between the two competitors. People wondered about the legitimate sponsor of the fiestas. The crisis passed, however, rectified at a later date. But the occasion served as an example of the continued Americanization of the Mexican community which simultaneously preferred allegiance to the United States while stubbornly paying its respect to its Mexicanness.[19]

Spanish language radio stations and television programs by the 1960s and 1970s furthered biculturalism. Television stations aired programs directed at the barrios, some with an entirely Spanish format while others opted for English only. Similarly, English-speaking radio stations allocated part of their air time for Spanish-language programming. But throughout the sixties and until the early seventies, radio station KLVL remained without major competition. It beamed its programming, which ran the gamut from radio *novelas* (radio serials) to programs featuring Mexican American artists, Mexican singers and orchestras and music from South and Central America, to a radius of 100 miles.[20]

With a solid following in the Houston community, Mexican music allowed for the continued popularity of Houston's own Lydia Mendoza, the singer who as a child in the Depression era had played with her family at popular spots in Magnolia Park. Since the 1930s, her career had seen both highs and lows, but her return to Houston and settlement in the Heights area in the 1960s had occurred while her fame was resurging. In the 1970s after five decades of performing, she was still making local, national and international appearances and being sought out by Hispanic record producers. She was regarded as one of the great performers of Norteño (northern) music, a unique, regional form of Mexican and American music.[21]

The Suburbs

The general shift in population from the inner core of Houston towards its outlying areas intensified during the 1960s. Beginning in the 1950s and continuing through the 1970s, extensive highway and freeway construction was undertaken. Six to eight lanes in width, with four lanes of access (feeder) along the sides, these freeways encroached upon formerly densely populated land, forcing residents, whether Anglo, Mexican, or black to move. Rapid expansion of the central business district also occurred about the same time; the process of expansion turned many of the low income residential areas in the inner city into commercial use, forcing and encouraging abandonment of close-in residences.[22] With racial barriers tumbling, Mexican Americans with new purchasing power and a desire to escape the rush of the inner city headed for the suburbs.

Also, many skilled workers or semi-professionals opted to purchase homes away from the inner city barrios. Some could not find suitable housing within the old barrios for their families and were lured by newer additions in other parts of town. Many of these Mexican American working class folks searched out predominantly or partly Mexican American areas where they could own their home, but still preserve a Mexican American atmosphere.[23] Such home-buying patterns acted to perpetuate and expand upon what may be termed "blue-collar suburbs." Such neighborhoods ordinarily were inhabited by a majority of residents having manual occupations, though a few of the workers therein had professional and managerial positions. Needless to say, these newer settlements of Mexican American concentration did not have a Mexicano cultural orientation comparable to that of the inner city barrios. By the 1970s, Baytown, Pasadena, South Houston, Jacinto City, and Galena Park in the eastern half of the city were examples of these blue collar suburbs in the Houston metropolis.[24]

Mexican Americans of means also chose the outer neighborhoods because of the popularity of suburban living. Professionals and semi-professionals made for the middle-class neighborhoods in the outer areas; they offered even greater conveniences and perquisites than did the blue collar suburbs, and certainly an escape from the cramped quarters characteristic of the older inner city barrios.[25] The trend increased during the 1970s, although Mexican American residency in "white collar suburbs" never compared to the levels found in their blue collar counterparts. Whereas in the 1970s Mexicans constituted an average of one-fourth of the population in blue-collar suburbs, they constituted less than half of this amount in white collar suburbs. The result was a sprinkling of Mexicanos here and there, and with few others to reinforce culture, increasingly assimilated Mexican Americans inhabited these white collar residential settlements.[26]

Social Classes

Table 8.1 points to the increased distinction in social classes within the Houston Mexican community during the decade of the 1960s. In 1970, the census was a bit more precise in identifying Spanish surnamed persons, making a difference between "total Spanish origin" workers and "Mexican origin" workers (the 1960 census listed the occupational distribution for "white persons of Spanish surname"). The figures used in Table 8.1 are for "Mexican origin" workers, and so while the difference between the distinctions made by the two censuses may skew a comparison somewhat, it is still evident that the Houston Mexican American middle class continued to expand. This enlargement, however, was not so much in the upper white-collar categories. For men, it was strongest in the craftsmen classification and for women in the clerical categories, the types of occupations that permitted Mexicanos to move into the "blue

Table 8.1
Occupational Distribution for
Employed Mexican Origin Workers
in Houston, 1970

	Males	Females
Professional, Technical, and Kindred Works	5.6%	6.6%
Managers & Administrators Exc. Farm	4.2%	1.1%
Clerical and Kindred Workers	6.3%	35.9%
Sales Workers	3.4%	5.5%
Craftsmen, Foremen, and Kindred Workers	27.7%	3.3%
Operatives, Including Transport	27.2%	17.3%
Private Household Workers	0.1%	2.1%
Service Workers, Exc. Private Household	12.6%	25.1%
Farms and Farm Managers	——	——
Farm Laborers and Foremen	0.4%	0.2%
Laborers, Except Farm	12.3%	2.7%
N	22,911	10,381

*Source: U.S. Census of Population: 1970, *Persons of Spanish Origin*, PC(2)–1C, Table 16, p. 186.

collar'' suburbs. Such a growth diversified the Houston Hispanic community further, making it one of ''many Mexicanos.''

Other evidence substantiates the presence of an expanding middle class during the 1960s and 1970s. While businessmen belonged to a Mexican Chamber of Commerce (one was founded in 1968; the pre-World War II Chamber apparently died) during the era, they had gone beyond that and founded more specialized organizations. Among the numerous such organizations existing in the early 1970s were Northside Businessmen Association, Pan American Jewelers, and Latin American Barbers Association. Businessmen were being encouraged further by Great Society programs such as the Business Resource Development Center and the Magnolia Business Center.

The burgeoning middle class was visible to contemporaries. Some of the aforementioned newspapers, for example, were published and aimed at the middle class, though of course, they did not disregard the other classes. *El Sol* editorialized in 1969:

> There is an ever-growing awakening among the masses of the people, originating at the grassroots and forming into a spearhead by aggressive, alert, intelligent and determined leadership made up of businessmen, lawyers, doctors, clergy, and other professionals. In our city we see the evidence of the dynamic strength within the Mexican Americans by the expansion of business, by the purchase of properties, by the establishment of new businesses, by the forming of new corporations, by the planning of new banks and even the projection of shopping centers and skyscrapers.[27]

The presence of classes was quite evident to observers of social life in the barrios. One study done in the 1960s characterized the community as ''segmented along three lines: an old aristocracy, a new middle class, and a low income mass.'' The small and thinning ''old aristocracy,'' according to the researchers, included early immigrants and refugees from the Mexican Revolution and their descendants. Members of this group were engaged in business or the professions within the barrios, and while not necessarily affluent, they commanded prestige and status by their social bearing and comportment. They carried themselves with gentility and emphasized their Mexican identity and traditions.

The middle class, noted the study, was a broadening segment of the community made up of the relatively acculturated who were bent on making their way in the larger society. By no means, however, were these people on the make rejecting their Mexicanness or severing ties with the Mexican American community. ''Rather,'' the study observed, ''the inclination was to forge a unified, self-conscious, and activist community led by the successful professional and business men of the new middle-class. Associationalism is vigorous and growing."

While the lower class was able to feed the middle class with achievers, this last stratum took in the greater portion of Mexicano laborers. Indeed, Table 8.1 shows that the majority of Mexican American workers in the city were solidly in lower blue collar occupations, most of them unskilled or at best semi-skilled. For most, mobility was limited to dead-end jobs. The researchers found that the low income mass was made up of the poor and the uneducated or minimally educated.[28] Herein included, of course, were immigrant folks whose dismal standing in income, occupation, and schooling magnified the portrait of poverty.

The bulk of Mexican American workers, therefore, fulfilled Houston's historic need for proletarian labor. Barrio residents frequently had to commute to their place of employment outside the community. They worked in construction, retail trade, and manufacturing. Others worked in the several hospitals throughout the city, especially the internationally famous Texas Medical Center, and for the railroads, or as helpers in warehouses, service stations, restaurants, small business enterprises, and the like. Many from Magnolia Park worked at the Ship Channel, just as their forefathers had. Those penetrating positions in industry found themselves overwhelmingly concentrated in the lowest paying occupations. A segment of working class was either chronically or seasonally unemployed.[29]

Which is to say that the while the city of Houston grew inexorably, the majority of Mexicanos remained poor. According to census figures, the median income in 1969 for "Mexican-origin" males sixteen years and older was $5,363. Comparatively, this did not compare well with the median income for Mexican-origin men in other metropolitan areas: in San Francisco, median income was reported at $6,580; in Orange, California, at $6,580; in Los Angeles, at $6,150; and in Denver, it was $5,410.[30] Even the middle class, whose members displayed more material things than their brethren in the lower class, did not earn the type of incomes that their Anglo professional colleagues made. Discrimination towards Mexican American workers still remained in high status occupations and the cost of ethnicity to wage-earners was literally hundreds of dollars annually.[31]

Barrio housing, needless to say, reflected the level of poverty. To be sure, residential districts, reflecting Houston's disdain for zoning ordinances, contained a motley array of family structures, poorly and hastily-constructed "shotgun shacks" at times situated in city blocks next to sturdily-constructed brick and frame homes. Many of the homes were of older construction, having been built for suburban living in early Houston, prior to the area of mass housing.[32]

In the Second Ward, Clayton Homes housed the poorest. By the early sixties, the 348-unit government housing project was home for more than 300 Mexican American families. As an artificially created area and not a normal neighborhood, it faced unique problems such a poor drainage, inadequate recreational families, ill-kept lawns or uncovered garbage. Neighborhood development, however, was attempted through the efforts of the residents, the Houston Housing Authority, and the Neighborhood Centers Association. The complex, therefore, radiated an aura of neighborliness and self-support. Tenents sponsored an annual fiesta for raising money which was then re-invested in improvements and equipment the Homes needed. They participated in various committees designed to upgrade conditions, such as education, beautification, washateria, and other committees.[33] Clayton Homes, moreover, offered various sorts of programs; among those being implemented there in the 1960s was one patterned after the "Little Schools of the 400" (indeed, it was Félix Tijerina, then a Houston Housing Authority board member, who sparked the move for the classes).[34] In the mid-1970s, the complex was in need of interior and exterior improvements, regrading of the grounds, improvements along the bayou, additional play equipment, and facilities and programs for teenagers.[35]

Schooling during the 1960s showed some improvement, but not enough. Mexican Americans were less likely to finish high school. The 7.4 median school years reported for Mexican-origin Houstonians twenty-five years and older in 1970 was only one grade of improvement over 1960, enough to Americanize the population further, but hardly enough to equip Mexicanos for a competitive society.[36] Rates of achievement were not uniform in all the barrios, either. Denver Harbor, for example, had a better record than El Segundo Barrio and Magnolia Park, both of which had high dropout rates.[37]

Visible in Houston:

This chapter makes apparent that Mexicans attained unprecedented visibility during the 1960s and 1970s. Of course, Mexican Houstonians had been around town for generations, and this book has sought to chronicle that presence. But why did Houston in general not recognize Mexicanos to the same degree before? Several factors may account for that "invisibility." First, Mexicans were twentieth century arrivals in the city; that is, they were not there to be acknowledged by Anglos as was the case in other South Texas cities of the nineteenth century where the settlement patterns were reversed. Also, Houston was among the largest cities penetrated by Mexicans. Despite the fact that the colonia grew incessantly, the number of Mexicanos in Houston never kept pace with the overall demographic increase. Until the growth of the last thirty years, they remained invisible numerically and were seen as "quaint" people to be heard but not necessarily accommodated.

After the 1960s, things took a new turn. The percentage of their numbers in the city began a transformation which took on unimagined proportions (by the 1980s, Hispanics comprised close to 40.0% of the student population in the city's school system, for example). The middle class expanded to wield new purchasing power; one result was the emergence of blue-collar suburbs populated heavily by Mexican Americans. The old barrios expanded further and the inner city became a minority geographic area—whites fled it to escape a ethnic density missing before the 1960s. The city acknowledged the growing mass of Mexicanos by extending needed social services to the colonia: clinics, employment referral programs, senior citizens services, schools, parks, to name a few. Social institutions recognized the growth and directed their attention to the barrios: churches added to their complexes or built anew and the media turned more attention to the Mexican American presence. Of course, many of the concessions of the post-1960 era came about because of protest movement. But that discontent was itself based on the new demography. As the following chapters show, Houston no longer looked at Mexicans as invisible.

NOTES

[1]Barry J. Kaplan, "Houston: The Golden Buckle of the Sunbelt," in Richard M. Bernard and Bradley R. Rice, *Sunbelt Cities: Politics and Growth Since World War II*, pp. 200–202.

[2]A comprehensive evaluation of urban and industrial change is presented in Christopher S. Davies, "Life at the Edge: Urban and Industrial Evolution of Texas, Frontier Wilderness—Frontier Space, 1836–1986," *Southwestern Historical Quarterly*, LXXXIX (April, 1986), 443–554.

[3]For a full discussion of the unrest of the 1960s, see Allen J. Matusow, *The Unraveling of America: A History of Liberalism in the 1960s*.

[4]Robert A. Calvert, "The Civil Rights Movement in Texas," in Ben Procter and Archie P. McDonald, *The Texas Heritage*, pp. 161–163.

[5]Rodríguez, "Patterns of Race and Ethnic Disparity and Conflict," p. 23, and Table 4.

[6]Mark Madera, et al., *The Barrios: Mexican Americans in Houston*, p. 17.

[7]Ibid., p. 22.

[8]Ibid., p. 30.

[9]"History of Our Lady of Guadalupe Parochial School, Houston, Texas," pp. 7–10; Houston *Post*, April 23, 1949, in HMRC, Juan P. Rodríguez Collection.

[10]*Immaculate Heart of Mary, Houston, Texas: Directory;* "Detalles Generales del Poblado de Magnolia y Su Incorporación a la Ciudad de Houston," HMRC, Mexican American Small Collection; Houston *Chronicle*, February 4, 1950, p. 3A.

[11]Magnolia Business Center, Inc., "Spanish Speaking Organizations and Precinct Judges of Houston (Harris County) Texas."

[12]Fiftieth Anniversary Program, HMRC, Club México Bello Collection; Houston *Post*, January 21, 1979, p. 8D; *El Puerto*, February, 1960, p. 8; Mary Ellen Goodman, *The Mexican American Population of Houston: A Survey in the Field, 1965–1970*, Rice University Studies, LVII (Summer, 1971), 97.

[13]Goodman, *The Mexican American Population of Houston*, pp. 96, 97; *Papel Chicano*, June 12, 1971, p. 11.

[14]Robert S. Guerra, "Political Fragmentation in a Mexican American Community: The Case of Houston, Texas" (M. A. Thesis, University of Houston, 1969), p. 50.

[15]Ibid., p. 41.

[16]*Semanario El Mexica*, Houston, Texas, 12 de Diciembre de 1974, p. 1.

[17]*Compass*, Houston, Texas, December 1967, pp. 3, 11; May 1968, p. 3.

[18]*Papel Chicano*, August 8, 1970, p. 2; December 20, 1972–January 5, 1973, p. 5.

[19]Houston *Post*, August 30, 1971, p. 1C; August 6, 1973, p. 4C; September 2, 1973, p. 8B; September 30, 1973, p. 4DD.

[20]Ibid., August 5, 1973, p. 6D; April 26, 1983, p. 1E.

[21]Ibid., October 24, 1976, p. 5D; "La Alondra de la Frontera," HMRC, Lydia Mendoza Collection; Gil, "Lydia Mendoza: Houstonian and First Lady of Mexican American Song."

[22]Goodman and des Jarlais, "The Spanish Surname Population of Houston," pp. 18–19.

[23]Madera, *The Barrios*, p. 32–33.

[24]Rodríguez, "Patterns of Race and Ethnic Disparity and Conflict," pp. 30–34.

[25]Goodman and des Jarlais, "The Spanish Surname Population of Houston," pp. 32–33.

[26]Rodríguez, "Patterns of Race and Ethnic Disparity and Conflict," pp. 30–34.

[27]*El Sol*, February 28, 1969, p. 2.

[28]Mary Ellen Goodman, *A Preliminary Report on Project Latin American*, pp. 4–5.

[29]Madera, *The Barrios*, p. 33; *Forward Times*, Houston, Texas, June 6, 1970, in *Hearings on Discrimination in Employment, Houston, Texas, June 2–4, 1970.*

[30]*U.S. Census of Population: 1970, Persons of Spanish Origin*, PC(2)–1C, Table 15, p. 176; Vernon M. Briggs, Jr., Walter Fogel, and Fred H. Schmidt, *The Chicano Worker*, p. 48.

[31]Tatcho Mindiola, Jr., "Core-Periphery Distinctions in Discrimination Against Spanish Surnamed Males in Houston, Texas," *The Borderlands Journal*, IV (Spring,

1981), 293–308; Tatcho Mindiola, Jr., "The Cost of Being a Mexican Female Worker in the 1970 Houston Labor Market," *Aztlán*, XI (Fall, 1980), 231–247.

[32]Madera, *The Barrios*, p. 21; Rodríguez, "Patterns of Race and Ethnic Disparity and Conflict," p. 26.

[33]Houston *Post*, July 27, 1961, n.p. (Section 8).

[34]Houston *Chronicle*, January 20, 1960, p. 2 (Section 1); February 14, 1960, p. 3 (Section 2); William A. Young, *History of Houston Public Schools, 1836–1965*, p. 83.

[35]*East End Neighborhood Plan*, pp. 44–45.

[36]*U.S. Census of Population: 1970, Persons of Spanish Origin*, PC(2)–1C, Table 13, p. 150.

[37]*Denver Harbor/Port Houston Data Book*, p. 3; *East End Neighborhood Plan*, p. 7; *Magnolia Park Neighborhood Plan*, p. 4; *Near Northside Neighborhood Plan*, p. 6.

CHAPTER IX
"EL MOVIMIENTO": DIVERGENT
POLITICAL DIRECTIONS, 1960–1970

Few could have failed to recognize by the decade of the 1960s that members of the Houston colonia were ideologically Americanized. Completely subordinated to this allegiance was the old loyalty to Mexico. "Lo mexicano" was observed and appreciated and it was carried on in people's biculturalism, but philosophically, Mexican Americans were what the label implied. The many aspects of culture and loyalty which had connected the colonia to Mexico were gone by the latter 1950s. Newer clubs and organizations invariably bore English names and their constitutions were written in that language. The baby crop of the post-1960 era characteristically was given English first names (or the children Anglicized their Spanish names, often in reaction to societal pressures). More and more, English became the dominant language and the form of ideological expression. When the Houston Texas-Mexican community plunged into the "militant" social movement of the decade—the so-called "Chicano Movement" (1965–1975ca)—the shibboleth of protest exposed Texas-Mexicans in the city as products of the acculturation process.

Ideological Transition, 1960–1965

Nationalist, class, and ethnic variety had ever characterized the Mexican community in Houston, and different ideological expressions continued being a staple of Mexican American life through the 1960s. By the early half of the decade, however, Houstonians showed greater spunk. A newer, bolder thinking arose, growing out of historical changes within the state, to internal class differentiation, and to varying degrees of ethnic adjustment. Simultaneously, it integrated remnants of thought traceable to the Mexican American Generation.

Among the several strands of thought during the first half of the 1960s which harked back to the Mexican American Generation was that of the old and venerable LULACer, Félix Tijerina, who had just relinquished his position as National President of the League in 1960. Still, his dream of Americanizing the young through the "Little Schools of the 400" lived on and the restauranteur worked tirelessly promoting the project. To this end he lobbied the Texas legislature, pushed the program within LULAC Council #60, and worked closely with major corporations to help them raise some of the needed funds for the program (one gimmick involved soda pop bottle caps: the Royal Crown Bottling Company of Houston would give the "Little Schools of the 400" half a cent for every bottle cap of R.C. turned in).[1] His stern belief in education prompted him, in 1960, to run for the Houston Independent School District, albeit unsuccessfully. Wishing to "give further service to the community that has been so good to me," he ran on an Independent platform promising, on the basis of his experience with educational matters (among his numerous accomplishments were working on the Hale-Aiken Education Committee of the State and on the White House Conference on Children and Youth), to represent fairly and honestly all his constituents. He promised no major innovations if elected to the school board, however, and his candidacy said nothing about ethnicity.[2]

Expressive of Tijerina's thinking was his stand on the rights of black people. As already noted, Tijerina, like so many others of the Mexican American Generation, separated the civil rights battles of Mexicanos and blacks. After all, Mexican Americans were white and thus had privileges coming to them: admittance to white schools and public places, for example. The segregation laws of the nation and state applied to black people, not they. Not surprisingly, then, Tijerina was only lukewarm about the desegregation efforts of blacks in Houston, opposing the tactics being employed in 1960. He had much sympathy for the plight of blacks, he noted, but such things as "sit-downs" at lunch counters antagonized a large segment of the population and created more difficult obstacles to overcome. He advised against a possible boycott of white owned businesses; a boycott could be counterproductive as whites might decide they did not need black customers or employees. "No law, fiat, or dictate exists," he reasoned, "that can assure social equality for white or black because everyone has their right and will to freely choose their friends and associates in business and social affairs."[3] Tijerina's own restaurants refused service to blacks, although he pointedly changed that policy with the passage of the Civil Rights Act of 1964.[4]

LULAC Council #60's activities in the latter years of the fifties and in the early sixties appear to have been somewhat of a mix of ups and downs. The council lacked the old spark. Membership was down. Projects were not pressed with the old conviction. The Junior LULACs had disbanded. The Rey Feo project lapsed. Ceremonies were poorly attended. The delegations sent to National Conventions were unable to sell the League on coming to Houston the Space City.

Stalwarts had carried on LULAC work, however, maintaining in the early sixties old ideas and notions about the proper vehicle for improving conditions for the colonia. Some had helped with the Félix Tijerina School Board race. Committees were assigned to go before governmental bodies to inquire about cases of discrimination or police harassment. The several fund-raising dances and projects continued. The council supported efforts made by historical groups wishing to convert the Lorenzo de Zavala Cemetery site into a State Shrine. The love of LULAC for the Lone Star State was expressed at every turn, most perceptibly every year on April 21 when John J. Herrera and a small delegation placed a wreath at the San Jacinto Battle monument and delivered a stirring patriotic speech. By the mid-1960s, then, things were on the upswing. The Junior LULACs were reactivated. The Rey Feo Contest was on again. More significantly, several new LULAC councils had been organized by 1965, among them #389 in the Northside, #402 in the east part of town, and Council #406 and #503. Additionally, Ladies' LULAC Council #22 persisted.[5]

LULAC Council #60's greatest coup was playing host to President John F. Kennedy during the LULAC State Director's Ball at the Rice Hotel while the president visited the city for a testimonial dinner in honor of a Harris County Congressman. Many of the LULACers in Houston had been active in "Viva Kennedy" clubs (to be discussed below), as had many from other parts of Texas who would be present at the LULAC Ball on November 21. Among the latter were fellow LULACers and members of the Political Association of Spanish-Speaking Organizations (also discussed below) who similarly had worked for Kennedy's election. Those writing to the President inviting him to "drop by and say hello" used the strategy that their efforts had been instrumental in the Texas Democratic victory in 1960. The President decided on the LULAC occasion over 1,000 other invitations extended to him by other Houston groups. The visit was to be short, taking in just a short span of time before the presidential party departed for the testimonial dinner.

An honor guard of five LULACers, among them Medal of Honor winner Macario García, met the president at the door of the Ballroom. John J. Herrera, who had been instrumental in persuading the President to visit, escorted him to the rostrum and, amid cheering and delight, presented him to the audience. The President spoke for three minutes about foreign policy in Latin America and about LULAC, then introduced Mrs. Kennedy who electrified the crowd by delivering her words in Spanish. The entire visit, which left the LULACers and their spouses drained and overcome by the historic visit, lasted some twenty-two minutes. Fifteen hours later, the President lay dead.[6]

The several hundred men and women who made up LULAC councils in Houston carried into the sixties the old ideas of the Mexican American Generation: appreciation for the institutions of the United States, a caution against protest demonstrations, and the goal of achieving equality through mainstream approaches. By no means, however, was every LULAC member inhibited by static notions by now a generation old. The many changes occurring within the community and outside of it touched them deeply, and many willingly adjusted to the new circumstances, voicing a philosophy and participating in activities which went against the grain preached by the LULACers of the pre-1960 era.

The new thinking of the early sixties emanated from structural changes occurring within Texas society, the continued development of classes within Houston's Mexican colonia, and the resilience of Mexicanos who could change with the times. As Professor David Montejano reminds us, many of the barriers and obstacles against which the LULACers and G.I. Forumeers had fought since their organization's inception had tumbled by the 1960s. The Mexican American Generation had succeeded, legally though not in fact, in desegregating the schools, in integrating juries, in doing away with the immigrant question, and so on.

Simultaneously, the question of "race" began an incipient decline sometime about the middle of the 1950s. Several historical factors brought that about. The election of political leaders such as Lyndon Johnson and Price Daniel who no longer showed the old interest in the conservatism of the McCarthy era, accelerated the decline of Jim Crow. The liberal wing of the Democratic Party was able to regroup by the latter 1950s, and it consciously recruited among labor unionists, minorities, and other liberal elements; the election of Ralph Yarborough to the Senate in 1957 was a sign of the liberal revival. The campaigning of John F. Kennedy, which directed itself to Mexican Americans, blacks, labor, and liberals diminished the tenacity of the old conservative block in Texas politics by winning over previously neglected elements. By 1964, the poll tax was gone. The next year, the U.S. Supreme Court invalidated legislative districting and the limiting provisions of the Texas Constitution. Mexican Americans in the state took a giant leap forward with the decision.[7]

Other features of the Houston colonia scene tempered the old-time racism and permitted for freer expressions than those of the post-War era. Among these were the recognition that Mexicanos were no longer the stepchildren of the city, the realization that the expanding middle class possessed purchasing clout, and the fact that more and more, an increased number of Mexicanos in the city were involving themselves politically. The latter, of course, was due to the perceptive abilities of Mexicanos in the city to grasp the opportunity of the changing times and plan a different strategy.

A catalyst for the newer directions of the early sixties was the gubernatorial race of Henry B. González in 1958. A liberal, González had fought segregation battles in the Texas legislatures during the 1950s and his race for the governorship had rallied elements within the ranks of Mexican communities, primarily from the membership of the G.I. Forum and LULAC. Though losing (González still retains the record for most votes given to a Mexican American gubernatorial candidate), González left a spirited group of Mexican American activists throughout the state. In Houston proper, the race inspired the formation of the Civic Action Committee (CAC) which had as its main function the push for increased Mexican American voter participation.[8]

Equally responsible for inspiring new thought was the presidential campaign of John F. Kennedy in 1960. Throughout the state, "Viva Kennedy" clubs had been organized by old-line LULACers, G.I. Formeers, and other Mexicanos inspired by the image which Kennedy projected (in Houston, the Civic Action Committee opened the first "Viva Kennedy" headquarters in Texas).[9] With the election won, the organizers of the Viva Kennedy Clubs attempted to preserve the mustered strength and parlay it into something more permanent. The Viva Kennedy campaign was thus transformed into a political partnership composed of Mexican American leaders from the established organizations (G.I. Forum, LULAC, and so on). This coalition was called the Political Association of Spanish-speaking Organizations (P.A.S.O.).[10]

The Harris County P.A.S.O., founded in 1961, promoted a philosophy that reflected the new middle class liberalism of the early 1960s. It attacked openly those who claimed to represent the Mexican American in Houston politics: Anglos came in for criticism, but so did Mexican American spokespersons.[11] And, it called for greater aggressiveness on the part of the rank and file.[12] For much too long, noted one of the P.A.S.O. leaders in 1965, Mexicanos had been humble and "you don't get anywhere being humble." By the mid-1960s, P.A.S.O. was accusing the national government, the state of Texas, and the city of Houston of promoting poverty.[13]

Such rhetoric, of course, was quite an intensification over what the Mexican American Generation preached. In actuality, however, it was in keeping with historical changes occurring throughout the state during that period and the community's own historical evolution. To be exact, most of the P.A.S.O. members were products of the expanding middle class in Houston. As such, many were members of LULAC and the G.I. Forum who saw new strategies possible for uplifting the masses and joined the P.A.S.O. movement. There had always been, as an example, members like John J. Herrera who were willing to employ confrontation. That is, they were resilient enough to adopt the P.A.S.O. approach. Others were middle class members who had not been satisfied with the older techniques of LULAC and the Forum.

As a middle class organization, however, P.A.S.O. in the early sixties exhibited a mix of the new and the old. From its inception, it had been divided between moderate and liberal lines. The former favored gradual progress using established avenues whereas the liberals urged more direct action. P.A.S.O. thus denounced society for promoting Mexican American poverty but asserted its patriotism; like LULAC and the G.I. Forum, it repeated that there had never been a Mexican American to turn traitor to the nation. It spoke for the neglected lower classes, but believed in "an ideal form of Government, wherein a 'numerous middle class' will always participate and make the decisions for the good that we seek."[14] In other words, even its liberalism was itself comprised of the several strains of ideological structure which existed within the middle class in the diverse Houston barrios.

El Movimiento: The Moderate Agenda

By the middle of the tumultuous sixties, therefore, elements with roots traceable to the expanding, yet diverse middle class, were poised in Houston to lead the community to grounds untrod by predecessors. What exactly moved the leaders of the mid-sixties and seventies to take bolder steps than had those of the Mexican American Generation? Part of the answer lies, seemingly, in the natural evolution of the community. Middle class leaders were products of Americanization, of the lessons learned by veterans during World War II, of a community capable of waging consumer power, and of a confidence borne out of civic action long before the sixties.

On the other hand, there were national currents underway during the epoch permitting for bolder actions. Liberals attained political power during the John F. Kennedy and Lyndon B. Johnson presidential administrations and sought to insure that the beneficence of American society reached all citizens. Liberals waged war on racism through civil rights legislation of every type and launched a War on Poverty through a multitude of programs, among them Medicare, the Job Corps, the Volunteers in Service to America (VISTA), and Head Start. But the liberal onslaught soon met resistance, not only from conservatives, but from a radical element. American capitalism and American democracy on which the liberals placed so much faith, now came to be denounced by the radicals. Hippies became alienated from American culture and new leftists were outraged over an American society which they labeled as corrupt. In other fronts, Black nationalists called for emancipation from American racism and peace advocates protested the American involvement in Vietnam. The period was convulsive, but it also provoked people of every political ilk to take an interest in one cause or another. Indeed, Mexican Americans in the 1960s, joined in—some championing the liberalism of the age, others the conservative cause, others the radical camp.[15]

Moreover, the period was also one of heightened expectations for Mexican Americans throughout the United States. In 1965, a labor activist named César Chávez led attempts to unionize farm workers in California. Closer to home, a "political coup" had been effected in Crystal City, Texas, by P.A.S.O. and the Teamsters union wherein an all-Mexican American slate was elected to the city council in 1963. The overthrow of Anglo rule there symbolized new possibilities for the political future of Texas-Mexicans. Then, a farm workers strike at La Casita Farms near Rio Grande City in the summer of 1966 catalyzed the "movimiento," igniting a broad resentment among all classes of the Mexican American community.

The explosion of political protest within Mexican American communities across the country is known historically as the "Chicano Movement" (*"el movimiento"*). In its extreme, the movimiento stressed the themes of cultural nationalism or the preservation of Chicano cultural heritage. Youth activists in the movimiento emphasized the themes of anti-assimilation and assailed white society for its racist practices—so much an enemy was the Anglo that the Brown Berets were formed in California to protect the barrios from outside threats. Protests and marches accompanied the political explosion and school walkouts in California and Texas became a common vehicle for highlighting educational inequities and demanding instruction in curricula relevant to Chicanos. In Texas, the Mexican American Youth Organization (MAYO) took the lead in trying to politicize communities while the Raza Unida Party (RUP) emerged as a strongly nationalistic third party in Texas; from there it spread to California, Colorado, and other states with smaller Mexican American populations. It talked about "Chicano Power" and assuming control of community institutions through the electoral process.[16] But in actuality, the movimiento encompassed several ideological strains, some moderate, some militant. Reflecting the historic differences within Mexican American communities, at times these various ideological blends overlapped; frequently they contrasted. The remainder of this chapter as well as the next deal with the "many" movimientos in Houston.

LULAC Before the Movimiento, 1965–1966

In Houston proper, the setting lent itself adequately for greater assertiveness. The accommodationist politics of Félix Tijerina had suffered a blow with his death in 1965, for one thing. Also, within the middle class leadership there were those advocating a more audacious course. LULAC Council #60 minutes for March 10, 1966, for example, show John J. Herrera thinking: "There is a lack of militancy in LULAC. Perhaps we should look into it."[17] Lastly, and more importantly, a newer example was set by Alfred J. Hernández of Houston, elected as LULAC National President in 1965.

Judge Hernández, as he was called by virtue of his appointment as a municipal court judge in 1960 (he was the first Mexican American in Houston to be so appointed), had a life history which mirrored that of so many others from the middle class ranks. Born in Mexico in 1917, he had arrived in Houston in 1921, finishing at Thomas Jefferson High School in 1935 and joining Council #60 in 1938. World War II called him to the African and European theatres. Veteran benefits helped him attend the University of Houston from which he graduated as a pre-law major before taking his LL. B. at South Texas College of Law in 1953. In the 1950s, he had been in the thick of LULAC projects, including helping Tijerina establish the "Little Schools of the 400."[18] Hernández was a protege of the Mexican American Generation but in a newer age, adjusted his speech and action.

On March 28, 1966, Hernández led, in conjunction with other Mexican American leaders from six Southwestern states, a "walkout" of delegates from an Albuquerque, New Mexico, federal Equal Employment Opportunity Commission (EEOC) conference; they charged that the Commission was indifferent to Mexican American needs and guilty of discrimination in its own hiring practices. A strident tone of boldness came to mark Hernández' subsequent speeches as the target of new strategy became the federal government and the President of the United States—the sixties generation was now broadening its tactics of dissent from the local and state to the greater national scene. Three weeks following the "Albuquerque walkout," Hernández attacked President Lyndon B. Johnson for producing "beautiful speeches and wonderful promises that never materialize." Programs established for Mexican Americans were little more than "token" projects designed to pacify Mexicanos, Hernández declared. "We are the stepchildren of the Great Society."

If necessary, Hernández warned, the LULACs and other groups were ready to employ more dramatic methods of protest—the types employed successfully by blacks in the Civil Rights movement. Mexican Americans were ready to start marching and picketing unless new action towards eliminating discrimination in employment and other fields were stepped up, he threatened. Practically acknowledging that the time was ripe for going beyond the tactics employed up to the 1950s, he observed: "We've been so quiet, patient and passive that we're being left out of everything. And we're going to do something about it."[19]

By the summer of 1966, Hernández was already among those in Texas leading a "moderate" version of social activism. Among other things, Hernández envisioned (along with other LULACers in Houston) federal programs which would uplift the disadvantaged Mexicanos for whom they spoke. A $2,000,000 federal grant to finance a Houston center which would help Mexican Americans find work in Texas and four other states had been sought in vain for some time, Hernández had noted in the famous "Latin Americans Ready to March Speech" of April 1966. The project had been approved by the Department of Labor and the Office of Economic Opportunity, but still no grant.[20]

The project to which Hernández referred was the future SER/Jobs For Progress, Inc. (SER stood for Service, Employment, and Redevelopment). The idea for job placement centers designed to find solutions to unemployment problems throughout the United States, as told in LULAC

Council #60 histories, was born during a general meeting held at "a dingy hall in the middle of the Houston barrio" in the summer of 1964. On April 10, 1965, the national LULAC office formally opened the Houston Job Placement Center at 3004 Bagby Street (LULAC Council #60's headquarters), and soon thereafter, the concept of a job referral service was being implemented in other parts of Texas, both by LULAC and the American G.I. Forum. Ultimately, President Lyndon Johnson earmarked $5 million for the job placement idea intended to eliminate poverty throughout the southwestern United States. SER/Jobs for Progress, Inc. thenceforth escalated into a major enterprise. In fiscal 1973, the nonprofit corporation operated on a budget of $18 million.[21]

The Farm Workers' March

Demonstrative of the middle class' inclination to move away from the tactics of their mentors of a previous epoch was the involvement of several Houston LULACers and P.A.S.O. people in the aforementioned farm workers strike and march in the summer of 1966. During the course of a melon strike against La Casita farms in Starr County, farm workers in the Rio Grande Valley had come face to face with the hated Texas Rangers, deputies, and imported Mexican laborers undermining their efforts. To dramatize the cause of the farm workers, strike leaders undertook a march from the Rio Grande Valley to Austin. According to standard explanations, the plight of the valley workers and the pathos of the march during the summer days of 1966 acted to militanize impatient youths and "radicalize" the middle class and their representative organizations. More correctly, however, the valley strike and march coincided with larger movements apace in the nation, ones which had inspired leaders such as Alfred J. Hernández to voice newer politics of protest. Said differently, LULACers and P.A.S.O. activists in Houston participated in the troubles of the Rio Grande Valley because those struggles fell into their changing perception that demonstration was a legitimate form of expressing discontent.

In fact, the Houston people took an interest in such a struggle months before the national media picked up the Valley episode. As early as March, 1966, just days before the time of the "Albuquerque walkout," one Eugene Nelson of the National Farm Workers Association visited Council #60 as part of an effort to organize a boycott in Houston against California grape growers. Nelson also visited with social and labor activists while in the city, then proceeded to the Rio Grande Valley to help in organizing farm workers. As the strike got underway in June, LULACers, P.A.S.O. members, Catholic church leaders, labor activists and other sympathizers commenced a drive in the Houston barrios to assist their rural cousins with food, clothing, and money. Guadalupe Catholic Church became the scene of a rally late that month; it was followed by other similar demonstrations of solidarity. A sense of unity in support of the striking farm workers quickly engulfed the Houston Mexican colonia.[22] An urban community found certain affinities with those in the rural regions of the state.

In late June, several Houstonians journeyed to South Texas to provide moral support to the farmworkers. So, when strike leaders decided upon a July 4 pilgrimage from Rio Grande City to San Juan Shrine Church to attract media attention, some forty Houstonians were part of the march. Included were Father Antonio González (assistant pastor at Immaculate Heart Church) and the Reverend James Novarro (pastor of the Kashmere Baptist Church in Houston, a member of LULAC, and state chaplain of P.A.S.O.) who emerged as co-leaders by the time the pilgrimage reached Mission, Texas. The Houston newspaper *El Sol* chronicled the peregrination with photos, related stories, and editorials. Also participating in the march was Alfred J. Hernández,[23] whose presence symbolized the shifting strategy of the Mexican American Generation. Whereas LULAC, for one, had counseled against large demonstrations up until the 1950s, it now endorsed the mass show of dissent. Previously, LULAC as a middle class organization had worked through legal channels for the good of the whole. Now, it sought to reel in the common man in the acceptable forms of mass demonstration, picketing, and boycotting.

After reaching San Juan, the Reverends James Novarro and Antonio González decided to continue the march by walking to the State Capitol, a distance of 490 miles and a sixty-five day march. As they travelled past the rich farmlands of South Texas, hundreds joined the caravan. Thousands showed up at rallies along some of the larger cities on the route to Austin. The refusal of Governor John Connally to meet them at the Capitol only aroused greater sympathy for the protestors. The governor's decision was to become a mobilizing political event for Mexican Americans in the state.

As the marchers entered Austin, a collection of P.A.S.O. people, LULACers, G.I. Forumeers, students, inspired citizens, and some 8,000 others escorted the peregrinators into the city. Some 10,000 demonstrators received the marchers on the south lawn of the capitol.[24] For those who witnessed the spectacle, the implications were not lost, and sure enough, the march left a mass Mexican American protest movement in its wake. Houstonians had played crucial roles in the singular event credited with igniting "el movimiento."

El Movimiento in Houston: Middle Class Style

The events of the summer of 1966 unleashed several movements (some cautious and tentative and others "militant") among Houston's middle class. Naturally, the several LULAC councils in the city kept apace of "the movimiento," though the rhetoric of Alfred J. Hernández lessened once the Judge stepped down as LULAC National President in 1967 (he was re-elected to the same office in 1969). But the cause ("la causa") was sustained by their stern commitments to programs emanating from Lyndon Johnson's Great Society; by so insisting on such programs, incidentally, the middle class was in the process of departing from the older commitment toward institutional integration—now, they condoned the establishment of special projects for Mexican Americans. LULAC members continued taking an interest in the politics of the city and political campaigns featuring Mexican American candidates drew them into the political arena. Rallies, demonstrations, school boycotts and other forms of discontent in Houston or emanating from other parts of the state often had the endorsement of Houston LULACers. Of course, the several councils carried on old interests: they continued to hold the traditional fund-raising dances for scholarship monies and the like, monitored cases of discrimination and police harassment, and kept up the annual ritual of presenting a wreath at the San Jacinto Monument every April 21.

P.A.S.O.'s contribution to the "movimiento" in Houston took avenues similar to those of LULAC, although it was more "political" than the latter organization. Its strategy for improving conditions for Mexicanos was clear: aggressive involvement in the political arena. Political action would allow sympathetic candidates to win elections to policy making positions, especially at the state level. P.A.S.O. believed that a coalition with other groups in the community was of prime importance in getting their candidates elected.[25]

So P.A.S.O.'s approach in the 1960s and 1970s conformed to these parameters. It endorsed political candidates, worked at the grassroots level conducting voter registration drives, established a student group at the University of Houston, issued strong statements against educational inequities in the city, passed resolutions at conventions supporting the farm workers and decrying conditions for Mexicanos generally, and dispatched delegations to protest in other parts of the state. Simultaneously, it toyed with the notion of going Republican, claiming the Democrats were taking Mexican Americans for granted. The organization, furthermore, assured the Houston public that P.A.S.O. condemned violence in the streets and that it in no way encouraged Mexican Americans in Texas to riot.[26]

The movimiento in Houston in turn engendered new organizations from more cautious and conservative elements within Houston's middle class. During the 1968 presidential campaign, for instance, Mexican American Republicans in Houston established "GLAD" (Good Latin American Democrats) in efforts to rally the vote for candidate Richard M. Nixon.[27] In early 1969 was founded the Mexican American Republican Club of Houston (MARCH) with the objective of building a substantial Mexican American electorate and improving the Republican Party's image.[28]

El Movimiento in Houston: The "Chicano" Agenda

The farm workers' cause of the summer of 1966 also unleashed movements in Houston with grass root foundations. Led by such groups as MAYO and RUP, this lower class- and youth-inspired movimiento (which itself was not monolithic) also expressed, like its middle class counterpart, the resentment felt by the Mexican American community. Its agenda was more militant, as already noted, and lashed out against the capitalists, the imperialists, and the establishment. Its rhetoric expressed the frustrations from within the barrios, calling for ethnic integrity, self-determination, and control of people's own destiny. Not unexpectedly, this phase of the movement chose its own self-designated label, fixing upon the word "Chicano" as a label for the new assertiveness. Long extant within the sanctions of the barrios, the word came to be brandished publicly as a symbol of pride in heritage. As the old resilient warrior John J. Herrera described it to the Houston *Chronicle* in the early 1970s:

> The word "Chicano" is a jailhouse, jive, pachuco short term for Mejicano or one of Mexican descent. The word "Chicano" had been part of the Mexican underworld idiom for almost thirty years before it became politically popular in referring to Mexican-Americans. Among us (and I refer to Mexican-Americans who use it toward each other) it is purely an affectionate term, a term of endearment. Many of the Mexicans from Mexico don't like it because it denotes an abbreviation of their nationality, and

175

to them, a Creolization of their origin which they do not appreciate. Chicano has now become part of the American language idiom through usage, just as Black jazz jive terms have seeped into our idiom through popular usage.[29]

Expressions of Chicanismo, while extreme in their militancy, nonetheless had their roots in the ideological evolution of the Houston Mexican community. Indeed, the members of this strain of the "Chicano movement" (Mexican American historiography refers collectively to the several strains of the movimiento as the "Chicano movement") were direct products of the Americanizing trends which intensified after World War II. Most tended to be young (late teens or early twenties) and English was frequently the medium of communication for them. Organizations carried Anglicized names (e.g. Mexican American Youth Organization and the mixed Spanish/English name "Raza Unida Party"). As assimilated bicultural/bilingual individuals, many of whom were college students, they were acutely aware of the other social movements afoot nationwide. Particularly relevant was the Youth Movement of the 1960s, and most were abreast of the anti-war, anti-establishment, pro-underdog currents of the period. Like other youthful Americans during the period, Chicanos opted for beards, long hair, and Hippie fashions. Independence and difference became a trademark. Chicanos placed emphasis on their Mexicanness—stressing their pre-Columbian heritage—while previous generations had been willing to minimize (at least publicly) that dimension of their heritage. Also, to the extent that they now identified with *"lo indio,"* they were shifting away from the whiteness that the Mexican American Generation had fought so hard to see recognized.

The farm workers' plight, as dramatized by the Minimum Wage March, acted to mobilize Chicano youths against dismal living conditions in Texas. The cause of the farm workers became "la causa" for Mexicanos everywhere, including Houston. But the youth movement contrasted visibly with the battle being waged simultaneously by the middle class. A number of features came to characterize the Chicano movement, not the least of which was ideological disagreement with the middle class, a fragmentation rooted in the historical differences of the Mexicano community.

By 1968, the old middle class order came in for vicious attacks by the younger militant members of MAYO and supporters of RUP. Some of the middle class and/or affluent Mexicans who took an interest in ethnic affairs did so for the purpose of self-aggrandizement, MAYO people declared. Most successful Mexican Americans were oblivious to the needs and problems of the disadvantaged, the militants cried out.[30] The indifference of businessmen "hurt La Causa much more than all the Bigoted and Biased Gringos in the country," editorialized a barrio newspaper. Understandable was the lack of attention mainstream society gave to such things as education, the paper continued, for school inequities assured posterity with "Beasts of Burden." But, it elaborated:

> How about our people who have made it, the Mexican-American Doctors, Politicians, Lawyers, Grocers and others who have used La Raza as a stepping stone for their own personal Gain. Does money or position make a person change color?? or have they simply assumed the characteristics of the coconut? Brown on the outside but white on the inside?[31]

Middle class leaders in Houston during these years came in for the same denunciation as the professionals. The older spokespersons were portrayed as "self-styled," complacent and opportunistic folks, aloof from the working class members of the community except when they thought it convenient to identify with the poor (special epithets hurled at them were *coyotes, cotorras, vendidos,* and *lidercillos*).[32] Consequently, the downtrodden in the barrios could not count upon any type of representation from within the community. "Nuestros lideres del pasado nos han vendido" ["Leaders of the past have sold us out."], editorialized the militant newspaper *Compass,* so that the Anglo continued to abuse Mexicanos as always.[33] Veteran activists like John J. Herrera and Alfred J. Hernández were not spared. They and others of their ilk were accused of being beholden to powers within the establishment such as government agencies. Their long struggles in middle class organizations had done little except to perpetuate a system dominated by the tyrants in Austin. After generations of living in the United States, the Chicano was still denied his rights, still faced Texas Rangers, and still taken for granted at the ballot box.[34]

The several social, benevolent, recreative, and civic organizations present in Houston, according to the militants' attacks, were mere "social-clubs," instead of social-action entities. Consequently, Houston lacked the political machinery with strength to demand the improvement of the masses. P.A.S.O., LULAC, and G.I. Forum were particularly denounced. LULAC had forfeited any leadership role in speaking for Chicanismo. Instead of producing men of action, they continued with the old custom of assisting one or two families, offering scholarships of small sums, and hosting fundraising dances, *tamaladas,* and the like. As for

P.A.S.O., it placed more emphasis on its social standing, on political manuevering, and on individual gains instead of looking into the real necessities of Mexicanos.[35] What was needed was an alternative leadership with sincere intents at erasing the poverty of the barrios. RUP represented such ambitions.[36]

The Juan Marcos Presbyterian Church Siege

Aside from ideological dissension with the middle class, the militant strain of the Chicano movement embraced radical measures such as grandstanding, takeovers, disruptions, and even violence to achieve means for social advancement. A MAYO leader, for example, in 1970 warned:

> If it takes violence, then that's what we'll use. That's an ugly word, but that's the way it is. We have been under this system 134 years. I would like to see that freedom and democracy we talk about one of these days.[37]

Such were means which the Mexican American Generation of a past era identified with disloyalty. Even LULAC and the G.I. Forum and the other middle class organizations which were willing to adopt harsher rhetoric and march for social justice during the 1960s found themselves having to disavow connection to some of the actions undertaken by Houston MAYO.

While Chicano militancy appeared in Houston by 1967, the physical manifestations of that militancy intensified by the latter years of the decade. In early 1970, a series of highly dramatic episodes occurred, among those attracting immense media attention being the occupation of the Juan Marcos Presbyterian Church on the Northside. A few days before the actual takeover, the Brazos Presbytery (regional governing body for the Presbyterian, U.S.), gave permission to the Juan Marcos Presbyterian Church at 1617 Johnson to move into a vacated church structure at 3600 Fulton Street. According to the agreement between the two church bodies, the Juan Marcos congregation would undertake a community center program to include a Spanish worship service, sewing and cooking classes, bilingual classes for adults, a Mexican history library, and recreational programs.

But Barrio MAYO members on February 15 moved into the vacant community center which adjoined the church, complaining that the Juan Marcos program was too spiritual and did not address the full needs of the barrios' hard core poor. The occupiers proposed to offer their own program of free breakfasts for neighborhood children, pre-school bilingual education, job training, and community meeting rooms. The takeover, according to MAYO, involved a cross section of organizations, among them P.A.S.O., LULAC, and SER but these groups denied any involvement in the occupation.

For the next two weeks, the MAYO militants held fast to their occupation and demands. Meantime, they negotiated with the Juan Marcos ministry and the Brazos Presbytery for acceptable terms concerning a relevant community program. Also, they implemented their own programs on a limited basis and familiarized the community with what MAYO hoped would become a community center. Ultimately, a court order was issued to remove them, but the militants threatened other tactics.[38] Indeed, they transferred their forces to the First Presbyterian Church, 5300 S. Main, the oldest and largest Presbyterian church (thus possessing symbolic value). There, they demonstrated on Sundays for some five weeks, a strategy which culminated on April 5, 1970, when the protestors marched down the center aisle (they had been invited into the church to worship with the congregation on the condition that they leave their signs outside) and back out the side aisles, shouting, disrupting the church service, and compelling the pastor to stop his sermon and halt the Church's live television coverage. To protect itself, the First Presbyterian Church filed a suit against MAYO members restraining them from coming near the church premises.[39]

More Disruptions, 1970

The politics of high-profile protest continued with equal intense drama throughout the rest of 1970. On April 2, representatives of MAYO had interrupted a LULAC political rally (where three U.S. Senate candidates were asking Houston's Mexican American community for support) at Our Lady of Guadalupe church to urge support for a "Chicano" party responsive to Mexican American needs.[40] Some three weeks later, MAYO members and sympathizers, carrying the red and black flag of the movimiento, assembled for the ceremonies at the San Jacinto Battleground on April 21, passing out leaflets charging that the Texas war for independence from Mexico was an "act of aggression by outside gringo invaders." When asked about their purpose there, a spokesperson replied that the group had in mind honoring Mexicans who had died on both sides of the battle of San Jacinto. Then, as the Governor of Texas Preston Smith attempted to deliver his speech, the demonstrators interrupted him several times with chants and slogans. Such conduct and point of view, of course, clashed with the ideology expressed by other Mexican American groups: while the LULACers, for example, still agreed with Governor Smith's lines that the Texas war for independence was "a way of freedom-loving people against tyranny," the militants perceived the war as one of victimization against the people of Mexico and those of Mexican descent in Texas.[41]

The day following the San Jacinto Day incident, the MAYO group showed up at the University of Houston Law School where they disrupted a major conference on Mexican American affairs which had been assembled under the planning hand of some very prominent Houston Mexican Americans. That evening, they rallied outside the Shamrock Hilton Hotel on South Main Street, then forcibly entered the Emerald Room of the hotel where the conferees were holding the evening's banquet. After some two hours of intermittent interruptions and the shouting of revolutionary slogans, the protestors left, leaving the Mexican American participants aghast at being criticized for the way in which they saw as the best avenue for the social improvement of Mexicanos.[42]

Other Protests

Further setting apart the militant strain of the Chicano movement from its middle class counterparts was a militant condemnation of the United States institutions. Mainstream society consisted of "gringos" who oppressed Chicanos, American institutions were plastic and rotten at the core, the U.S. was a greedy capitalist society which stole Mexico's land in 1836 and subsequently that of Texas-Mexican landowners. Moreover, as an imperialist power, it was conducting an unjust war in the Far East, using Chicanos to fight a white man's struggle.

In Houston, the anti-war posture of the Chicano movement was expressed as part of a nationwide series of Chicano moratoria. On July 26, 1970, for example, over 1,000 persons marched on the streets near Hidalgo Park in Magnolia Park, carrying a coffin and white crosses representing the deaths of Chicanos in Vietnam. At the moratorium's rally, fiery speeches against a "gringo's war" rang out from a succession of speakers. References to the spirit of Chicanismo, the need for new alternatives, the right to self-determination and the like provoked responses of clenched fists and cries for "Chicano Power."[43]

To be sure, the militancy of Chicano youths differed in degrees, so even this phase of the movimiento represented different agenda. Many sympathized with the ideology of Chicanismo, embraced the label of

"Chicano," resented the approach of the middle class, displayed their dissent by the clothes they wore or the leftist philosophy they adopted, yet directed their energies in directions other than advocating violence or takeovers. At the University of Houston, for example, students organized the League of Mexican American Students (LOMAS) in 1967, but changed its name to MAYO in accordance with a decision by a statewide convention of campus Chicano organizations held in Austin in 1968. The U.H. MAYO chapter, however, was more campus-minded than it was community-oriented. It undertook work among public school students such as tutoring them or visiting school campuses to recruit seniors to college. Even though their record of community involvement included work in health clinics, organizing marches, and making up the staff of the barrio newspaper *Papel Chicano,* an uneasy alliance developed between them and the more activist "Barrio MAYO" which saw the U.H. counterpart as representing an ivory tower, "non-barrio" group whose thinking did not understand the real needs of the barrios. Moral support for "the cause" could be found among these various strains, however, and the U.H. MAYO often endorsed the actions of its community counterpart, as it did during the takeover of the Juan Marcos community center.[44]

Efforts at Consensus

As the discussion in this chapter makes plain, the Chicano Movement in Houston (as it was throughout Texas) was multi-faceted, competing, and contrasting. Ideology may have differed and the tactics used may have ignited condemnation by the different elements, but it was readily apparent that Movement people shared a similarity of goals, to wit, to coerce mainstream society into opening up and allowing for the betterment of *la raza.* Further, the various elements agreed on common areas: the need for unity in the community, the desirability for political activism, and the need to effect change through the vote. An organization which sought to present a united front among thirty-seven Mexican American organizations was the United Organization Information Center (UOIC), founded in 1966 or 1967 to "develop, promote, and encourage, by the preparation and distribution of literature, pamphlets, magazines, periodicals, tokens, and otherwise to act as a clearing house of information."

Among projects the UOIC assumed were ones related to employment and education but most importantly, others designed to secure a share of the poverty program funds for the Mexican American neighborhoods. The UOIC also attempted to coordinate the various programs of other Mexican

American organizations. Among its undertakings was sponsoring a Raza Unida Conference in April 1968 at St. Thomas High School. This was the third state-wide Raza Unida conference held in Texas, and intended to bring the problems of the Mexican American before the local, state, and federal governments. Other topics discussed included employment discrimination, the education role of the Catholic Church, the Mexican Americans' self image, and the anti-poverty programs.[45]

Membership in the UOIC tended to be diverse and included grass roots people, though many were of the professional class motivated to civic and political action by the local war on poverty. Some were LULAC-ers who joined UOIC feeling they could work more effectively since LULAC's non-political posture restrained them. UOIC activists were fully informed of the many local issues that arose in the community, and they were usually an articulate and outspoken group, not patronizing to American society, but more militant than the members of other middle class organizations. As UOIC's sponsorship of the Raza Unida conference indicated, the organization could embrace the nationalistic thrust of the militants. Ultimately, UOIC became an organization in its own right, a specific pressure group.[46]

The New Politics

Sometime around the middle of the 1960s, the Houston Mexican community broke with the politics of the Mexican American Generation. Harris County P.A.S.O.'s birth in 1961 marked the transition and that organization's role, along with LULAC's, in the protest politics of the mid-1960s served to divide old political stands from the newer ones. That the rhetoric of MAYO and RUP gained adherents among youths and the poorer working class confirms the political evolution of the community. If the middle class and the militant movements clashed, it only highlighted the rift long extant within Mexican American communities elsewhere in the country. The cleavage, of course, did not brand the Chicano movement as singularly disunified; similar splits touched other movements of the period. In this respect, the Chicano community in the city was showing a diversification akin to that found among the rest of the population in the greater United States.

NOTES

[1]Houston *Chronicle,* April 16, 1960, p. 1 (Section 1); Form Letter, HMRC, LULAC Council #60 Collection.

"El Movimiento"

[2]Houston *Chronicle*, October 21, 1960, p. 14 (Section 1); Houston *Press*, November 2, 1960, p. 4.

[3]Houston *Chronicle*, May 13, 1960, p. 11 (Section 1). Also, HMRC, Félix Tijerina Collection.

[4]Statement of Policy at Felix Mexican Restaurant, HMRC, Félix Tijerina Collection.

[5]"Minutes," July 6, 1961, January 31, 1965; "Minutes," July 3, 1962, February 7, 1963; and Letter, November 9, 1965; all in HMRC, LULAC Council #60 Collection.

[6]Letter, October 24, 1963: "They Have Killed My President!" HMRC, John J. Herrera Collection; Houston *Chronicle*, November 22, 1963, p. 22 (Section 1).

[7]Montejano, *Anglos and Mexicans in the Making of Texas*, pp. 275–277.

[8]Bulletin, Civil Action Committee, Houston, Texas, March 9, 1960, September 1960, in HMRC, Hector García Collection; Houston *Chronicle*, January 21, 1960, p. 12 (Section 1); *The Harris County PASO Fact Book*, p. 8, HMRC, John Castillo Collection.

[9]*The Harris County PASO Fact Book*, p. 9; newspaper clippings, HMRC, Mexican American Small Collection.

[10]"Political Association of Spanish-speaking Organizations, Harris County," HMRC, LULAC Council #60 Collection; *The Harris County PASO Fact Book*, p. 9.

[11]Form Letter, October 26, 1961, HMRC, LULAC Council #60 Collection.

[12]"Political Association of Spanish-speaking Organizations, Harris County," HMRC, LULAC Council #60 Collection.

[13]Houston *Chronicle*, October 31, 1965, p. 7 (Section 2).

[14]Ibid.; "Political Association of Spanish-speaking Organizations, Harris County," HMRC, LULAC Council #60.

[15]See Matusow, *The Unraveling of America*.

[16]Rodolfo F. Acuña, *Occupied America: A History of Chicanos*, Chapter 9 and pp. 366–368.

[17]Minutes, March 10, 1966, HMRC, LULAC Council #60 Collection.

[18]HMRC, Oral History Collection, interview with Judge Alfred J. Hernández; Houston *Chronicle*, June 27, 1965, p. 4 (Section 2); February 6, 1970, p. 5 (Section 4); *LULAC News*, June 1969, pp. 5–6; July 1969, p. 1; October 1970, p. 3; "The Minority No One Knows," San Antonio *Express*, April 23, 1972; various newsclippings in HMRC, Alfred J. Hernández Collection.

[19]*El Sol*, 1 abril 1966, p. 1; Houston *Post*, April 21, 1966, p. 12 (Section 1); San Antonio *Express*, April 23, 1972.

[20]Houston *Post*, April 21, 1966, p. 12 (Section 1).

[21]Houston *Chronicle*, April 11, 1965, p. 21 (Section 1); Houston *Post*, June 27, 1966, p. 2 (Section 1); *LULAC Extra*, October 1966, p. 1–2; *LULAC News*, May 1974, pp. 24–27; Minutes, January 19, 1967, HMRC, LULAC Council #60 Collection; "Certificate of Incorporation, Jobs For Progress, Inc.," HMRC, Alfred J. Hernández Collection.

[22]*El Sol*, 17 junio, 1966, p. 1; Minutes, March 10, 1966, August 1, 1966, September 22, 1966, and September 29, 1966, in HMRC, LULAC Council #60 Collection.

[23]*El Sol*, 8 julio 1966, p. 1; 9 septiembre 1966, p. 3; Minutes, September 29, 1966, HMRC, LULAC Council #60 Collection; Marilyn D. Rhinehart and Thomas H. Kreneck, "The Minimum Wage March of 1966: A Case Study in Mexican American Politics, Labor, and Identity" (unpublished manuscript).

[24]Houston *Post,* July 8, 1973, p. 4DD.

[25]Guerra, "Political Fragmentation in a Mexican American Community," p. 77.

[26]Newsclippings, HMRC, Mexican American Small Collection; "Constitution and By-Laws of P.A.S.O.," HMRC, John Castillo Collection; *The Harris County PASO Fact Book,* HMRC, John Castillo Collection; Houston *Chronicle,* March 27, 1969, p. 17 (Section 1).

[27]*El Sol,* March 28, 1969, p. 1.

[28]Ibid., February 14, 1969, p. 1.

[29]Letter to Houston *Chronicle,* August 16, 1973, HMRC, John J. Herrera Collection, published in Houston *Chronicle,* August 23, 1973, p. 7 (Section 2).

[30]*El Sol,* March 28, 1969, p. 1, 3.

[31]*Papel Chicano,* February 29, 1972, p. 11.

[32]*El Sol,* March 28, 1969, p. 1.

[33]*Compass,* June 1968, p. 4.

[34]Ibid., November 1968, pp. 2, 8.

[35]Ibid., August 1968, p. 6; December 1968, p. 3.

[36]Ibid., August 1968, p. 6; June 1968, p. 4; December 1968, p. 3; *El Sol,* March 28, 1969, p. 1.

[37]*New York Times,* June 5, 1970, newsclippings in *Hearings on Discrimination in Employment, Houston, Texas, June 2–4, 1970* (Equal Employment Opportunity Commission, 1970).

[38]Houston *Chronicle,* February 16, 1970, p. 1 (Section 1); February 17, 1970, p. 7 (Section 1); February 18, 1970, p. 1 (Section 4); February 19, 1970, p. 4 (Section 3); February 20, 1970, p. 1; February 26, 1970, p. 1; February 27, 1970, p. 1, 2.

[39]Houston *Chronicle,* April 6, 1970, p. 7 (Section 1); April 7, 1970, p. 5 (Section 1); April 11, 1970, p. 11 (Section 1); April 28, 1970, p. 5 (Section 1); and June 8, 1970, p. 24 (Section 1).

[40]Ibid., April 3, 1970, p. 2 (Section 1).

[41]Ibid., April 22, 1970, p. 1 (Section 3).

[42]Ibid., April 5, 1970, p. 6 (Section 1); April 23, 1970, p. 10 (Section 6).

[43]Houston *Post,* July 27, 1970, p. 3A (Section 1); *Papel Chicano,* August 8, 1970, p. 4.

[44]Houston *Post,* March 4, 1979, p. 6B; conversation with Tatcho Mindiola, Director, Mexican American Studies Center, University of Houston, July 8, 1987.

[45]*El Sol,* 5 abril, 1968, p. 2; *Compass,* June 1968, p. 4.

[46]Guerra, "Political Fragmentation in a Mexican American Community," pp. 32, 36–39, 74–78.

CHAPTER X
POLITICS OF DIVERSITY, 1970–1975

The several ideological currents floating throughout the Houston barrios swelled at every front during the early years of the 1970s—the "height" of the Chicano Movement in the city. These were years during which the community became politicized to an unprecedented extent. As the colonia rallied on pertinent issues, ideologies converged, but sometimes clashed. MAYO, RUP, LULAC, P.A.S.O., the G.I. Forum and newer organizations spinning off the Movimiento found common ground on certain issues, but vied for public support on others. Unity mixed with disharmony. Such diversity reflected the historical absence of commonality in the Mexican American experience, for one thing. But for another, the Chicano movement resembled other social movements throughout the country seeking to win followers for their respective agendas.

During this period, also, the community carried on cultural expressions with roots in the new awareness of the 1960s. Creative writers produced literary pieces extolling Chicanismo and artists painted works in support of the movimiento. At the intellectual level, students and professors, political leaders and grass roots activists, and others with a penchant for critical inquiry engaged in discourse pertinent to the themes of the era. Women raised their voices to higher levels in their own struggle against sexism.

The "Huelga" Schools

Among the events of the early 1970s coalescing the Houston Mexican community against a common foe was the issue of school desegregation. Pressured by the federal government into integrating the city's school, Federal Judge Ben C. Connally in 1970 presented a desegregation plan[1] designed to bring about a semblance of racial equity in the inner city (in 1969, the HISD statistical breakdown for students was: 124,451 Anglo, 79,043 black, and 31,605 Mexican American).[2] The plan immediately incurred opposition from the NAACP and Mexican American groups, as did an alternative plan submitted by the HISD. For one, the Mexican American Legal Defense and Education Fund (MALDEF), a new actor in desegregation cases since its founding in 1968, filed an amicus curiae (friend of the court) brief with the Fifth Circuit Court of Appeals in New Orleans asking that the Houston desegregation plan take into account the Mexican American students. The MALDEF brief alluded to the decision of Federal District Judge Woodrow Seals of Houston in *Cisneros* v. *Corpus Christi ISD* (June, 1970) that Mexican Americans were an "identifiable ethnic minority," meaning that they could not be denied the equal protection of the law under the Fourteenth Amendment (segregation violated those rights). By the 1960s, as school districts cleverly used the old classification of "white" Mexicans to desegregate the schools or to justify the retention of "Mexican schools," Mexican American lawyers throughout Texas began moving towards the equal protection argument.[3] Now in the 1970s, the Texas-Mexican community was departing from the historic insistence that Mexican Americans were white. The newer classification would help avoid school integration when practically no Anglos attended Mexican American schools.

In August 1970, the U.S. Fifth Circuit Court of Appeals overruled Connally's order. Then in *Ross* v. *Eckels,* however, it rejected the argument advanced by Mexican Americans and blacks that mixing these minorities did not provide the equal educational opportunity of a unitary school system. Instead, it proposed another plan which "paired" twenty-five elementary schools—two-thirds of these were predominantly black and about one-third were Mexican (only one Anglo elementary school was part of the plan). Under this design, all pupils of certain grades would attend one of the paired schools and pupils in the other grades would attend the other school. Theoretically, one of the schools was predominantly white and the other predominantly black, but as noted, the white schools in the pairing plan were predominantly Mexican American.[4]

The Fifth Circuit's plan did not please the Mexican American community either, for Houston school officials could now desegregate blacks with Mexican Americans while leaving the all-Anglo school intact.[5] Consequently, Mexican American groups and committees from different barrios hastily came together to form a loose confederation called the

Mexican-American Education Council (MAEC) to protest the order. MAEC asked that the HISD school board appeal the U.S. Fifth Circuit Court of Appeals' ruling to the Supreme Court, but more forcefully, it threatened to advise Mexican American parents to keep their children home from school on opening day to protest the pairing of the elementary schools.[6] Disparate groups, galvanized by the blatant subterfuge being employed by the Court and school districts, readied for a hard struggle. But the younger activists forming MAEC wanted to act immediately and on August 29 called a news conference at the North Side People's center, 1501 Brooks, to announce plans for a boycott of the Houston schools. Seasoned activists in MAEC advised reason, however, among them being Leonel Castillo (the community relations director of the Galveston-Houston Roman Catholic Diocese) who at the news conference articulated, amid militant youths in khaki fatigues, the Mexican American community's outrage. The pairing plan used Mexican American children (themselves educationally disadvantaged) to keep Anglos from busing and integration, Castillo argued. "If we are mixed with blacks simply to say Houston's schools are integrated, this is not justice," he noted.[7]

The threatened boycott had the promise of success given the disgust of the people over the pairing order and the fact that, on this particular issue, so many of the Mexican American organizations in Houston were willing to work in unison for the good of the "Mexican American community." Among the most prominent organizations were P.A.S.O, MAYO (which promised to cover the "political aspects" of the boycott), and LULAC (which adhered to the LULAC tradition of handling the issue through legal channels). Additionally, there was help from the Catholic Church as well as a cadre of inspired personnel who did not belong to any particular group.[8]

On opening day, August 31, 1970, hundreds of students stayed out of school as their parents abided by the recommendations of MAEC. Additionally, pockets of dissent, protest, and picketing marked the start of the school year. Parents and family members marched outside several of the schools marked for pairing while others demonstrated in front of the School Administration Building.[9] The public display of anger, like the MAYO takeovers of the same year, departed radically from what previous generations strove for: dissent through the system, not mass demonstration, a wish to be recognized as white, not as brown, and faith in American institutions, not rejection. The protest was carried in English, Spanish, and a combination of the two.

To assist in the educational needs of the boycotting students, MAEC (under the chairmanship of Leonel Castillo) during the first days of the boycott went about establishing *"huelga"* schools—Castillo translated the concept of the huelga ("strike") schools to "freedom" schools, for the benefit of the Anglo media—and setting up tutoring and other programs. [10]

For some two weeks, the huelga schools, staffed by volunteers from the Catholic schools, from the public schools, and from the University of Houston, functioned according to a structure set up by MAEC. It handled from some 2,000 students during this period while another 3,500 stayed home during the boycott. [11] In mid-September, a pivotal turn in the confrontation occurred when the HISD school board voted unanimously to appeal the *Ross* case to the United States Supreme Court. School officials recognized that Houston, then with the sixth largest school district in the United States, had a tri-racial rather than a bi-racial student population. [12]

Soon after the HISD's decision to appeal the case to the Supreme Court, the MAEC decided to end its boycott of the public schools and urged children to return to their regular school by September 21, 1970. By now school officials and MAEC had reached substantive agreement on seventeen of twenty MAEC demands, among them the delay of pairing or grouping of the schools while the *Ross* case was under appeal, the consideration to recognize Mexican Americans as an identifiable ethnic minority group for educational purposes, the acceptance of a plan to hire more Mexican American administrators, the willingness to integrate Mexican American participants on a proportional basis on all HISD public school committees, the adoption of an intensive program to correct the serious shortage of Mexican American teachers, counselors, and other personnel, and the development of textbook and curriculum material which adequately reflected Mexican American cultural heritage. [13] MAEC nonetheless remained in existence, working to assure compliance and acceptance of the points agreed to with HISD, pursuing legal action to secure full protection under the law for Mexican American school children, and continuing the huelga schools as tutorial and supplementary education centers. [14]

The optimism of the Mexican American community over its apparent victory with the school board proved premature. Things turned against MAEC and the protestors when the U.S. Fifth Circuit Court of Appeals in December refused to grant a delay in the pairing decision until the United States Supreme Court could address the question. At a board meeting held on December 15, 1970, therefore, the school board approved a plan for pairing twenty-one elementary schools. This proposal, a compromise submitted by the administration, called for lottery selection of children to be transferred. But Mexican Americans found this newer approach as unacceptable as the original one in September.

In late January 1971, the MAEC unanimously agreed to adopt a policy of non-cooperation in regard to the federal court-ordered pairing of black and Mexican American schools. For the next weeks, a "stay-at-home" policy unfolded, and parents picketed the elementary schools chosen for pairing.[15] Ultimately, the United States Supreme Court turned down the *Ross* appeal and the school board, which in September of 1970 had agreed to have the pairing decree reconsidered, now declared the entire matter of school desegregation closed.[16]

At the start of the 1971–1972 year, therefore, the Mexican American community continued to fight a battle already won in other parts of the state where school districts were being compelled to abide by the *Cisneros* case. MAEC, which turned to new leadership when Leonel Castillo resigned in the early summer of 1971 to pursue election to City Controller, announced a boycott of all HISD schools for August 26, 1971.[17] When school opened, about 2,000 Mexican Americans stayed away, and the number of students attending the huelga schools was about 200. As the year wore on, Mexican Americans and black spokesmen decided to cooperate on legal and political challenges to the desegregation plan.[18]

But pairing continued according to the HISD designs as the struggle taxed the stamina and tenacity of the Mexican community. The MAEC itself underwent evolution. The "huelga" schools after May 1972 no longer were under the MAEC; instead, the schools became incorporated under the name of Centro-Escolar México-Americano.[19] By mid-1973, the MAEC had become the Educational Advancement for Mexican Americans (EAMA) and had widened its scope to include services to both white and black students. Financed by grant money, it worked for integration through tutorial and cultural programs, dropout prevention and career orientation and continued to work for parental involvement with the schools.[20]

By then, the crisis atmosphere under which MAEC had been conceived had vanished. In 1973, the United States Supreme Court also acknowledged the separate legal status of Mexican Americans as an identifiable minority group in the Denver case of *Keyes* v. *School District No. 1.*[21] The HISD would now attempt new plans to bring about desegregation. That is discussed in the next chapter.

Politics of Diversity

Several observations may be made about Houston Mexican American politics during the period between 1966 and 1975. To begin with, that era was not the first time during which Mexican Americans from the city pursued political positions. Among the most prominent office seekers had been John J. Herrera, who had sought a seat as early as 1947 in the state legislature and two others who had attempted to gain seats in the School Board, namely A. D. Azios in 1954[22] and Félix Tijerina, the Independent who had run in 1960.

Secondly, the heightened politicization that occurred following the mid-1960s was inspired in part by the aforementioned historical changes which were occurring state wide. These included the inexorable dismantling of Jim Crow traditions and the abolishment of the poll tax. Further, there existed those other movements transpiring nationwide. Equally, if not more significant in creating increased interest in the 1960s was the Movimiento itself. As stressed, the Chicano movement touched the barrios profoundly and sparked old organizations onward or ignited the birth of new ones.

A last thing which may be said about Mexican American politics during the period of the Chicano movement is that those politics were a product of the population which nourished them. That is, the same social-economic differences displayed by the Mexicano community were manifest in Chicano politics. As an "American" community of long-standing in the city, the colonia showed a political diversity not unlike that which voters in the rest of Houston displayed.

An Early Victory, Many Failures, 1966–1970

The Houston Mexican community's first victory to a major office came in 1966, right on the eve of the famous Farm Workers' March of that summer. With the support from P.A.S.O., LULAC, and the G.I. Forum, Magnolia Park's Lauro Cruz won the State House Legislative District 23, Position 5 election.[23] Then in the latter 1960s, as the Chicano Movement unfolded in force, political fervor accelerated. Increased politicization among the masses had produced new organizations such as MAYO and created the UOIC. Simultaneously, the older middle class organizations perceived the opportunity for new gains. Candidates who had long worked the trenches at the precinct level within the Democratic party, had worked with labor unions, or had been part of LULAC or P.A.S.O., saw fresh possibilities to cash in on election. The year 1969, expectedly, saw an unprecedented number of Mexicanos running for political office simultaneously—one for the City Council and four others for the HISD school board. The school board election, especially, reflected the diversity and fragmentation of the Mexican American colonia. With only four positions open for election, two Mexican American candidates found themselves running against each other and vying for the support of the several political groups in the barrios. Not one of the four candidates won.[24] Elections in the 1970s would turn out more favorably.

Many Movimientos, 1970–1975

In 1970 and 1971, the Houston colonia had shown commendable cohesiveness and tenacity as it faced the school pairing controversy. Why could this solidarity not be transferred to other issues relevant to the Mexican American as a community? First, the pairing issue was unique in that it touched every parent in the barrios individually. Not only was one's family being tampered with, but children were being manipulated by outsiders in charge of an institution which Mexican Americans held dear. Second, the whole pairing plan smacked of such blatant prejudice that even the most indifferent Mexican American, whether in the inner city or the suburb, was touched by the injustice of the scheme. Third, the MAEC people who came to lead the boycott proved to be especially skillful at uniting the diverse elements within the community. Leonel Castillo, in particular, intelligently and carefully articulated the anger of the barrios, led the establishment of the huelga school structure, and by forcing the school board to back off from its pairing plan (at least temporarily), won the people's trust and could thus convince them to maintain a united front. Finally, this one issue of education did not provoke the divisiveness that politics do universally. In effect, the unity displayed during the pairing controversy disguised the differences historically present in the Houston colonia.

These differences were manifest in the presence of several organizations in the city, some of which were old, others of them growing out of the hype of the Movimiento. LULAC remained, and while non-political, the several councils did produce activists who had particular notions about the best means to approach problems for the good of the people. P.A.S.O.

was still looked up to for feelers on the Mexican Americans' sentiment, although the candidates it endorsed did not always gain the support of the Mexican American voters.[25] The UOIC, which had been born of the need in the late 1960s to have a unifying organization, apparently did not survive the early 1970s.

Younger groups (that is, those born during the Chicano Movement) representing other ideological strands within the Mexican American community competed to represent specific constituencies. Ideologically conservative in the 1970s was the Latin American Political Association (LAPA), born in 1968. This organization, with its headquarters in the heart of the barrio, consisted of a core of some 100 self-made businessmen and about 600 rank-and-file. Believing that the Democratic party was conservative, conservatism was then the proper tactic to take in penetrating the party. LAPA renounced government programs; instead it believed that Mexicanos with gumption could uplift themselves.[26]

On the political left by the early 1970s was La Raza Unida Party (RUP). As the political arm of the militant phase of the Chicano Movement (MAYO people were generally RUP members), it characteristically mirrored the idealism of the era. RUP leaders generally were of grassroots origins, ordinarily young, included prominent women activists, and were bilingual, though perhaps English-dominant.[27] The party (el partido they called it) directed its energies to the working class, calling on them to reject the established parties and vote Raza Unida. By so doing, Mexican Americans could determine their own destiny instead of entrusting their fate to the Democrats and Republicans who had yet to come through on age-old promises.[28] To those inclined to support RUP, even Lauro Cruz was not delivering for Mexican Americans.[29]

At election time, therefore, Mexican American politicians running at-large not only had to campaign before the white constituency but had to vie for the Mexican American voters which they could not take for granted. The campaigns waged during the first half of the 1970s sought to mold such a difficult coalition. Some succeeded; others did not.

The most prominent case of coalition politics involved the election of Leonel Castillo as City Controller. Castillo had won media attention in 1970 as spokesperson and chairman of MAEC and as the organizer of the huelga schools. As already noted, he had resigned his position as MAEC chairman in the early part of the summer of 1971 in order to run for the City Controller position that November (1971). Such a city-wide race required, of course, appealing to the larger community, but Castillo had already made a good impression on the voters. His sincerity, geniality, and flexibility when it came to compromise during the pairing controversy had projected an image of a person who could be trusted as a representative of all Houstonians instead of a firebrand able to speak for only one element, namely the Mexican Americans. Also helping the campaign along was Castillo's competitor: the seventy-one year old incumbent was disabled by a recent stroke which, to voters, impaired his ability to work (he died a few months after the election). The race, furthermore, required a polished campaign machine; this was done by taking the MAEC structure which included a cadre of bright, capable, and hard-working Mexican Americans, and transferring it to the new campaign. The organizational concept of MAEC, which involved representatives from each of the several Houston barrios, was duplicated all over the city. The result was a Castillo victory in a runoff election in December 1971.[30] As time would show, Castillo took a relatively unknown political position—city controller—and gave it visibility and in the process proved that such a nondescript office could be used to enhance minorities.

Also successful in ringing in the several elements during the campaign of November 1971 was HISD school board candidate David López. His selection for candidacy was the work of a coalition between the Citizens for Good Schools (CGS would put up slates of candidates against such other organizations as Committee for Sound Education, though other candidates ran as Independents) which wanted to appease the demands of the Mexicanos, and leaders within the Mexican American community (endorsed by P.A.S.O.) who wanted representation in the school board which was then implementing the controversial desegregation plan. López' election meant Mexican American representation for the next four years.[31]

The next year, another victory for the barrios came with the election of Ben Reyes to the state legislature (the new representative profited from recently drawn single member districts). Reyes was in several ways a product of the era. He was young (twenty-five years old), a Vietnam veteran who had returned to the Houston barrios to find things as he had left them. As representative of District 87, he spoke for the barrios of Magnolia, Second Ward, Northside, Denver Harbor and the Third Ward. He was replacing Lauro Cruz who had resigned his position to run for state treasurer (Cruz was defeated in the primaries).[32]

The Castillo, López, and Reyes elections were among the successes which the Mexican American community scored during the years of the Chicano Movement. But voters in the barrio remained independent for the most part, pursuing different courses reflecting ideological thoughts of long standing. That individualism nagged at political leaders desperately wanting cohesiveness. Every organization appeared to recognize the need for unity. It was self evident that Mexican Americans were a minority in Houston, and even if they voted solidly their numbers paled in a city where a quarter of a million voters cast ballots on election day. But in the end, these organizations found themselves competing for the support of the same pool of voters. P.A.S.O., LULAC, LAPA, and RUP all were coming from the same place and heading toward the same direction, noted a RUP spokesperson. "It's the methods and tactics to get there that we differ on. And here's where we lose our unity."[33]

Thus, Mexican American politics during the first half of the 1970s were both united, as displayed in the support of MAEC and the successful candidates, and disjointed. In some of the races, leaders campaigned for different political parties, two or more Mexican Americans ran against each other, or the different organizations divided on their endorsements. In the gubernatorial election of 1972, for example, 20.8% of the Mexican American population of Harris County voted Raza Unida, 56.1% voted Democratic, and 21.5% went to the Republican runner.[34] In the District 87 legislative race of 1972, Ben Reyes was able to fend off the challenge of another Mexican American.[35] In 1974, Reyes brushed back an opponent from RUP, then at its high-mark in Houston politics.[36] In a City Council election in November 1973 involving two Mexican Americans, P.A.S.O. endorsed one candidate (RUP gave him lukewarm support) and LAPA the other.[37]

El Movimiento in Retrospect

The current historiographical wisdom holds that the Chicano Movement declined sometime around the mid-1970s and that Mexican Americans passed into another historical phase. Several factors worked to end that era. The exhaustion which touched the other social movements of the sixties and seventies nationwide caught up with the Texas-Mexican community as well. Many of the issues impelling the several strains of the movimiento to action waned, victims of the changing times. Segregationist laws against which the Mexican American Generation inveighed disappeared by 1969 when the Texas legislature rescinded old laws separating white and black school children. Similar statutes allowing cities to segregate the races, mandating railroads to provide separate facilities for whites and blacks, and empowering society to forbid sports events between persons of different color were repealed that same year. True, laws had black folks in mind, but Anglos always extended them to

Mexicanos.[38] The federal courts did their share to dismantle Jim Crow throughout the South; in Houston Ben Reyes by 1975 talked about redistricting which would assure greater Mexican American representation in the Texas legislature.[39] An unwritten prohibition against expressing racist feeling publicly appeared by the 1970s.

If the above were enough to undermine the Movimiento of the middle class, the militant phase took its licks from a reactionary Texas society suspicious of leftist traditions. Texas Rangers and the FBI kept watch over the activities of MAYO and RUP throughout the state. Public opinion was mobilized against a philosophy which called for self-determination. In-fighting also set in among the militants' ranks as they quibbled over leadership and direction. One chapter of MAYO in Houston, as an example, dissolved itself in 1971 because state MAYO had become a "reformist" group instead of evolving into a more revolutionary organization.[40] Demoralization overcame the ranks after indefatigable work did not produce the anticipated unity. In Houston, RUP began its decline following its losses in 1974. Most of the party members had been University of Houston students attending there from other parts of the state or the suburbs, and thus suffered from inexperience. The urban metropolis was something with which they were not familiar and their interaction with the working poor posed problems. As upwardly mobile collegians, several found it difficult working with "Chicanos," especially common people who distrusted them for their assimilated demeanor.[41]

In its wake, the Movimiento in Houston left its mark. Most obviously, there were three elected officials in major positions as of 1975; Castillo and Reyes won re-election and López was serving a four-year term. In mid-1973, the Harris County Commissioners' Court, with a new liberal majority working with Mexican American leaders, redrew justice of the peace precincts and the predominantly Mexican American precinct 6 was carved out. This led to the appointment of the first two Mexican American county justices of the peace and a constable.[42] As of 1975, there were twenty Mexican American precinct judges whereas there were hardly any before the Movimiento.[43] Similar gains were scored in education. MAEC's efforts produced visible changes in the school system. The number of Mexican American administrators had tripled by the start of the 1973–1974 school years, the number of teachers doubled, the number of counselors increased, and efforts were underway to improve upon this policy.

New forms of cultural expressions also rose alongside the political manifestations of the Movimiento. Nationwide, the Chicano Movement had contributed to cultural awareness and this was also evident in Houston. The stress on ethnic integrity produced renewed confidence in elevating "lo mexicano" with "lo americano" instead of subordinating it to the former as before. Creative writers took up the newer topics of Chicanismo and experimented with mixing languages in their prose and poetry; this is evident from reading the extant barrio publications of the era (primarily newspapers) and from the literature still being produced in the contemporary period. Artists incorporated Chicano motifs into their drawings although Houston apparently did not develop a tradition of extensive mural paintings such as that which characterized other cities in colonias across the United States. The new intellectual discussion as carried out at conferences and symposia left its imprint in the several public schools, and, at the University of Houston, the MAYO chapter, along with fellow activist students, successfully pressed for the establishment of a Mexican American studies program in 1972.[44] *Revista Chicano-Riqueña*, a journal of creative literature, saw Houston as a promising setting for further Hispanic-American literary expression and transferred its offices to the University of Houston in 1980.

Equally expressive of the cultural and ideological trends was the rethinking that went on concerning the role of *"la mujer"*—the Mexican American woman. Like their counterparts elsewhere, Houston Chicanas exhorted a more assertive stance for women—one which moved away from the "submissive" role dictated historically by male society, by the standards of the "proper" middle class, and the traditional societal norms of Mexico. In Houston, women were not without an activist history before the Movimiento, and repeated references have been made herein concerning the roles played by women as guardians and transmitters of familial traditions, contributors to family finances, founders of self-help groups and recreative clubs, and as movers of such organizations as Club Chapultepec, Ladies LULAC, and Junior LULACers. With the emergence of the Chicano Movement, Mexicanas had renewed their efforts and taken leadership roles in MAYO and in the activism at the University of Houston. Indeed, an active MAYO member was elected vice-president of the UH Student Association in the spring of 1971. Later she succeeded to the presidency of the campus student groups,[45] and in 1974 ran as the Raza Unida candidate for the District 87 legislative race.[46]

Philosophically, the Chicana feminist movement of the 1960s and 1970s at the national level touched upon such issues as leadership roles for women in the community, racism, educational opportunities, sex-based wage deferentials, job training, legal rights, birth control, abortions, welfare, day care, *"machismo,"* and the double standard. In keeping with these goals, the Houston women of the Magnolia Park Branch YWCA hosted the *Conferencia de Mujeres por la Raza* on May 28–30, 1971 (sometimes, this conference is referred to as the National Chicana Conference). The gathering represented the "militant" strain of the Movimiento, and so far as is known, was the first national conference ever held for and by Chicanas in the United States.

The *Conferencia de Mujeres* attracted several hundred Chicanas from all parts of the country, some of them among the most active in the nation. The convention addressed such things as the distinction between the problems of Chicanas and those of other women, attacked male chauvinism and sexism for oppressing women and for accusing the Chicana Movement of being an "Anglo thing" and anti-male and thus divisive of the Movimiento, and denounced critical stereotypes such as the assumption that the only place for the woman in the Movimiento was in the home. Being a woman in Houston, one of the speakers noted, meant learning how best to please the men in the Church and the men at home. The resolutions produced by the delegates were poignant and uncompromising. One of the largest workshops "Sex and the Chicana" issued resolutions demanding "Free legal abortion and birth control for the Chicano community, controlled by the Chicanas. As Chicanas, we have the right to control our own bodies." The workshop on "Marriage—Chicana style" declared:

> We as *mujeres de La Raza* recognize the Catholic Church as an oppressive institution and do hereby resolve to break away and not to go to them to bless our union. So be it resolved that the national Chicana conference go on record as supporting free and legal abortions for all women who want or need them.

Despite the stridency of the resolutions, not everyone at the conference was in unison over the meaning of the convention. Some of the delegates saw the proceedings as an effort by mainstream society to divide the entire Chicano Movement (since the conference was sponsored by YWCA, whites sought to separate Chicanas from Chicanos, it was argued) and they boycotted the proceedings. In walking out, they showed that the feminist movement was itself fractured, or at least comprised of different strains, just as was the overall Chicano Movement. [47]

But the feminists at the *Conferencia de Mujeres* were not the only ones pushing the issue of equality in Houston. Indeed, the moderate middle class wing had not been left behind. In November 1972, Houston played host to the first state convention of LULAC's Women's Affairs Committee, an organization founded at a national LULAC meeting in Phoenix in March of that year for the purpose of giving proper attention to the needs of women at a time of flux. The delegates sought to change the image of the Mexican American women simply as housewives and to project them into active community service and political life, a national spokesperson said, and the effort towards achieving such goals was to be done through means within the system, for the group did not believe in militancy. Some 250 women from all over Texas plus national members from Arizona and California attended the Houston conference where several resolutions were passed, among them one calling for LULAC to engage in a more active role to give "Chicanas" (their term) a greater voice in government by calling for their appointment to all branches of government.[48]

Women hardly gained equal status with men in Houston or elsewhere after the frenzy of the Movimiento, and the litany of examples which bespeak of their second class status need not be repeated here. But Chicanas during the era had taken their stand and previous limitations were reduced after the 1960s and 1970s. To be sure, such forces as the Civil Rights Act of 1964, court decisions, and state laws designed to erase sexism, had contributed to newer conditions. But the "Chicana Movement" left its imprint. Mexican American women are now acknowledged to have an equal right to pursue a higher education, are now accepted as part of the sexually integrated professions, are granted the power to determine family size and children's upbringing, and are conceded numerous rights denied them before the modern era. The Movimiento guarded against future obstacles which might deprive Mexican American women of their own right to pursue sexual equality.

The Houston Movimiento in Comparison

Not enough studies yet exist on the Chicano Movement for a careful comparison between the Movimiento in Houston and other parts of the country. From what has been discussed in the last two chapters, it is apparent that it resembled its counterparts elsewhere in a number of ways. But in what ways did it differ? A few features appear to differentiate it from the more "radical" movimientos of South Texas, at least the ones that have been studied by the scholarly community.[49]

Compared to some of the movements in the more rural communities of the Winter Garden and the Coastal Bend of Texas, the Houston movimiento appears to have leaned towards the middle class. In parts of South Texas, "takeovers" of communities were engineered by groups belonging to the militant strain of the Chicano movement. Leaders of these factions were able to play upon the emotional suspicion Mexican Americans had for Anglos as ruler and manipulators. In those towns, however, Mexican Americans were a demographic majority of the community and thus had the numbers to support a Chicano slate. Moreover, the population in those towns was less heterogenous than it was in Houston. Much more of the population was concentrated in the lower classes, and thus ripe for Raza Unida political philosophy. It was in the East End, for example, where Houston's RUP sought to concentrate its efforts.[50]

Once the coalitions inspired by the militants gained influence in the above communities, they were able to exercise control of mainstream institutions. School boards, city councils, police departments came to have either a majority of Mexican Americans or were staffed completely by them. These new incumbents, however, did not always belong to the militant faction, for indeed, several strains within the lower, working class movement competed for supremacy of community governments. Factionalism and petty infighting ensued in many cases; this tended to alienate middle-aged voters or produce counter political philosophies, to say nothing of Anglos who fled those communities in classic white flight. By the mid-1970s, as already noted, the Chicano Movement in these communities also faded. But it left an imprint not visible in Houston. It destroyed the old Anglo control over the Democratic Party and produced government by Mexicanos who once more returned to the fold. Mexican Democrats now abided by mainstream methods in governing communities either as an ethnic group or in coalitions with Anglos.

The Houston case was much different from those examples. Mexican Americans composed such a minority in the city that a "takeover" of government was an impossibility even if the community was homogeneous. The relative solidarity expressed during the huelga schools showed that Mexican American numerical and organizational strength was not enough to produce change. The fact was that Mexican Americans did not gain concessions from HISD in 1970 through any power they themselves possessed. Rather, it was by causing the suspension of federal funds to HISD that they exerted any influence over the school administration. The move for recognition as an "identifiable ethnic group" was won in the courts, not on the streets.[51] Change might be effected by coalition politics, as indeed the election victories of the early 1970s showed.

Further present to weaken any "fringe" movement in the city was the climate pervasive in the "Golden Buckle of the Sunbelt." Mexican American impoverishment and inequality were not the only problems besetting Houstonians during the era of the Chicano movement. Yet few other dramatic displays of discontent were heard. Houston, as observed, lacks a history of grassroot agitation to address major social problems; the reasons for this absence of organization activity are reviewed in the Preface. Houston has not been a good place for labor, community, or ethnic organizing, especially of a radical sort.

As noted above, the middle class strain of the Movimiento overshadowed that of the MAYO/RUP persuasion. While RUP's showing at the polls certainly made the veteran Mexican American politicos re-evaluate their political thinking, neither MAYO nor RUP seriously challenged the authority the middle class had staked out in the Houston barrios. MAEC organizers and many of its leaders were middle class. Those who won elections or were appointed to newly created offices in the early 1970s were veteran civic activists, many of whom traced their earlier involvement in Mexican American matters to the Viva Kennedy movement or LULAC, the G.I. Forum, or P.A.S.O. Almost all were college educated, professional men. The radical organizations which spun off the Chicano movement in California, moreover, were manifestly absent in Houston.[52]

The above observations are tentative at best. More studies need to be undertaken of the Chicano movement as it unfolded under different circumstances. How does the Houston movement, which itself merits an in-depth study, resemble or differ from that in the larger Texas cities such as Dallas, Fort Worth, Corpus Christi, or El Paso where Mexican Americans are also a minority? How does it compare with the Chicano movement in San Antonio where Mexicanos hold a numerical edge? What of Brownsville, Laredo, and other South Texas towns where Mexican Americans ruled alongside Anglos long before the Chicano movement?

NOTES

[1]Houston *Chronicle,* September 2, 1970, p. 1 (Section 1).
[2]Ibid., August 16, 1970, pp. 1, 22 (Section 1).
[3]Guadalupe San Miguel, "Mexican American Organizations and the Changing Politics of School Desegregation in Texas, 1945–1980," *Social Science Quarterly,* 63 (December, 1982), 710.
[4]Houston *Chronicle,* August 28, 1972, p. 1 (Section 1); August 30, 1970, p. 1 (Section 1); August 31, 1970, p. 1 (Section 1); September 2, 1970, p. 1 (Section 1);

The Houston Council on Human Relations, *Black/Mexican-American Project Report*, pp. 25–26.

[5]San Miguel, "Mexican American Organizations and the Changing Politics of School Desegregation," p. 710.

[6]Houston *Chronicle*, August 28, 1970, p. 1 (Section 1); August 28, 1970, p. 1 (Section 1).

[7]Ibid., August 30, 1970, p. 1 (Section 1); "Will Success Spoil Leonel Castillo?" *Texas Monthly*, August 1976, p. 106.

[8]Houston *Chronicle*, August 30, 1970, p. 22 (Section 1); September 3, 1970, p. 1 (Section 1); October 11, 1970, p. 3 (Section 2); *Papel Chicano*, August 12, 1971, p. 1.

[9]Houston *Chronicle*, August 31, 1970, p. 1 (Section 1).

[10]"The Mexican American Educational Council," HMRC, John Castillo Collection; Houston *Chronicle*, September 3, 1970, p. 1 (Section 1).

[11]Houston *Chronicle*, October 11, 1970, p. 3 (Section 2); "Will Success Spoil Leonel Castillo?" p. 106; Houston Council on Human Relations, *Black/Mexican-American Project Report*, p. 26.

[12]Guadalupe Salinas, "Mexican Americans and the Desegregation of Schools in the Southwest," *The Houston Law Review*, VIII, 943.

[13]MAEC, "Statement of Leonel J. Castillo," September 17, 1970, in HMRC, John Castillo Collection; *Papel Chicano*, October 10–October 23, 1970, p. 8.

[14]*Papel Chicano*, October 10–October 23, 1970, p. 8.

[15]Ibid., February 3, 1971, p. 1; February 20, 1971, p. 1.

[16]Houston Council on Human Relations, *Black/Mexican-American Project Report*, p. 27.

[17]*Papel Chicano*, August 12, 1971, p. 1; September 2, 1971, p. 1.

[18]Houston Council on Human Relations, *Black/Mexican American Project Report*, p. 28.

[19]Letter, May 25, 1972, HMRC, Huelga Schools Collection.

[20]Houston *Post*, October 28, 1973, p. 3DD; Letter, January 25, 1974, HMRC, John Castillo Collection.

[21]San Miguel, "Mexican American Organizations and the Changing Politics of School Desegregation," p. 711.

[22]Houston *Chronicle*, November 1, 1954, p. 10A.

[23]*El Sol*, 13 de Mayo, 1966, pp. 1, 3; 10 Junio, 1966, p. 1; 4 de noviembre, 1966, p. 1; Houston *Post*, December 6, 1970, p. 6B.

[24]*El Sol*, 24 octubre, 1969, p. 1; 21 de noviembre, 1969, p. 1.

[25]Houston *Chronicle*, August 19, 1973, p. 1 (Section 4).

[26]Ibid.

[27]Houston *Post*, December 8, 1974, p. 20A.

[28]Houston *Chronicle*, August 19, 1973, p. 1 (Section 4).

[29]Houston *Post*, December 6, 1970, p. 6B.

[30]"Will Success Spoil Leonel Castillo?" pp. 134–136; "Bio-Data—Leonel Castillo," HMRC, Leonel Castillo Collection.

[31]Houston *Post*, March 17, 1974, p. 4B; *El Sol*, 24 de octubre, 1969, p. 1; 26 de noviembre, 1971, p. 1.

[32]Houston *Post*, November 8, 1972, p. 17 (Section 1); January 19, 1975, p. 5D; Campaign flyers, HMRC, John Castillo Collection.

[33]Houston *Chronicle*, August 19, 1972, p. 1 (Section 4).

[34]Ibid.

[35]*La Vida Latina en Houston*, Houston, Texas, Abril, Mayo, Junio, 1972, p. 10.

[36]Houston *Post*, March 4, 1979, p. 6B.

[37]Houston *Chronicle*, October 9, 1973, p. 3 (Section 1).

[38]Montejano, *Anglos and Mexicans in the Making of Texas*, pp. 289, 285–287.

[39]Houston *Post*, January 19, 1975, p. 5D.

[40]*Papel Chicano*, March 12, 1971, p. 1.

[41]Houston *Post*, March 4, 1979, p. 6B; conversation with Tatcho Mindiola, Director, Mexican American Studies Center, University of Houston, July 8, 1987.

[42]Ibid, December 23, 1973, p. 7B; Houston *Chronicle*, August 19, 1973, p. 1 (Section 4).

[43]Houston *Post*, January 19, 1975, p. 5D.

[44]Ibid., May 13, 1973, p. 2DD.

[45]Ibid., March 17, 1971, p. 1B.

[46]Samples of the sources indicating women activism in the 1970s would be Houston *Chronicle*, February 19, 1970, p. 4 (Section 3); April 22, 1970, p. 1 (Section 3); September 14, 1973, p. 19 (Section 1); Houston *Post*, March 17, 1971, p. 1B; May 13, 1973, p. 2DD; March 4, 1979, p. 6B; *Papel Chicano*, March 12, 1971, p. 1, April 1, 1971, p. 5.

[47]Mirta Vidal, *Women: New Voices of La Raza*, pp. 3–15; *Papel Chicano*, April 1, 1971, p. 4, June 12, 1971, p. 8; Martha P. Cotera, *Diosa y Hembra: The History and Heritage of Chicanas in the U.S.*, p. 184; Alfredo Mirandé and Evangelina Enríquez, *La Chicana: The Mexican American Woman*, pp. 236–238.

[48]*El Sol*, 17 de marzo, 1972, p. 1; "Resolutions Passed at The Women Affairs Committee LULAC State Meeting, November 18, 1972"; Houston *Post*, November 19, 1972, p. 3B; "Minutes," Council No. 402, July 18, 1972. All sources in HMRC, Mamie García Collection.

[49]See as examples, John Staples Shockley, *Chicano Revolt in a Texas Town*; Douglas E. Foley, et al., *From Peones to Politicos: Ethnic Relations in a South Texas Town*; and José Villarreal Martínez, Jr., "Internal Colonialism and Decolonization in El Centro: A Sociohistorical Analysis of Chicanos in a Texas Town" (Ph. D. Dissertation, University of Texas at Austin, 1981).

[50]Houston *Chronicle*, August 19, 1973, p. 2 (Section 4).

[51]Houston Council on Human Relations, *Black/Mexican-American Project Report*, p. 25.

[52]See Barrera, "The Historical Evolution of Chicano Ethnic Goals," 27–36.

CHAPTER XI
MODERATION AND INCLUSION,
1975–1980s

Since the mid-1970s, Texas-Mexicans have found it necessary to moderate their politics. Throughout the country, a slide to the political right and a return to consensus politics has been obvious. This drift had its origins in the late 1960s when the liberal politics of the Lyndon Johnson era began to erode before an uprising by Hippies, members of the new left, black nationalists, anti-Vietnam War demonstrators, and other elements. A backlash from middle America against radicalism, ethnic chauvinism, the counterculture, welfare programs, and other aspects of liberal politics insured a decline of a historical epoch and produced a new direction for the 1970s. By the 1980s, there seemed present in American politics a genuine sentiment to replace the cultural and political legacy of the sixties and early 1970s with moderation.[1]

A greater willingness among Mexican Americans to work with the Democrats and Republicans, therefore, replaced the confrontational style of the Chicano Movement after 1975. Yet, it was during this period of moderation that the Houston community registered its most significant socio-economic and political gains. It seems ironic that inclusion occurred during such a time of moderation. But the progress made was a direct consequence of the historical changes which took place in Texas before the mid-1970s: among these were federal legislation to prod mainstream society to act in behalf of the downtrodden and a mitigation of racial attitudes since the 1950s. It was also due to the legacy left by the Chicano Movement discussed in the last chapter and to the emergence of the middle class confident in its economic stability. Once this latter segment felt secure, its attention turned to issues relevant to the Mexican American community as a whole.[2] The role of the middle class in the politics of recent times makes up part of the discussion in this chapter.

A Bottleshaped Social Structure

Historians wanting to describe the contemporary socio-economic conditions for Mexican Americans throughout the United States have used the analogy of a bottle. In this description, the growing Chicano population is prevented from upward mobility by several factors, among them racism, the need for a pliable labor force, the lack of skills among Mexican Americans for the newer technology, as well as structural shifts in the contemporary economy. Consequently, the majority of Mexicanos find themselves packed at the bottom part of the bottle. On the other hand, there is a segment at the neck; it is comprised of a small but vocal middle and upper class.[3]

The Bottle's Bottom

Houston, as noted throughout this text, has been a major oil-industrial center in the capitalist world system for much of the twentieth century. As businesses of every sort proliferated, more and more Mexican Americans made their way to Houston. Most, however, did not share in the city's boom. Like their counterparts in other parts of the country, Houston Mexican American laborers earned their livelihood as low-status workers.

As of the 1980s, Mexican Americans were most likely to work as laborers than blacks or whites. As to income and poverty conditions, the 1980 census revealed that Mexican Americans in the Houston area were a little better off than blacks but lagged measurably behind whites. The family median incomes for Mexican Americans was $16,617; this compared to $25,699 for Anglos and $15,260 for blacks. If the income of undocumented Mexicans and Central Americans was considered, however, it is likely that the family median income for Mexicanos would be lower than for blacks. Furthermore, Mexican Americans continued having the lowest educational achievements. While 70.0% of the total metropolitan population age 25 or older had graduated from high school in 1980, only 40.0% of Mexican Americans of the same category had finished all their public education. Such figures portended a pessimistic future of slight upward mobility for those caught in jobs which offer little future.

A Houston area survey conducted in 1985 by researchers at Rice University in Houston reported similar conditions as revealed by the 1980 census. The level of full-time employment for Mexican American respondents was 57.0%; for Anglos it was 62.0%, while blacks came in last with 51.0%. Household incomes corresponded to the same stratification: 35.0% of Hispanic households reported earnings below $15,000; only 12.0% of whites did so compared to 33.0% for blacks. Conversely, 51.0% of whites had household incomes above $35,000. Mexican Americans ranked second with 23.0% while 17.0% of black households reported salaries that high.[4]

At the Neck

The percentage of Houstonians at the bottle's neck continued to expand, nonetheless. While the Houston economy's need for lower class labor may have stifled ambition for so many at the bottom, the city's dynamic growth provided economic opportunity for many others. Houston's free enterprise environment and the labor market's higher quality permitted the determined, ambitious, and more fortunate within the colonia to climb far and fast. Mexican Americans living in the white-collar suburbs, to use an example, contrasted sharply with those residing in blue-collar suburbs. In one particular white-collar suburb two miles southwest of the city, the population of about 2,000 had a college education rate that was five times higher than in any of the blue-collar suburbs. The number of people in the professional and managerial category there was three times greater than in the blue-collar suburbs. At $28,317, the median family income of the white-collar suburbanites was $10,000 more than the highest median family income of counterparts in the blue-collar suburbs. The Houston area survey of 1985 showed that even the disadvantaged in Houston shared the belief that hard work in their city would eventually bring success. No wonder so many preferred staying in the "Golden Buckle of the Sunbelt" where the status symbol of the Chicano mover and shaker was the BMW or the Mercedes Benz.

In contemporary Houston, members of the middle and upper class have penetrated just about every niche in the private and public sectors. Hispanic owned businesses are abundant. The Mexican Chamber of Commerce, founded in the late 1960s (the pre-World War II Chamber had apparently died) include members who own or operate anything from auto body shops to multi-million dollar restaurants. Fourteen of the 500 largest Hispanic companies in the United States and Puerto Rico are located in

Houston. Since 1980, the business community has been advertised through the publication of a handy directory called the *Páginas Amarillas* (the *Spanish Yellow Pages*). Lawyers, doctors, architects, college professors are conspicuous by their numbers when compared to South and West Texas communities. The media boast of a number of star personalities, especially television with several reporters, anchor people, and features program hosts. An Hispanic Business and Professional Women's Club meets the needs of middle-class professionally oriented women; indeed, Mexican American females in Houston were among the most accomplished within the middle class. This sampling is not to be understood as meaning that middle and upper class Mexican Americans have attained economic parity with Anglos. The majority of those in white collar occupations, for example, were in sales and clerical jobs.[5] Moreover, there continued to be a "cost" to being of Mexican ancestry in the Houston labor market in the 1980s.

The Politics of the 1980s

Mexican American society in Houston has reached a stage wherein members of the successful middle class look out for the concerns of the lower class. That, of course, had historically been the case, but more recently, a significant cadre of middle and upper class Mexican American businessmen, doctors, lawyers, educators, and the like attend to the less privileged in the Chicano community, much in a manner envisioned by LULAC founders in the 1930s. Despite economic and social gains, moreover, many within the more privileged classes take advantage of their education, their position within mainstream institutions, and their political astuteness in efforts to hoist those below them.

The training ground for middle class politicos is involvement in LULAC, P.A.S.O., the Harris County Hispanic Caucus (an offspring of P.A.S.O.), the Democratic or Republican parties or a combination of these groups. Gone from the Houston scene by the late 1970s was RUP which reeled from continued defeats after 1974.[6] Additionally, numerous civic and social associations produced spokespersons from their ranks. Such clubs included IMAGE de Houston, a national organization concerned with government employment for Hispanics (it moved closer to community issues in the 1970s); PADRES, an organization of local priests which tried to fill basic community needs like emergency food, clothing, medical aid, and employment assistance; the Houston Mexican Chamber of Commerce; as well as the Mexican American Socialworkers

Organization, the Hispanic Forum, the Hispanic Postal Workers, the Mexican American Bar Association, the Association of Spanish Speaking Accountants, and the faculty and student groups at the University of Houston.[7] Efforts at bringing about these several groups under one umbrella association continue. In 1977, several of the organizations made efforts at subordinating themselves under something called El Concilio de la Raza.[8] This effort bore no fruit, seemingly, for in 1985, a *Concilio de Organizaciones de Houston* (Council of Houston Hispanic Organizations) was founded to serve as a Coordinating Council for the various organizations and Hispanic public officials as it addressed issues affecting the Hispanic community.[9]

What the presence of so many civic clubs makes evident is that Mexican American leadership is diverse, just as is the constituency which it seeks to represent. What binds leaders together, of course, is their goal of social improvement for Mexicanos. In pursuing such an ambition, middle class politicians join institutions outside the barrio (e.g., the city council, the school board, the state legislature) as spokespersons for the community's needs. In so doing, they have developed a network which uses mainstream channels to protect the interests of the barrios.

Generally speaking, leaders in Houston until now have run as "ethnic Mexicans." Unlike some of the politicians of the northeastern or midwestern United States who can run as "Americans" of a particular ethnic descent, Mexican American politicians in Houston have found it difficult to run as anything besides candidates espousing Mexican American causes. Coalition politics have been difficult; the media inevitably label them as Mexicans, and in the modern era of single-member districts, it is easier to win in Mexican American strongholds. Many of the issues which these politicians address are ethnic in nature and are debated in that context. But other points are of class interest and ethnicity is therefore discarded.

Ethnic Issues

The HISD

Because school pairing implemented in the HISD during the early 1970s had met with such adverse reaction, the school district in November 1974 created a twenty-one member committee to recommend alternative desegregation plans. In the spring of 1975, the task force presented a voluntary desegregation plan to the HISD board; this was the so-called "Magnet School Plan" which provided special programs not offered at most schools. The plan aimed at attracting students across neighborhood lines, thereby increasing integration and forestalling white flight (whites were leaving the HISD in droves and heading for the suburbs which were outside court-mandated integration). The committee's recommendations to the board called for twenty-five special programs to be placed in more than twenty-five schools, all of which would be located within the 610 Loop where much of the minority population resided. Transportation in the form of busing was to be essential so that students outside walking distance of the magnet schools could have access to them. Attendance at these schools embodying the new concepts would be voluntary.

Spokesmen for the Mexican American community immediately criticized the recommendations although the controversial plan won approval in a federal court in the summer of 1975. The well-established middle class organizations argued the side of the Mexican American community. Heading the initiative was MALDEF which saw litigation as the primary instrument to affect educational policy. In the magnet plan, it argued, there existed little chance of achieving integration and its implementation would essentially leave the district a dual school system.

But by the latter part of the 1970s, it seemed as if the colonia was growing weary of the desegregation controversy. Mexican Americans leaders noted that Mexican Americans did not want any more desegregation than already existed under voluntary programs. MALDEF itself shied from recommending further desegregation plans. Such an attitude was not unique to the Houston barrios; throughout the entire country by the latter 1970s, desegregation no longer held priority among activists. Concerns shifted to other issues, such as bilingual education and increased hiring of teachers and administrators. [10]

During the 1980s, desegregation continued to be controversial, especially as the exodus of white families to the suburbs intensified, leaving the HISD with large numbers of minority students. But of prime concern now were such things as integrating the HISD administratively. Again, middle class groups led the fight for equal representation for teachers, principals, and administrators. LULAC and MALDEF, for example, filed charges of employment discrimination against the school district. [11]

Equally important to community activists was the implementation of a sound bilingual program. The number of students enrolled in the bilingual classes continued climbing, yet the program was inadequately staffed (the HISD countered that it could not recruit enough teachers qualified to teach in bilingual education). [12] Mexican American organizations also pressed for appointment to some of the most powerful posts within the district,[13] and in September 1979, Agustina ("Tina") Reyes, a Houston native, won appointment as Director of Bilingual Education.[14] Other concessions were made during the 1980s to lobbying groups and in 1986, Mexican American activists sought the position of Superintendent of Schools when it became vacant. A coalition of twenty-five Hispanic groups (the aforementioned Council of Houston Hispanic Organizations) led the drive, which ultimately proved unsuccessful.[15]

Politics were another avenue pursued in the campaign to achieve educational change in Houston. The term of David López expired in 1975 (he declined to run for re-election) but a strong bid for a position in the school board was made by the above mentioned Tina Reyes, a Harvard graduate and an experienced educator. That race was lost, but in February 1979, Reyes was considered for a vacancy on the school board. A number of Mexican American, black, and Anglo community leaders and organizations pleaded with the HISD board to appoint a Mexican American, but the efforts proved of no avail. In 1981, however, Reyes, by then the Director of Bilingual Education, captured a seat on the school board. During the middle of the 1980s, she served as the board's president.[16]

The Joe Campos Torres Affair

In the contemporary era, the Houston Mexican American community has continued to have difficulties and misunderstandings with the Houston Police Department (HPD). This, of course, follows a historic pattern of mixed relations with the law enforcement authorities. Ambivalence toward policemen is not limited to Mexican Americans, however, for Houston continues to display a tendency toward violence matched by few cities in the entire United States. In 1970, Dallas ranked second and Houston third among the twelve largest standard metropolitan areas in the United States for the per capita rate for murders and non-negligent homicides, by far exceeding rates for places like New York, Chicago, Detroit, and San Francisco.[17] In 1977, Houston's mayor confessed: "This is still a frontier city with a lot of law-and-order mentality. Many people support the police no matter what."[18]

But the murder of Joe Campos Torres on May 6, 1977, by HPD officers was so callous that it became a cause célèbre in the ethnic politics of the period. According to what investigating authorities were able to piece together, twenty-three year old Joe Campos Torres was arrested by police in a lounge disturbance on Canal Street. While in custody, he was taken to Buffalo Bayou and beaten severely. Then, Torres either fell, jumped, or was pushed seventeen feet into the waters. Two days after his arrest, Torres' body was found floating on Buffalo Bayou near the McKee Street Bridge.[19]

A roar of protest resounded from all quarters of the Mexican American community. On the one hand, LULAC and other middle class organizations took the mainstream route in pursuing the matter. This element fixed its strategy on appealing and working with the police and the Justice Department, as Torres' death represented a violation of civil rights. Other middle class leaders and groups taking a deep interest in the case included State Representative Ben Reyes, the Coalition for Responsible Law Enforcement, P.A.S.O., The American G.I. Forum, MALDEF, and IMAGE of Houston.

Other quarters of the Houston Mexican community hit the streets,[20] inspired by a grass roots committee called *Barrios Unidos*. The group, tied to the fledgling RUP, sought to represent "the community" on the grounds that the LULACers and other middle class spokespersons were unrepresentative of the colonia. Barrios Unidos organized marches at the police station and City Hall and looked upon LULAC as too mainstream in its approach at bringing justice for Torres' family. In their suspicion of LULAC, Barrios Unidos members represented the historic social rift in the barrios between "la gente pobre" and what proletarian members of the barrios referred to derisively as the *"jaitones"* (high-toned people), the upwardly mobile, culturally assimilated Mexican Americans. But as the LULAC District 8 Director countered, such an image was a skewed one which people traditionally held of LULAC. In her case, she had been born and raised in Clayton Homes, was the director of senior citizens at Ripley House in the East End, and served twelve years as a volunteer for LULAC in the Canal Street area. "How much more barrio-oriented can you get?" she asked. Explaining the difference between the two tactics, the Director noted, "We work differently. LULAC believes in diplomatic channels. Barrios Unidos believes in demonstrations. While they're marching, we're working with lawyers."[21]

As time passed, the middle class organizations clearly displayed the edge in efforts to bring justice for Joe Campos Torres. While grassroots organizations expressed the concern of the masses, they were unable to generate the finances and influence to prod a complex legal system into responding to their needs. Middle class organizations such as LULAC, re-energized by the Chicano Movement of the sixties and early 1970s, could. They had the structure and legal counseling to do it, especially as the case took ominous twists and turns. First, only two of the six police officers accused of the Torres death were indicted for murder and a third for misdemeanor assault.[22] A state jury in Huntsville in October 1977 found the two policemen accused of the murder as being guilty, but only of negligent homicide—a misdemeanor—and assessed them probation.[23]

When the federal system did pass judgment on the three accused policemen, the sentences were no more satisfying. A federal jury found the officers guilty of conspiring to violate Jose Campos Torres' civil rights in February 1978, but the federal judge presiding over the case handed down suspended ten-year sentences and placed each man on five years' probation. The decree provoked new spurts of protest—three different marches to City Hall were held on April 2; among those participating were IMAGE of Houston, LULAC, G.I. Forum, and P.A.S.O.[24] Finally, in October 1979, a federal appeals court rejected the suspended sentences for the officers. Many in the Houston community were pleased, but they remained suspicious of the HPD.[25]

The Moody Park Disturbance

The resolution of the Joe Campos Torres case never settled well with too many Mexican Americans in Houston. Its legacy in the year following the episode was a bitter one. The HPD had incurred an extremely negative image in the wake of the Torres murder and barrio residents felt deep mistrust and fear of the police.[26] Frustrations with the legal system whose verdicts seemed to confirm the generations-old belief that there was no law against the killing of a Mexican, mounted. People fumed at seeing the courts consistently rule in favor of the policemen, or at least, not applying appropriate punishment to them. Also, anxiety lent encouragement to fringe groups whose militancy were a bit out of date with the increasing political moderation occurring in the latter 1970s. An organization named People United to Fight Police Brutality (PUFPB), a committee within the Revolutionary Communist Youth Brigade, for example, formed shortly following the Torres incident.[27]

Almost a year later, on May 7, 1978, picnickers celebrating the Cinco de Mayo on a typical Sunday afternoon at Moody Park on the Northside, released inflamed passions. Without warning, some revelers began destroying and vandalizing the Park; quickly a mob mentality spread to others enjoying the afternoon. The disturbance (or riot) spilled over into the Northside business district along Fulton Street as small groups of people took out their anger on the businesses. The mob of about 1,500, according to police (other estimates say 150–300), set stores

211

aflame and vandalized them. As the police arrived, they were greeted with insults and obscenities ("kill the pigs") from the rioters who rained them with stones and bottles. Television crews were mistreated as they sought to film the rioting. Damage to buildings, cars, and equipment caused by the riot (which continued sporadically into Monday night) totaled into the millions of dollars.[28]

In the aftermath of the Moody Park Riot, the city sought to find explanations for the affray. According to one version (which the police endorsed), the rampage was a spontaneous one caused by too much beer on a hot Sunday afternoon. According to some of the eyewitnesses, an argument between several young men and the brother of a young woman to whom they made advances apparently triggered the disturbance. The youths started fighting near the park bathrooms at 7:30 p.m. and the struggle turned into a melee after one young man was cut. When the Park police arrived, the toughs ganged up on the interlopers. Then, bystanders started protesting the arrest. A rowdy crowd formed and made for a police car and overturned it.[29] This versions of affairs held further that the PUFPB, the committee connected with the Revolutionary Communist Youth Brigade, had incited people to riot in the park by shouting encouragement over bullhorns as the disorder unfolded.[30]

The middle class organizations, which had been urging nonviolence in the year following the death of Joe Campos Torres, took its own stand. The HPD certainly bore a good part of the responsibility for the disturbance given its mistreatment of Mexicans in Houston, a LULAC spokesman declared. But other leaders came down hard on militant elements, namely the people involved with the PUFPB. According to this explanation of the riot, members of the PUFPB had "incited the kids and the boozed-up folks in the park." Leaders in the community labeled the PUFPB participants as outside agitators, revolutionary Communists, and non-Chicanos (the group was integrated, but was not a "Chicano" organization).[31]

The PUFPB, for its part, hailed the meaning of the riot. In actuality, they said, the PUFPB was not at the park when the melee began. When PUFPB members returned, they tried to direct people's anger not at the stores, but at the police. As the Communist group saw it, however, the episode was "a powerful action of the Chicano people rising up to throw off their oppressor in a violent act. The rebellion in Houston was, in fact, a revolutionary struggle, a glimpse of the future, when the masses of people led by the working class will take up arms and seize state power."[32]

The Moody Park Affair ended almost as mysteriously as it started. The following Sunday, May 13, a protest march held at Moody Park demanding justice for Joe Campos Torres and release of those jailed in the Moody Park disturbance went without incident.[33] Three members of the PUFPB (the whole group together consisted of about fifteen active supporters) were arrested, tried, and eventually given probated jail terms.[34] The middle class organizations, in their traditional way, launched their campaign for change through channels. P.A.S.O. met with the mayor at City Hall. LULAC, IMAGE of Houston, the American G.I. Forum, the Padres of Texas, and Chicano Human Service Workers petitioned the U.S. Civil Rights Commission to hold hearings in Houston on the incident.[35]

The Moody Park disturbance, in retrospect, seems to have been an unplanned outburst (instead of a ground swell popular uprising) of resentment kindled by a sense of inflicted wrong, especially in the wake of the Joe Campos Torres indignity. Several factors buttress the thesis of spontaneity. First, the tumult never did spread to other barrios—the rioting was confined to the Northside. Even if the frustration was felt by other Mexican Americans throughout Houston, the era of violence in American history was past and an impulse in one barrio did not trigger mass demonstrations as might have been expected in the 1960s or early 1970s. Secondly, the incident and its aftermath did not galvanize the barrios as did the desegregation controversy of the early 1970s. The MAEC had successfully united people in a common struggle and preserved that momentum for more than a year. Third, no leader or group was catapulted into the role of the new spokesperson for Mexican American Houstonians. The PUFPB, for all its rhetoric, was neither an indigenous group to the barrios nor a Chicano-oriented organization. Mexican Americans did belong to the PUFPB, but the Communist branch hardly contained the spiritual base which fed MAYO or RUP, for example. By the latter 1970s, as the community had passed into another historical phase, few rallied to a philosophy that contradicted their wisdom of making the current system work for them as effectively it worked for Anglos.

Class Issues

In the era of moderation, many of those leaders who act as spokespersons for the larger Mexican American community generally have middle class ties; in several respects their basic values resemble those of their white contemporaries. But they continue to play the role of intermediaries for the working class, feeling a responsibility to help those beneath them.

In the new ethnic politics, however, they do not narrowly voice the sole interests of their Mexican American constituents. Instead, they address issues which are important to the group to which Mexican Americans belong. Some of these issues are non-ethnic and so appeals to the ethnicity and nationalism of Mexicanos appear irrelevant. Nonetheless, the theme of the "power structure" against "us" (the Mexicans) is unavoidable.

City Council Redistricting

Among the issues fought on class grounds during the late 1970s was that of redistricting the city to achieve fair representation. In November 1975, the majority of voters in Houston voted, in a nonbinding referendum, for the concept of having city council members elected by district instead of the citywide method. Despite the vote (54.0% cast ballots to see the system changed), city fathers were recalcitrant to implement the wishes of the majority. But white, black, and brown leaders had been asking for election by district for years and a group of Houston organizations and civil rights people were already working through the judiciary; indeed, by November 1975, they had already filed suit seeking a court order requiring single member districts. They complained that the current system diluted the minority vote and was discriminatory. A legal mandate or a charter revision were the only ways to change the citywide system.

By 1977, the winds of change were overcoming the old arrangement. In the fall of that year, hearing were held in federal court on the suit seeking to have the at-large method of electing city councilmen declared unconstitutional. According to State Representative Ben Reyes, one of the witnesses, the system of representation as it existed contained nine elected members who cared little about barrio concerns. Consequently, the East End had inferior parks, streets and sewer lines. An uneasy relationship existed between barrio residents and non-Spanish speaking policemen, firemen, and ambulance attendants, he declared.[36]

In the end, the Justice Department of the United States ordered the city of Houston to implement a fairer method of representation. The 9–5–1 plan, submitted to voters in August 1979, called for charter amendment to authorize the election of nine of the city council members from designated districts and five of the members and the mayor to be elected in a city-wide vote. Mexican American leaders opposed the plan, suspecting that it was intended to maximize the incumbents' chances for re-election and to minimize the impact of minority representation. Under the 9–5–1 plan, the citywide councilmembers would require the support of only three district representatives to obtain a majority. More importantly, the 9–5–1 plan did not allow for fair representation for the barrios. They sought, therefore, the defeat of the plan and worked to place an alternative version on a November ballot through petition. This other plan (the 16–4 plan), drawn up by a coalition of minority and civic groups, would assure at least five black and two brown members on a council of sixteen single-member districts and four at-large seats. In a case where redistricting affected so many, Mexican American leaders appealed to class interests and not necessarily to ethnicity.[37]

Ultimately, the 9–5–1 plan won out. Special interest groups marshalled their forces and money effectively and waged a clever campaign while the Mexican American voters responded faintly to appeals; less than 7.0% of Mexican American voters went to the polls. The plan allowed for gerrymandering one huge Mexican American district, insuring the election of one Mexicano. As things turned out, therefore, city government continued to function as it had before federally mandated redistricting. The councils of the 1980s were more diverse than they had ever been, including several blacks and women in addition to the one Mexican American representative. But a coalition of at-large members and some district members have worked to block any dramatic changes.[38]

Adversely, the 9–5–1 plan for the Chicano community meant infighting for the one Mexican American position, or compelling Mexican American politicians to run at large. That scenario was played out in the first election under the new plan that November 1979. Running for the predominantly Mexican American District I were three candidates; former State Representative Ben Reyes won out. Another Mexican American ran at-large, though she went down to defeat against an incumbent who ran a well-financed campaign.[39]

The Metropolitan Transit Authority

Another city-wide drive which drew the middle class Mexican American leadership into action was the proposed establishment of the Metropolitan Transit Authority (MTA). By the late 1970s, Houston was ready to revamp its mass transit system and thus endorsed the creation of the MTA, a bus transportation plan spearheaded by the city's business establishment. The cost would be a one-cent sales tax. Mexican American leaders, like others in Houston, felt this a fair and equitable method of financing such a proposed system.

By the time that the referendum on the creation of the system neared in August 1978, practically all Mexican American political leadership had been brought behind the MTA idea. A group called Mexican Americans for Better Transit led the campaign. Judges, constables, former city controller Leonel Castillo, and others announced support for the project. LULAC, the greater Houston American G.I. Forum, and P.A.S.O. all joined the effort to mobilize the Mexican American community and rally support for the MTA election; P.A.S.O. received promises from the political establishment in the form of appointments to MTA in return for its endorsement. New jobs, promised representation on the MTA Board, and guarantees of equitable representation of Mexican Americans at all levels of employment, planning, implementation, contracting, sub-contracting, supplying, and purchasing in the MTA network through a sure-proof affirmative action plan, were trumpeted. Additionally, MTA would result in cross-town routes connecting the Northside and the East End, bilingual and Spanish information centers to better serve Mexican American riders, and improved thoroughfares as a result of street repairs initiated by the city for the good of MTA. The expectations rang promising, and Houston Hispanic voters approved the MTA election by a three-to-one ratio according to the Mexican Americans for Better Transit.[40]

Political Incumbents in the 1980s

The political standing of Mexican Americans in the Houston community in the 1980s stands in marked contrast to the period before 1970 when only Lauro Cruz held any significant elected office. As ever, at-large elections are difficult to wage and the Mexican American voters continue being independent. In 1979, Leonel Castillo, who in 1977 resigned his position as city controller to become head of the Immigration and Naturalization Service in Washington D.C., returned to Houston to run for mayor, but saw defeat. Two years later he attempted to regain his old seat as city controller, but failed.[41] P.A.S.O. continued to screen candidates, convincing the voters of the wisdom of their choice some times, but falling short at others. In 1981, for example, it endorsed and campaigned hard for the incumbent mayor (as did black leaders and the city's powerful white conservatives), but the barrios went with a challenger along with the rest of Houston.[42]

Political incumbency, then, is restricted to those positions representing predominantly Chicano areas. As is the pattern throughout most of the state in the 1980s, middle class persons represent those districts. Elected offices having Mexican American incumbents include the judiciary (justice of the peace court, criminal court-at-law, municipal court, and court of civil appeals), law enforcement (constables), the city council, the school board, the state legislature (two Mexican American representatives as of 1987: Al Luna from District 143 and Román Martínez from District 148). Additionally, there are numerous Mexican Americans working in positions of political appointment and influence.

Inclusion?

Such unprecedented achievements merit applause, but they do not represent equality. The fact of the matter is that they are "accomplishments" only when compared to the slimmer record of the pre-1970s when various obstacles stifled major steps forward. Indeed, the good fortune of a few has eluded the majority of Mexican American Houstonians. Too many find themselves relegated to the lower paying jobs in the city's labor market. Students continue going to schools in increased numbers—in the fall of 1985, Hispanic students made up 36.0% of the overall student population in the HISD; comparatively, the white population in the district was 17.6% and blacks made up 43.0%—but reality sheds a different light on what the increased numbers may augur. First, white flight to the suburbs accounts in part for the diminished percentage of Anglo Americans in the school district (it was pointed out that as time progressed, there would not be enough Anglos left in the district to integrate the schools). Second, and more significantly for the community, a high dropout rate nullified the gains made in numbers.[43] Conditions of poverty, furthermore, have been exacerbated with an incredible rise of illegal and undocumented immigration from Mexico and from Central American countries. Consequently, the struggle within the Mexican American community for social justice continues.

NOTES

[1]Read, for example, Matusow, *The Unraveling of America.*
[2]Montejano, *Anglos and Mexicans in the Making of Texas,* pp. 290, 299–300.
[3]Saragoza, "The Significance of Recent Chicano-Related Historical Writing."
[4]Rodríguez, "Patterns of Ethnic Disparity and Conflict," pp. 35, 37–39, and Table 6; Houston *Post,* April 26, 1974, p. 20D; January 13, 1985, p. 3B.
[5]Rodríguez, "Patterns of Ethnic Disparity and Conflict," pp. 32, 45, and Table 6; Houston *Post,* January 13, 1985, p. 3B; February 15, 1985, p. 4D; February 18, 1979, p. 8B; *La Voz de Houston,* Houston, Texas, 31 de marzo, 1983, p. 4.

217

[6]Houston *Post*, June 13, 1979, p. 3A; March 4, 1979, p. 6B; Houston *Chronicle*, May 21, 1978, p. 10 (Section 1).

[7]Houston *Chronicle*, May 21, 1978, p. 10 (Section 1).

[8]"Concilio de La Raza, Minutes," HMRC, Hector García Collection.

[9]"Concilio de Organizaciones de Houston," Mamie García Collection.

[10]Houston *Post*, July 11, 1975, p. 1A; May 1, 1977, p. 4D; San Miguel, "Mexican American Organizations and the Changing Politics of School Desegregation in Texas," pp. 709–710.

[11]Houston *Post*, April 26, 1974, p. 20D; December 18, 1977, p. 2D; June 18, 1978, p. 9A; February 4, 1979, p. 4B.

[12]Houston *Post*, May 1, 1977, p. 5D; October 18, 1976, p. 3A; June 19, 1977, p. 13A; December 18, 1977, p. 2D.

[13]Newsletter, June 1978, Image de Houston, HMRC, LULAC Council #60 Collection.

[14]Houston *Post*, May 5, 1978, p. 3B; *Semanario El Mexica*, 6 de septiembre 1979, p. 1.

[15]Houston *Chronicle*, June 28, 1986, p. 21 (Section 1).

[16]*Semanario El México*, 21 de agosto, 1975, p. 1; 27 de noviembre, 1975, p. 1; Houston *Post*, March 17, 1974, p. 4B; February 4, 1979, p. 4B, 8B; Houston *Chronicle*, June 28, 1986, p. 21 (Section 1).

[17]Richard Maxwell Brown, *Strain of Violence: Historical Studies of American Violence and Vigilantism*, p. 285. See also, David G. McCombs, *Houston: A History*, pp. 152–154.

[18]*Time* Magazine, September 19, 1977, p. 30.

[19]Houston *Post*, May 10, 1977, p. 1A; June 29, 1977, p. 1A; February 9, 1978, p. 1A.

[20]Ibid., May 13, 1977, p. 16A; May 18, 1977, p. 1A; October 5, 1979, p. 4A.

[21]"Call for Unity," HMRC, Mamie García Collection.

[22]Houston *Post*, June 29, 1977, p. 1A, 15A; Houston *Chronicle*, August 21, 1977, p. 1 (Section 1).

[23]Houston *Post*, February 9, 1978, p. 1A; October 7, 1977, p. 3A; "Attention: Friends of Joe Campos Torres," HMRC, Mamie García Collection.

[24]Newsletter, April 1978, Image de Houston, HMRC, LULAC Council #60 Collection.

[25]Houston *Post*, October 5, 1979, p. 4A.

[26]Ibid., May 13, 1978, p. 23A.

[27]Leaflet, "Demonstrate October 29," HMRC, Mexican American Small Collection; Houston *Post*, February 9, 1978, p. 1A.

[28]Houston *Post*, May 8, 1978, p. 1A, 23A; May 9, 1978, p. 1A; May 10, 1978, p. 1A.

[29]Ibid., May 8, 1978, p. 1A, 23A; May 9, 1978, p. 23A.

[30]Ibid., May 10, 1978, p. 1A.

[31]Ibid., May 9, 1978, p. 1A, 23A.

[32]Ibid., May 9, 1978, p. 1A, 23A; May 10, 1978, p. 1A; May 11, 1978, p. 28A; Leaflet, "Viva Cinco de Mayo: It's Right to Rebel," HMRC, Hector García Collection; Leaflet, "Free the Moody Park Three!," HMRC, Mexican American Small Collection; *Revolution*, IV (April, 1979), 7–9; *Revolutionary Communist Youth*, II (May, 1979), 3, 7.

[33]Houston *Post*, May 14, 1978, p. 1A.

[34]Ibid., May 13, 1978, p. 1A, 23A; January 18, 1979, p. 13A; *Revolution*, IV (April, 1979), 7–9; *Revolutionary Communist Youth*, II (May, 1979), 3, 7.

[35]Houston *Post*, May 10, 1978, p. 23A; May 13, 1978, p. 23A; Newsletters, May 1978 and June 1978, IMAGE de Houston, HMRC, LULAC Council #60 Collection.

[36]Houston *Chronicle*, November 5, 1975, p. 13 (Section 1); *La Voz del Barrio*, August/September 1977, p. 5; Houston *Post*, August 5, 1979, p. 6B.

[37]Houston *Post*, August 5, 1979, p. 6B; Kaplan, "Houston: The Golden Buckle of the Sunbelt," pp. 206–207.

[38]Houston *Post*, September 9, 1979, p. 3D; Kaplan, "Houston: The Golden Buckle of the Sunbelt," pp. 206–207.

[39]Houston *Post*, November 25, 1979, p. 21A; *Semanario El México*, 8 de noviembre, 1979, p. 1.

[40]*Semanario El México*, 3 de agosto, 1978, p. 1; *La Prensa*, Houston, Texas, 4 agosto, 1978, p. 2A; 11 de agosto, 1978, p. 1A; Houston *Post*, August 1, 1978, p. 18A; August 6, 1978, p. 4B; Kaplan, "Houston: The Golden Buckle of the Sunbelt," p. 208.

[41]Houston *Post*, November 25, 1979, p. 21A; November 8, 1981, p. 25A.

[42]Houston *Post*, November 8, 1981, p. 25A; November 25, 1979, p. 21A.

[43]Houston *Post*, October 28, 1977, p. 3A; August 20, 1982, p. 1A; November 1, 1984, p. 19A; November 9, 1985, p. 25A.

CHAPTER XII
LA COLONIA HISPANA IN THE 1980s

Partly guiding this book is the thesis that the Mexican American community in Houston from the time of its inception in the city has undergone persistent change in ethnic identity and culture. By the 1980s, indeed, several traits characteristic of mainstream American society were integral to Mexican American life. English was the primary language for a large segment of the colonia, for example (many Mexican Americans were not enrolled in bilingual programs in the 1980s—that was left to the children of the immigrants). Such a pattern of cultural adjustment has been the experience of the other immigrant groups in the United States, of course, and so the historical evolution of Mexicanos in Houston resembles the process of immigrant acculturation.

But the Mexican American experience in the United States has departed from the European immigrant experience in its success at preserving the cultural past. Retention may be attributed to the geography of the colonia: barrios bounded by segregation and poverty have engendered cultural enclaves as well as residential enclaves. Cultural tenacity also owes to the contribution made by recent arrivals from Mexico who nourish Mexican culture. It may further be due to the fact that cohorts do not acculturate uniformly, especially in a circumstance where low rates of educational achievement exist. Mixing with bicultural Mexicanos in the Houston barrios, thus, are less acculturated members of the working class. They are the clientele of so many Mexican oriented stores in the barrios, the preservers of the Spanish language, and the carriers of a Mexican American culture. Also contributing to cultural preservation is the notion that "lo mexicano" is something to be appreciated. The fact that the Mexican American community in Houston is the product of

220

historic cultural adjustment, therefore, does not imply the repudiation of old cultural ways. To the contrary, "lo mexicano" lives alongside "lo americano" in the Houston Mexican community. Moreover, barrio residents work to improve their distinct way of life, not dismantle it.

Mexican Americans in a Sunbelt City

Indeed, the Houston colonia continues to preserve a link to its Mexican past. This is a preference expressed by the community in general, and so, even those being seduced by assimilative gestures from mainstream society do not completely lose their identity. Some of the more obvious tenets of Mexican culture perpetuated are language and religious traditions. These are preserved in the home and through familial relationships. Mexican culture is maintained through some of the clubs already discussed. The connection of Mexican Americans to the history of Mexico is remembered during the fiestas patrias celebration every Cinco de Mayo and Diez y Seis de Septiembre.[1]

But institutional means are also employed to maintain "lo mexicano." Presently, there are several newspapers which publish in Spanish, among them *El Sol*. Television in Houston provides Spanish programming on a limited basis. More important as a medium is Spanish-language radio which permits different segments of the community to learn about each other. In the 1980s, the status of Spanish-language radio had grown past an older age when KLVL dominated the airwaves. At least seven stations served non-English speakers and those who enjoyed the mother culture. Radio stations carried programming and advertisements by which business people reached their customers. Aside from news and public service announcements, they broadcast *"radio novelas,"* or soap operas. In efforts to accommodate the diversity of the population, the stations offered slightly differing formats. Some played mostly *música norteña* (the music popular in northern Mexico) while others tried to cater to other tastes by presenting Latin disco and the sounds recorded by international music stars from Mexico, Latin America, and Spain.[2]

Crucial to perpetuating Mexican culture in Houston is the persistent, and since the 1970s, increased influx of people fleeing poverty in Mexico. During the mid-1980s, estimated figures for the number of undocumented immigrants from Mexico were placed at around 150,000.[3] Naturally, they inject cultural ingredients that prevent dilution of the colonia's ethnicity. Certain foods are more popular among the immigrants than among the indigenous group, for example. Restaurants and barrio stores offer these delights and the loss of the dish is forestalled. Spanish-language magazines from Mexico are demanded and are stocked. Businesses advertise in Spanish instead of switching to the more appropriate English. In the colonia, therefore, barbershops, insurance firms, and law offices prominently display signs reading *"Se Habla Español."*

On the negative side, the *inmigrantes* pose dilemmas. They are vulnerable to labor exploitation. Stories carried by the news media about single men and women being at the mercy of the law and the system are tragically common. Many young girls work as domestics in the city's most opulent sections, but often fall prey to misfortune, including blackmail from those who know of their presence in the country. Illegals suffer through illnesses and other calamities lest they be picked up by the Immigration and Naturalization Service and deported. Given their precarious status, the undocumented are relegated to the most menial occupations. According to figures from the late 1970s, Mexican men earned less than $9,500, compared to the Houston work force median of slightly more than $14,500. For undocumented women, salary was $4,500 compared to the Houston median estimated at about $9,200.[4]

The *inmigrantes* in the 1980s also contributed to the rise in crime in the colonia as many became homicide victims. Why so many of them fell prey to murder was open to debate. Some blamed it on the environment of the bars, others on the impersonal nature of the city, the trying quarters under which the immigrants were compelled to live, the lack of cohesive community and healthy social control outlets, or to the economic class from which they descended.[5] For the most part, however, most came to work in Houston and the great majority remained peaceful, seeking to establish order in their lives, just as previous generations of Mexicanos had done.

Furthermore, the *inmigrantes* did not represent a welcomed ingredient to the barrios. Working class residents thought them to have adverse effects on the community. They viewed Mexican nationals as an economic threat and believed their presence to give Mexican Americans "a bad image." Since the great majority of people living in Houston are already Americanized, moreover, they see a cultural gulf between themselves and the newcomers. United States born Mexicanos distinguished themselves from the recent immigrants. In the schools, the conflict was tense. Junior high students verbally and physically taunted the children of the *inmigrantes*, casting upon them epithets such as *mojos*, a derogatory derivation of the Spanish term *mojados* ("wetbacks"). Numerous physical altercations resulted from such resentment.[6]

Still, it is instructive that the immigrants have their defenders. Ironically, those most interested in the treatment and status of Mexican nationals in Houston, as throughout the United States, come from segments of the middle class. Why would the more Americanized members of the Mexican American community, who have less in common with the *inmigrantes,* want to speak for illegals? Several reasons have been posited. For one, the middle class may feel continued discrimination at the hands of mainstream institutions. Educational equality with Anglos may still not lead to expected gains at the workplace; this realization may prompt assimilated Mexicanos to take action against the system, in the form of say, attacking it for its treatment of the completely disadvantaged Mexican nationals. Secondly, the middle class Mexican American may have more to gain from destroying discriminatory barriers. By so doing, it could more easily sustain itself as a class, especially if able to transfer middle-class opportunities to its progeny. Thirdly, the middle class has an interest in expanding its constituency. Lastly, it has ever aspired to being the spokesperson for the needs of the Mexican American community, and this would include newly arrived Mexican nationals who are part of barrio life. Already familiar with the proper channels and resources available for dealing with Houston's power structure, the middle class carries out its historic role.[7]

Of course, the irony of the middle class acting as intermediaries for the immigrants lies in the historical opposition taken by their organizations toward immigration. In contradistinction to the stand taken through the 1950s, civic organizations have come full circle and are now pro-immigrant rights. As mentioned, this shifting sense of responsibility is part of the continued and complex evolution of the Mexican American community, and may be one of the aftereffects of the Chicano movement which dramatized the needs of the most poverty stricken in the barrios. Whatever the case, civic groups have done the most in behalf of the immigrants. LULAC, for example, has consistently spoken out for the immigrants' rights, has opposed government efforts to control immigration through a policy of mandatory registration of workers, and has decried the wholesale deportation of Mexican nationals.[8] Other allies have set up a network of self-help for the immigrants. During the 1970s, such organizations as *Centro Para Inmigrantes* in the Northside and *Centro Aztlán* were conducting programs to assist Mexican nationals in Houston.[9]

Education for children has been of utmost importance to the immigrants' defenders. LULAC, for one, has consistently supported the right of children to acquire an American education. Sympathetic groups in the

1970s also assisted the immigrants. Through the efforts of various members of the Houston colonia, alternative schools such as *Escuelita Guadalupe Aztlán* and the *Instituto Mexicano* were set up for schooling Mexican undocumented children during the 1970s when the HISD refused them a free education.[10] Then, the most significant case in immigrant education in Texas, *In Re: Alien Children Education Litigation* (1980), was initially heard in Houston, and handled by committed Mexican American Houston lawyers working in conjunction with fellow attorneys from other parts of the country.

At heart for those wishing equality to be extended to immigrant children was a change made in the Texas Education Code by the Texas legislature in 1975. The revision allowed free education only to citizens of the United States or those who were legally admitted aliens. But in 1979, U.S. District Judge William Wayne Justice of Tyler, ruled that public schools had to admit illegal alien children without tuition. That ruling led attorneys in the Houston area to file suit against seventeen school districts, including HISD. The suit challenged the constitutionality of the 1975 law and HISD's policy of charging the children of undocumented workers a monthly enrollment fee.[11]

In a bitter fight before the court of U.S. District Judge Woodrow Seals (Houston), the plaintiffs emerged the victors. Judge Seals ruled that free education should be extended to the estimated 7,000 to 9,000 foreign-born children who lived in the Houston area. He based his opinion on the concept of equal protection of the laws and the premise that denying an education to the immigrants would only create a dependent underclass of people. But this decision was overturned on appeal and went to the Supreme Court. In *Plyler* v. *Doe* (December 1982), however, the high court reinstated Judge Seals' decision (*In Re: Alien Children Litigation,* 1980).

This landmark decision was significant in several terms. Primarily, of course, it handed to undocumented immigrant workers rights previously denied them. But other things of importance came out of the effort. According to some of the major participants in the case, the litigation coalesced and united the Houston Mexicano community behind the effort to improve the lot of the Mexico-born Houstonians. Furthermore, Mexican governmental agencies allied themselves with the Chicano campaign, among them the Relaciones Exteriores de México and the Mexican Consulate in Houston. The Houston consul came to the assistance of the attorneys for the immigrant children and fulfilled his obligation to protect the civil rights of Mexican nationals.[12]

Less relevant to the perpetuation of a Mexican culture but significant in making up the "Hispanic" community in Houston is the presence of immigrants from the Caribbean countries and from Central and South America. The term "Hispanic" has presently emerged as an all embracing term for those having cultural roots in the Latin American countries. Mexican Americans, in fact, have gravitated toward the use of the term as part of the moderation of the 1980s, though in using the label they ordinarily have themselves in mind. In Houston, such a use would be correct since Mexican Americans make up more than 80.0% of the entire Spanish-origin, Spanish-surname, and/or Spanish-language population. Also, users of the term realize that historically, the label "Hispanic" has the Mexican American community as its base since the above groups from Latin America are late arrivals to Houston.

But the fact of the matter is that other groups comprise the "Hispanic community" of Houston. Cuban refugees are small in numbers but are conspicuous by their presence in the business community. Puerto Ricans appear to fare little better than the *inmigrantes* from Mexico. Some South Americans have found a nest in Houston, but they are almost invisible. The most prominent foreign element within the Hispanic community in the 1980s, therefore, is the one comprised of Central American migrants and refugees who have come to Houston to escape domestic turmoil in their native lands or find a better standard of living than is possible in their country of origin.

Social workers and other observers familiar with immigration from Latin America estimated the number of undocumented Central Americans at over 100,000 in 1986. This figure put Houston second only to Los Angeles in the number of Central American migrants. Statistically, those from El Salvador constituted the largest population of immigrants from Central America, numbering as high as 50,000. They were followed by those from Guatemala, who figured at a population of between 10,000 to 15,000, and the Hondurans who amounted to a number of about 5,000 to 10,000.

For the most part, these Central Americans settled in three types of Hispanic zones. First, they moved into the traditional barrios. Almost half of the undocumented Central Americans in Houston resided in these areas, thus adding their own brand of Hispanicization to the persistent Mexicanization occurring in the colonia. Also, the Central Americans drifted into transitional zones, that is, areas which were undergoing a change from Anglo to Hispanic neighborhoods. Thirdly, these Central Americans emerged to establish new ethnic pockets in predominantly white areas, mainly in rows of apartment complexes.

Like their counterparts from Mexico, the Central Americans faced a difficult and uncertain life in Houston. Employment was not always forthcoming but those working were concentrated in construction and maintenance work, transportation and wholesale industries, and personal service occupations which relegated them to the lower levels of income distribution. Despite the cheap labor they provided, however, the larger society did not respond favorably to their presence. Most Houstonians, including Mexican Americans, saw them as welfare cases, criminals, and usurpers of jobs. [13]

Preserving a Distinct Mode of Living

Presently, Mexican Americans make up 17.0% of Houston's population (this does not include the undocumented population from Latin America). [14] As has been indicated, Mexican Americans live all over town, but the majority remain in the barrios. They live there not only because so many of them are poor, but because many prefer the cultural ambience therein. From means such as establishing self-help organizations and the transplantation of traditions and cultural institutions from Mexico, Mexican Americans have sought to preserve a distinctive mode of living. That lifestyle is guarded by a network comprised of activists who work through mainstream channels and strive to improve living standards in the barrio. Internally, this informal web also tries to protect Mexican American life as inhabitants of the barrio define it.

Thus, Mexican Americans in Houston continue seeking to make the colonia an improved place to establish and raise families. In the mid-1980s, for example, a movement was undertaken by barrio members to ensure the preservation of the East End. Fearing that it would become an industrial section of warehouses and storage yards, several hundred volunteers came together under The Metropolitan Organization (TMO). Through TMO, they organized ten primarily Hispanic Roman Catholic parishes in the East End into a united community improvement group. They hoped to revitalize the East End with homes, small businesses, good schools and city services. That was to be done, in part, through capital improvement bonds approved by voters in 1984. [15]

Also about the same time, Mexican American leaders succeeded in getting the Houston Planning and Development Department to invest public and private development resources into a Mexican-style market in the Segundo Barrio. El Mercado del Sol, as the market was called, promised to enhance inner city redevelopment and be an economic stimulus to Mexican American businessmen and workers.[16]

Schooling remained an issue of foremost importance. One success came with the naming of a school in the East End at 1601 Sherman after Félix Tijerina.[17] Also, efforts were made to rescue some of the many children falling victims to dropout. A most successful attempt to rectify this loss was undertaken by the Association for the Advancement of Mexican-Americans (AAMA), founded in 1970 by young teachers, businessmen and students reared in the Houston barrios. AAMA operated a federally funded alternative education program for Mexican American junior and senior high school students experiencing troubles in the public schools. By adapting the learning process to student needs and by providing personal attention to the enrollees, AAMA successfully dealt with those harboring low self-esteems, inferiority complexes, and fixations that they sprung from backward cultures. In 1979, AAMA was successful enough that its program spurred an alternative school, the George I. Sánchez Junior and Senior High School.[18]

At a higher level, Mexican American activists organized Houston's Hispanic International University in 1970 with the intent of offering a program that would relate to the personal, cultural, and professional needs of the Mexican American community. A member of the national University Without Walls program since 1974, the Hispanic International University by the 1980s had outlived its original design. Relocated at 2102 Austin and renamed Houston International University in 1984, it was no longer geared exclusively to Mexican Americans and its 400 students included sizable numbers of Anglos, blacks, and Asians. Its Mexican American board by then sought state certification and regional accreditation.[19]

The Ideological and Socioeconomic Development
of the Mexicano Community in Houston

The generational changes in self-identity and the gradual but incessant development of a diverse social structure in twentieth century Houston could not have been too much of a departure from the experiences of Mexicano colonias in Texas in the same era. The way by which the community underwent a transformation from one of immigrant origins to one of many socio-cultural stripes is a lesson in the makings of urban Chicano communities elsewhere. This section summarizes the totality of the history of Mexican Americans in Houston as an example of historical flux in ethnic identity and culture.

In the era before the Depression, the Houston Mexican community inclined towards retaining cultural accouterments imported from Mexico. This was the case for a variety of reasons, among them the fact that white society erected barriers inhibiting integration into mainstream institutions. Put another way, Anglo Houston defined the role of Mexicanos as outsiders and foreigners who were ill-equipped and unprepared for social equality; in this perception, whites were not singling out Mexicans; people of color had been similarly ostracized since the 1830s. Prevention from attending schools, moving into Anglo neighborhoods, and gaining access to the political machinery insured the survival of the foreign culture. Like other immigrant groups in the U.S. experience, on the other hand, the Mexicans exhibited their own preference for the preindustrial, premodern ways of their native land. In Houston as elsewhere, Mexicans revealed a desire to reconstitute the flavor of the colonia in accordance with the old country's origins. In this, they re-established such things as *tedajos* which existed along Congress Avenue, the *periódicos* of that epoch, and the several types of clubs and organizations. Given this combination of limitations and personal tendencies for "lo mexicano," society remained somewhat ideologically homogeneous, even though "lo americano" was already making inroads.

Socially, the colonia on the eve of the Depression was not greatly fragmented. True, some of the exiles of the Revolution transferred their skills to the new setting, but overall, residents of the colonia faced poverty. In the eyes of many, all they had done was to exchange one barrio for another. Yet, energy was not directed at struggling for political equality, agitating for better wages, and demanding better services for the barrios. Rather, the immigrants placed priority on survival, providing needed assistance to their compatriots, and preserving their identity, values, and social behavior. In taking this direction, the Houston community resembled most other Chicano urban communities in the United States during the 1910s and 1920s. Forms of resistance were not blatant and were expressed in subtle means, such as rejecting aspects of the American ethos, insisting that "lo mexicano" take primacy over "lo americano," and within the confines of the barrios, questioning the sincerity of an America that spoke of bountifulness yet deprived it of so many.

It is evident that by the early 1930s in Houston there existed an expanding element receptive to the newer thinking being advanced throughout several parts of the state by the Mexican American Generation. The roots of this developing and assertive segment of the population in the city could be found in the schooling of the 1920s, in the adaptations (conscious or otherwise) taking place among those who had decided to stay in Houston, and the natural osmosis that occurs when a group interacts with societal institutions. By the late 1920s, social agencies had established themselves amidst the colonia, and Mexican schools and Mexican churches acted as agents of Americanization. Still, people of the colonia were not completely sold on Americanisms and may have rejected them for undermining ethnic culture. For example, the schools were not so powerful assimilating intermediaries so as to erase the Spanish language, and the Mexican churches were dominated by the parishioners who helped conduct affairs in a manner which strengthened ethnic identity. In the 1930s, therefore, there existed in Houston a mix of interests and offerings for those who yearned for "lo mexicano," for those making the transition from Mexican to American, and for those who were severing ties of allegiance with Mexico.

Among those who came to be spokesmen for the community in the latter half of the Depression decade and the immediate post-World War II era, a niche in integrated schools, public places, and white neighborhoods was to be pursued. But the struggle was to be carried on in a dignified and moderate manner. In opting to disregard more dramatic and radical approaches for bringing about improvement, the leaders of the era, namely the LULACers and the G.I. Forumeers, were agents of their times and were not less assertive than their American contemporaries. The era, it must be remembered, became one of increasing intolerance from the 1920s through the 1950s. At mid-century, the stress throughout the country was on conformity and consensus. The cohorts of the era did not incur the label of the "silent generation" arbitrarily. Protest and dissent attracted unwelcomed attention from reactionaries, McCarthyites, and the FBI. Mainstream society skirted confrontation—intellectuals refrained from social criticism, literary rebellion was virtually nonexistent, and even labor organizers made little headway in an atmosphere of redbaiting. It would have been ahistoric for the Mexican American Generation to have behaved otherwise.

The post-war era, also, was one of continued biculturation. Ethnic parishes, foreign-language movies, Spanish-language radio stations, fraternal and other organizations, foods, music, entertainment, familial and kinship ties, neighborhood and community all sustained lo mexicano. Inequality, segregation, name calling were all reminders that white society still considered those of Mexican descent to be "Mexicans" whether they were native born or not. Still, Mexican Americans could not help but to be swayed to American ways of thinking and behaving and accepting the values of the only country they now knew. Resisting accommodation was no easy task given the seductive nature of Anglo American life in the 1950s. Mexicanos were heirs to advances in public health and profited from the development of wonder drugs which did away with polio, tuberculosis, whooping cough, and diphtheria. Consumer goods made their way into homes, as businesses sought to tap the purchasing power of Mexicans who, like everyone else, bought on credit. Television promoted mass culture while radio and record players brought the rebelliousness of youth culture in American right into the colonia. The fads of the country became crazes in the barrios as well.

Such a way of life, of course, did not seduce everyone similarly. Nor had everyone profited from society's beneficence in the same way. As a whole, the Mexican American Generation looked back over the previous thirty years with a sense of accomplishment. Some strides had been made in education, job advancement, income, and social acceptance. But of course, these were superficial advances for they were gains only in comparison with those of their parents. In fact, they did not measure up to strides in comparison to the rest of society, nor did improvements trickle down to everyone in the barrios. An expanding middle class might have claimed a new mobility, but the large segment of the Mexican American Houston population remained concentrated in a lower class status.

Historically speaking, the period since 1960 may be considered the modern era for Mexican Americans in Houston. That is to say, the forces which energized biculturism in the 1960s were the same ones shaping the identity of Mexicanos in the 1980s. During that period, assorted types of influences penetrated every segment of the Mexican American population, from those in the suburbs to those in the most desperately poor sections of the barrios. Compulsory education insured that just about everyone receive at least a junior high education, and since the 1960s, efforts have been made by government and private agencies to subsidize the college instruction of ambitious young people. Only the most sheltered residents would have been inured to political media blitzes brought into homes by television. The War in Vietnam won over the most patriotic, alienated the most cynical, but imposed invaluable lessons and experiences upon young boys who served in the armed services. The Great Society programs, if not uplifting many, certainly were interpreted as tokens of a caring government—Medicare and Head Start remain benefits which are taken for granted. Birth control, leisure time, rock concerts among other privileges of American life seemed to transform Mexico into an unfortunate, Third World land of *mojados*.

In part, the above forces took a bicultural community and diversified it more than it had been heretofore. The decline of Jim Crow, furthermore, allowed room for Mexican Americans to define their own self-identity; no longer did de facto segregation stigmatize them as undeserving of the accommodations previously reserved for whites. But the times and resources which permitted self-analysis produced no consensus as to what it was to be Mexican American—instead, the community was one of "many Mexicanos." Some were led to embrace unequivocally the high ideals of equality and democracy. But those same circumstances compelled others to reconsider their fortunes, especially since the Chicano community lagged far behind in living standards. At a time when Mexican Americans never had it better, the Movimiento emerged in a tide of rising expectations. Militants challenged the status quo, attacked societal inequities which still left many Mexican Americans below the poverty line, and they harked back to the idyllic past of their ancestors, the Aztecs who had come from a mythical land called Aztlán. The middle class liberals voiced the same concerns about their constituents in the barrios, though the notion of self-determination appeared not to have excited them.

These differences reflected not only the ideological diversity that had unfolded since immigrants arrived in Houston to assume jobs in the railroads and the oil industry, but also the social diversification springing from an economy and ambient which simultaneously exploited workers yet permitted the more ambitious to rise far and fast. Still, it is to the credit of the Houston Mexican American community that it has persisted as a bicultural organism to this day. Even the most accomplished and socially mobile in the growing middle class do not present themselves as non-ethnics. In the political front, it is the acculturated among the ranks of the middle class who currently assume the role as spokesmen for the problems of inequality, slum blight, inadequate wages, medical care, and immigration. When the Mexican American community retreated along with the rest of the nation into a world of diversion and material consumption in the 1980s, the most ardent supporters of the new conservatism did not negate their Mexicanness. It is this persistence of a mother culture co-existing with the culture of the host country which differentiates the process of Mexican immigration, adjustment, and assimilation from that of Europeans nationals.

NOTES

[1]Houston *Post,* September 14, 1984, p. 1E; May 6, 1985, p. 11A.

[2]Ibid., October 19, 1980, pp. 1BB, 12BB.

[3]Rodríguez, "Patterns of Race and Ethnic Disparity and Conflict," p. 18.

[4]Houston *Post,* June 13, 1979, p. 3A; Rodríguez, "Patterns of Race and Ethnic Disparity and Conflict," p. 38.

[5]Houston *Post,* September 9, 1979, p. 1A.

[6]Tatcho Mindiola, "A Personal Comment on Assimilation," *The Houston Review,* III (Summer, 1981), 261–262.

[7]Ibid., p. 263.

[8]Ibid., pp. 262–263.

[9]Personal correspondence with Attorney Isaias D. Torres, August 14, 1986; Houston *Post,* September 9, 1979, p. 1A.

[10]Personal correspondence with Attorney Isaias D. Torres, August 14, 1986; Houston *Chronicle,* February 3, 1980, p. 4.

[11]Houston *Post,* November 2, 1979, p. 7A; August 25, 1979, p. 8A; Houston *Chronicle,* February 3, 1980, p. 4; July 25, 1982, p. 6 (Section 6).

[12]Personal correspondence with Attorney Isaias D. Torres, August 14, 1986.

[13]Rodríguez, "Patterns of Race and Ethnic Disparity and Conflict," and Nestor P. Rodríguez, "Undocumented Central Americans in Houston: Diverse Populations" (unpublished manuscript).

[14]Kaplan, "Houston: The Golden Buckle of the Sunbelt," pp. 201–202; Houston *Post,* July 17, 1981, p. 8F.

[15]Houston *Post,* October 21, 1984, p. 2D; June 15, 1985, p. 7B.

[16]Houston *Post,* June 6, 1984, p. 5A; June 9, 1984, p. 1B; May 30, 1985, p. 1D; August 16, 1985, p. 1E; September 6, 1985, p. 2B; Houston *Chronicle,* July 9, 1986, p. 1 (Section 1).

[17]*Semanario El México,* 30 de Junio de 1977, p. 1.

[18]Houston *Post,* November 18, 1971, p. 1 (SW) "Closeup"; April 13, 1975, p. 4D; March 31, 1976, p. 3A; May 13, 1979, p. 6B.

[19]Houston *Chronicle,* May 26, 1986, p. 12 (Section 1); Memo, April 5, 1977, University Without Walls, HMRC, Leonel Castillo Collection; *Semanario el México,* 1 Abril, 1976, p. 1.

NOTE ON SOURCES

The best collection presently available for the study of Mexican Americans in Houston is the one held by the Houston Metropolitan Research Center (HMRC) in the Houston Public Library. Amassed by Thomas H. Kreneck, Assistant Archivist at HMRC, it is a wonderful collection of primary material of vast range, covering numerous subjects that embrace a gamut from original pieces of creative literature to letters and documents of public figures. Some of the sources are of wider importance, having much relevance to the broader field of Chicano history. The content of the Collection is discussed fully in Thomas H. Kreneck, "Documenting a Mexican American Community: The Houston Example," *American Archivist*, 48 (Summer, 1985). Any study on Mexican Americans in Texas would be incomplete if it did not tap this treasure lode.

Complementing the Mexican American Collection are the holdings in the Texas Room, also situated at the HMRC. Public documents, reports, histories, city directories, maps, newspapers, and censuses are only a sampling of the immense holdings here. Since this collection specializes in the study of Texas history, researchers can count on finding almost any book or article pertinent to the study of Texas.

The M. D. Anderson Memorial Library at the University of Houston holds its own valuable sources. There are Master of Arts theses and some doctoral dissertations which provide fruitful insight into the experience of Mexican Americans in Houston. Its own newspaper collections, especially complete runs of the Houston *Post* and *Chronicle* and a partial holding of the Houston *Press,* are invaluable. Naturally, it is a repository for most secondary materials related to Mexican Americans.

Unfortunately, no major guides, bibliographies, or indexes are available to provide scholars with a head start. An effort to provide some relief, however, has been made with the compilation of two research tools completed in 1986. They are "An Index of Items Relating to Mexican Americans in Houston as Extracted From the Houston *Chronicle*" and "The Mexican American Collection at the Houston Metropolitan Research Center: An Inventory," both by Arnoldo De León and Roberto R. Treviño. The two research tools are held as part of the Mexican American Collection at HMRC.

BIBLIOGRAPHY

Because of the need to economize on publishing costs, the decision was made to reduce the length of the end notes. Full citations are included in the bibliography. For anyone interested in determining with precision which documents from the HMRC were used, a fully cited draft is in deposit at the Mexican American Collection, HMRC, Houston Public Library, 500 McKinney Avenue, Houston, Texas 77002.

Primary Sources

Archival Collections (from Houston Metropolitan Research Center, Houston Public Library, Houston, Texas):

John Castillo Collection.
Leonel Castillo Collection.
Chairez Family Collection.
Club "México Bello" Collection.
Carmen Cortez Collection.
Hector García Collection.
Mamie García Collection.
Melesio Gómez Collection.
Alfred J. Hernández Collection.
John J. Herrera Collection.
LULAC Council #60 Collection.
Lydia Mendoza Collection.
Mexican American Family History Collection.
Mexican American Small Collection.

Félix Morales Collection.
Newspaper Microfilm Collection.
Juan P. Rodríguez Collection.
Juvencio Rodríguez Collection.
Félix Tijerina Collection.

Oral History Collections (all interviews with Thomas H. Kreneck, Houston Metropolitan Research Center, Houston Public Library, Houston, Texas):

Carmen Cortez Interview, December 16, 1983.
Ramón Fernández Interview, September 5, 1979.
Isidro García and Primitivo L. Niño Interview, April 9, 1979.
Rodrigo García Interview, July 10, 1979.
Refugio Gómez Interview, March 24, 1980.
Alfred J. Hernández Interview, January 15, 1979.
Juan C. Hernández Interview, November 19, 1978.
John J. Herrera Interview, May 22, 1981.
Mrs. Félix H. Morales Interview, February 5 and February 19, 1979.
Santos and Ester Nieto Interview, July 7, 1983.
Primitivo Niño Interview, March 16, 1979.
María Puente Interview, October 26, 1976.
Juvencio Rodríguez Interview, August 14, 1980.
Alfredo Sarabia Interview, February 16, 1979.
Ralph and Mary Villagómez Interview, April 16, 1979.

Newspapers:

Compass, Houston, Texas, 1968.
El Observatorio Latino, Houston, Texas, n.d.
El Puerto, Houston, Texas, 1935, 1938, 1959–1960.
El Sol, Houston, Texas, 1966–1972.
El Tecolote, Houston, Texas, newsclippings 1924–1938ca.
Galveston *Daily News,* Galveston, Texas, 1911.
Houston *Chronicle,* Houston, Texas, 1904–1986.
Houston *Post,* Houston, Texas, 1934–1986.
Houston *Press,* 1933, 1943–1960.
La Gaceta Mexicana, Houston, Texas, 1928.
La Prensa, Houston, Texas, 1978.
La Vida en Houston, Houston, Texas, 1972.
La Voz del Barrio, Houston, Texas, 1977.

La Voz de Houston, Houston, Texas, 1983.
LULAC News, 1933, 1945–1956, 1969, 1974, and Twenty-Fifth Anniversary Issue.
The Morning Star, Houston, Texas, 1839.
Papel Chicano, Houston, Texas, 1970–1972.
Semanario El México, Houston, Texas, 1974.

Census Schedules:

Fifteenth Census of the United States: 1930: Population.
U.S. Census of Population: 1960, Persons of Spanish Surname. Final Report PC (2)–1B.
U.S. Census of Population: 1970, Persons of Spanish Origin. PC(2)–1C.

Government Documents:

Congressional Record. 71st Congress, 3rd Session (1931), 74 (Part 4).

Reports:

Denison, Lynne W. and L. L. Pugh. "Houston Public School Buildings: Their History and Location." n. p., 1936.
Denver Harbor/Port Houston Data Book. Houston: Houston City Planning Department, 1976.
East End Neighborhood Plan. Houston: Houston City Planning Department, 1975.
First/Sixth Wards Data Book. Houston: Houston City Planning Department, 1976.
Houston Council on Human Relations. *Black/Mexican American Project Report.* Houston: Houston Council on Human Relations, 1972.
Magnolia Park Neighborhood Plan. Houston: Houston City Planning Department, 1974.
Moody Park Area Neighborhood Plan. Houston: Houston City Planning Department, 1974.
Near North Side Neighborhood Plan. Houston: Houston City Planning Department, 1975.
The People of Houston vs. Slums, Annual Report. Houston: Housing Authority of the City of Houston, 1947.
"This is HCCAA." Houston: HCCAA Planning Department, 1971.
University of Texas Bulletin, No. 2328: July 22, 1923. *A Report on Illiteracy in Texas,* Bureau of Extension.

Weir, L. H. "Public Recreation in Houston." Houston: Houston Recreation Department, 1927.

Directories:

Directory of the City of Houston, 1900. Houston: Morrison and Fourmy, 1900.
Directory of the City of Houston, 1910. Houston: Morrison and Fourmy, 1910.
Directory of the City of Houston, 1920. Houston: Morrison and Fourmy, 1920.
Directory of the City of Houston, 1930. Houston: Morrison and Fourmy, 1930.
Immaculate Heart of Mary, Houston, Texas: Directory. Houston: Immaculate Heart of Mary Parish, 1979.

Personal Correspondence:

Letter, August 14, 1986. Isaias D. Torres to Arnoldo DeLeón

Books:

Allen, Dr. O. F. *The City of Houston From Wilderness to Wonder.* Temple, Texas: n. p., 1936.
Freund, Max, ed. *Gustav Dresel's Houston Journal: Adventures in North America and Texas, 1837–1841.* Austin: University of Texas Press, 1954.
Muir, Andrew Forest, ed. *Texas in 1837: An Anonymous Contemporary Narrative.* Austin: University of Texas Press, 1958.

Articles:

Harby, Lee C. "Texan Types and Contrasts." *Harper's New Monthly Magazine.* Vol. 81 (June, 1890).

Secondary Sources

Books:

Acuña, Rodolfo F. *A Community Under Seige: A Chronicle of Chicanos East of the Los Angeles River, 1945–1975.* Los Angeles: Chicano Studies Research Center Publications, UCLA, 1984.

Acuña, Rodolfo. *Occupied America: A History of Chicanos.* 3rd edition; New York: Harper & Row Publishers, 1987.

Agatha, Sister M. *The History of Houston Heights, 1891–1918.* Houston: Premier Printing Company, 1956.

Allsup, Carl. *The American G.I. Forum: Origins and Evolution.* Austin: Center for Mexican American Studies, University of Texas, 1982.

Balderrama, Francisco. *In Defense of La Raza: The Los Angeles Mexican Consulate and the Mexican Community, 1929–1936.* Tucson: University of Arizona Press, 1982.

Branda, Eldon Stephen, ed. *The Handbook of Texas: A Supplement.* Austin: The Texas State Historical Association, 1976.

Briggs, Vernon M. Jr., Walter Fogel, and Fred H. Schmidt. *The Chicano Worker.* Austin: The University of Texas Press, 1977.

Brown, Richard Maxwell. *Strain of Violence: Historical Studies of American Violence and Vigilantism.* New York: Oxford University Press, 1975.

Camarillo, Albert. *Chicanos in a Changing Society: From Mexican Pueblos to American Barrios in Santa Barbara and Southern California, 1848–1930.* Cambridge: Harvard University Press, 1979.

Corwin, Arthur F. ed. *Immigrants—and Immigrants: Perspectives on Mexican Labor Migration to the United States.* Westport, Conn: Greenwood Press, 1978.

Cotera, Martha P. *Diosa y Hembra: The History and Heritage of Chicanas in the United States.* Austin: Information Systems Development, 1976.

Davidson, Chandler. *Biracial Politics: Conflict and Coalition in the Metropolitan South.* Baton Rouge: Louisiana State University Press, 1972.

De León, Arnoldo. *San Angeleños: Mexican Americans in San Angelo, Texas.* San Angelo: Fort Concho Museum Press, 1985.

De León, Arnoldo. *The Tejano Community, 1836–1900.* Albuquerque: University of New Mexico Press, 1982.

Estep, Raymond. *Lorenzo de Zavala: Profeta del Liberalism Mexicano.* Mexico, D. F.: Librería de Manuel Porrúa, 1952.

Foley, Douglas, et al. *From Peones to Politicos: Ethnic Relations in a South Texas Town, 1900–1977.* Austin: University of Texas Press, 1977.

García, Mario T. *Desert Immigrants: The Mexicans of El Paso, 1880–1920.* New Haven: Yale University Press, 1981.

Giles, Robert. *Changing Times: The Story of the Diocese of Galveston-Houston in Commemoration of Its Founding.* N. p., 1970ca.

Goodman, Mary Ellen. *A Preliminary Report on Project Latin American.* Houston: Rice University, 1966.

Goodman, Mary Ellen. *The Mexican American Population of Houston: A Survey in the Field, 1965–1970.* Houston: Rice University Studies, LVII, Summer, 1971.

Griswold del Castillo, Richard. *The Los Angeles Barrio, 1850–1890: A Social History.* Berkeley: University of California Press, 1979.

Hernández, José Amaro. *Mutual Aid for Survival: The Case of the Mexican American.* Malabar, Florida: Robert E. Krieger Publishing Company, 1983.

Houston and Harris County Facts: Yesterday, Today, Tomorrow. Houston: Facts Publishing Company, 1939.

Kibbe, Pauline. *Latin Americans of Texas.* Albuquerque: University of New Mexico Press, 1946.

McComb, David G. *Houston: A History.* Austin: University of Texas Press, 1981.

Madera, Mark., et al. *The Barrios: Mexican Americans in Houston.* Houston: Rice University, 1971.

Matusow, Allen J. *The Unraveling of America: A History of Liberalism in the 1960s.* New York: Harper & Row Publishers, 1984.

Mazón, Mauricio. *The Zoot-Suit Riots: The Psychology of Symbolic Annihilation.* Austin: University of Texas Press, 1984.

Melville, Margarita. *Mexicans in Houston.* Houston: Houston Center for the Humanities, 1982.

Miller, Thomas Lloyd. *Bounty and Donation Land Grants of Texas, 1835–1888.* Austin: University of Texas Press, 1967.

Mirandé, Alfredo and Evangelina Enríquez. *La Chicana: The Mexican-American Woman.* Chicago: Chicago University Press, 1979.

Montejano, David. *Anglos and Mexicans in the Making of Texas, 1836–1986.* Austin: University of Texas Press, 1987.

Paredes, Américo. *"With His Pistol in His Hand": A Border Ballad and Its Hero.* Austin: University of Texas Press, 1971.

Peña, Manuel. *The Texas-Mexican Conjunto: History of A Working Class Music.* Austin: University of Texas Press, 1985.

Romo, Ricardo. *East Los Angeles: History of a Barrio.* Austin: University of Texas Press, 1983.

Rosenquist, Carl M. and Walter Gordon Browder. *Family Mobility in Houston, Texas, 1922–1938.* Bureau of Research in the Social Sciences, University of Texas Publications No. 4224. Austin: University of Texas Press, 1942.

San Miguel, Guadalupe Jr. *"Let All of Them Take Heed": Mexican Americans and the Campaign for Educational Equality in Texas, 1910–1981.* Austin: University of Texas Press, 1987.

Sheridan, Thomas E. *Los Tucsonenses: The Mexican Community in Tucson, 1854–1941.* Tucson: University of Arizona Press, 1986.

Shockley, John Staples. *Chicano Revolt in a Texas Town.* Notre Dame: University of Notre Dame Press, 1974.

Sibley, Marilyn McAdams. *The Port of Houston: A History.* Austin: University of Texas Press, 1968.

Talbert, Robert H. *Spanish-Name People in the Southwest and West.* Fort Worth: Texas Christian University, 1955.

Thomas, Jesse O. *A Study of the Social Welfare Status of the Negroes in Houston, Texas.* Atlanta: National Urban League, 1929.

Tsanoff, Corinne S. *Neighborhood Doorways.* Houston: Neighborhood Centers Association of Houston and Harris County, 1958.

Valdez, Sister Mary Paul. *The History of the Missionary Catechists of Divine Providence.* N.p., 1978.

Vidal, Mirta. *Women: New Voices of La Raza.* New York: Pathfinder Press, 1971.

Weber, David J. *The Mexican Frontier: The American Southwest Under Mexico, 1821–1846.* Albuquerque: University of New Mexico, 1982.

Works Projects Administration. *Houston: A History and Guide.* Houston: The Anson Jones Press, 1942.

Young, William A. *History of Houston Public Schools, 1836–1965.* Houston: Gulf School Research Development Assoc., Inc., 1968.

Articles:

Álvarez, Rodolfo. "The Psycho-Historical and Socioeconomic Development of the Chicano Community in the United States." *Social Science Quarterly,* LIII (March, 1973).

Barrera, Mario. "The Historical Evolution of Chicano Ethnic Goals: A Bibliographic Essay." *Sage Race Relations Abstracts,* X (February 1985).

Calvert, Robert A. "The Civil Rights Movement in Texas." In Ben H. Procter and Archie P. McDonald, *The Texas Heritage.* St. Louis: Forum Press, 1980.

Clark, Victor S. "Mexican Labor in the United States." From Department of Commerce and Labor, Bureau of Labor *Bulletin*, No. 78, Washington D.C., 1908. Reprinted in Carlos E. Cortés, ed. *Mexican Labor in the United States.* New York: Arno Press, 1974.

Davies, Christopher S. "Life At the Edge: Urban and Industrial Evolution of Texas, Frontier Wilderness—Frontier Space, 1836–1986." *Southwestern Historical Quarterly*, LXXXIX (April, 1986).

De León, Arnoldo. "Tejanos and the Texas War for Independence: Historiography's Judgment." *New Mexico Historical Review*, LXI (April, 1986).

De León, Arnoldo. "Tejano History Scholarship: A Review of the Recent Literature." *West Texas Historical Association Yearbook*, LXI (1985).

García, Mario T. "Americans All: The Mexican American Generation and the Politics of Wartime Los Angeles, 1941–1945." *Social Science Quarterly*, LXV (June, 1984).

García, Mario T. "La Frontera: The Border as Symbol and Reality in Mexican American Thought." *Mexican Studies/Estudios Mexicanos*, I (Summer, 1985).

García, Mario T. "Mexican Americans and the Politics of Citizenship: The Case of El Paso, 1936." *New Mexico Historical Review*, LIX (April, 1984).

García, Richard A. "The Mexican American Mind: A Product of the 1930s." In Mario T. García, ed. *History, Culture, and Society: Chicano Studies in the 1980s.* Ypsilanti, Michigan: Bilingual Press/Editorial Bilingue, 1983.

Gil, Carlos B. "Lydia Mendoza: Houstonian and First Lady of Mexican American Song." *The Houston Review*, III (Summer, 1981).

Gómez-Quiñones, Juan. "Piedras Contra La Luna, México en Aztlán y Aztlán en México: Chicano-Mexican Relations and the Mexican Consulates, 1900–1920." In James W. Wilkie, ed. *Contemporary Mexico: Papers of the IV International Congress of Mexican History.* Berkeley: University of California Press, 1976.

Goodman, Mary Ellen and Don des Jarlais. "The Spanish Surname Population of Houston: A Demographic Sketch." Houston: Rice University, 1968.

Kaplan, Barry J. "Houston: The Golden Buckle of the Sunbelt." In Richard M. Bernard and Bradley R. Rice. *Sunbelt Cities: Politics and Growth Since World War II.* Austin: University of Texas Press, 1983.

Kaplan, Barry J. "Race, Income, and Ethnicity: Residential Change in a Houston Community, 1920–1970." *The Houston Review,* III (Winter, 1981).

Kreneck, Thomas H. "The Letter From Chapultepec." *The Houston Review,* III (Summer, 1981).

Limón, José E. "El Primer Congreso Mexicanista de 1911: A Precursor to Contemporary Chicanismo." *Aztlán,* V (Spring and Fall, 1974).

Manuel, H. T. "The Mexican Population of Texas." *The Southwestern Social Science Quarterly,* XV (June, 1934–March 1935).

Miller, Thomas Lloyd. "Mexican Texans in the Texas Revolution." *Journal of Mexican American History,* III (1973).

Mindiola, Tatcho Jr. "Core-Periphery Distinctions in Discrimination Against Spanish Surnamed Males in Houston, Texas." *The Borderlands Journal,* IV (Spring, 1981).

Mindiola, Tatcho Jr. "The Cost of Being a Mexican Female Worker in the 1970 Houston Labor Market." *Aztlán,* XI (Fall, 1980).

Mindiola, Tatcho Jr. "A Personal Comment on Assimilation." *The Houston Review,* III (Summer, 1981).

Platt, Harold L. "Houston at the Crossroads: The Emergence of the Urban Center of the Southwest." *Journal of the West,* XVIII (July, 1979).

Rosales, F. Arturo. "The Mexican Immigrant Experience in Chicago, Houston, and Tucson: Comparisons and Contrasts." In Francisco A. Rosales and Barry J. Kaplan. *Houston: A Twentieth Century Urban Frontier.* Port Washington: Associated Faculty Press, Inc., 1983.

Rosales, F. Arturo. "Mexicans in Houston: The Struggle to Survive, 1908–1975." *The Houston Review,* III (Summer, 1981).

Rosales, F. Arturo. "Shifting Self-Perceptions and Ethnic Consciousness Among Mexicans in Houston, 1908–1946." *Aztlan,* XVI (1985).

Salinas, Guadalupe. "Mexican Americans and the Desegregation of Schools in the Southwest." *The Houston Law Review,* VIII.

San Miguel, Guadalupe Jr. "Mexican American Organizations and the Changing Politics of School Desegregation in Texas, 1945–1980." *Social Science Quarterly,* LXIII (December, 1982).

San Miguel, Guadalupe Jr. "The Struggle Against Separate and Unequal Schools: Middle Class Mexican Americans and the Desegregation Campaign in Texas, 1929–1957." *History of Education Quarterly,* XXIII (Fall, 1983).

Saragoza, Alex M. "The Significance of Recent Chicano-Related Historical Writings: An Appraisal." *Ethnic Affairs,* No. 1 (Fall, 1987).

Shelley, George. "The Semicolon Court of Texas." *Southwestern Historical Quarterly,* XLVIII (April, 1945).
"Will Success Spoil Leonel Castillo?" *Texas Monthly,* August 1976.
Zarefsky, Joseph L. "Spanish Americans in Houston and Harris County." Houston: Research Bureau Community Council, 1953.

Dissertations and Theses:

García, Richard A. "The Making of the Mexican American Mind, San Antonio, Texas, 1929–1941: A Social and Intellectual History of an Ethnic Community." Ph. D. Dissertation, University of California at Irvine, 1980.
Guerra, Robert S. "Political Fragmentation in a Mexican American Community: The Case of Houston, Texas." M. A. Thesis, University of Houston, 1969.
Jackson, Mary Susan. "The People of Houston in the 1850s." Ph. D. Dissertation, Indiana University, 1974.
Maas, Elaine H. "The Jews of Houston: An Ethnographic Study." Ph. D Dissertation, Rice University, 1973.
McKay, R. Reynolds. "Texas Mexican Repatriation During the Great Depression." Ph. D. Dissertation, University of Oklahoma, 1982.
Maroney, James C. "Organized Labor in Texas, 1900–1929." Ph. D Dissertation, University of Houston, 1975.
O'Donnell, Sister Mary Brendan. "Annunciation Church—Catholic Mother Church of Houston." M. A. Thesis, University of Houston, 1965.
Rocha, Rodolfo. "The Influence of the Mexican Revolution on the Mexico-Texas Border, 1910–1916." Ph. D. Dissertation, Texas Tech University, 1981.
Zamora, Emilio. "Mexican Labor Activity in South Texas, 1900–1920." Ph. D. Dissertation, University of Texas at Austin, 1900–1920.
Zeigler, Robert E. "The Workingman in Houston, Texas, 1865–1914." Ph. D. Dissertation, Texas Tech University, 1972.

Unpublished Papers:

Armstrong, Rev. Walter W. "A History of Houston Methodist Missions, 1815–1963."
Feagin, Joe R. and Beth Anne Shelton. "Community Organizing in Houston: Social Problems and Citizen Response."

Feagin, Joe R. "The Socioeconomic Base of Urban Growth: The Case of Houston and the Oil Industry."

Fisher, Robert. "Houston, Texas: A Working Paper on the Interrelation of Economic Growth, Ideology, Power, and Community Organization Since 1920."

"Hispanic Persons in the Federal Census of 1900, Harris County, Texas." Held in HMRC.

"Hispanic Persons in the Federal Census of 1910, Harris County, Texas." Held in HMRC.

Rhinehart, Marilyn D. and Thomas H. Kreneck. " 'In the Shadow of Uncertainty': Texas Mexicans and Repatriation in Houston During the Great Depression."

Rhinehart, Marilyn D. and Thomas H. Kreneck. "The Minimum Wage March of 1966: A Case Study in Mexican American Politics, Labor, and Identity."

Rivera, Julius, et al. "Society, Culture, and Health in Two Houston Barrios: A Comparative Study." Houston: Department of Community Medicine, Baylor College of Medicine, 1975.

Rodríguez, Nestor P. "Patterns of Race and Ethnic Disparity and Conflict: Hispanic Communities."

Rodríguez, Nestor P. "Undocumented Central Americans in Houston: Diverse Populations."

INDEX

Index

Index

Index

Index

251

Index